GROWING OLDER WITH *Jane Austen*

By the same author

Jane Austen's Family through Five Generations

Jane Austen's England

A Charming Place: Bath in the Life and Novels of Jane Austen

A City of Palaces: Bath through the Eyes of Fanny Burney

Jane Austen and Food

Jane Austen's World

Jane Austen and Lyme Regis

Understanding Austen: Key Concepts in the Six Novels

Celebrating Pride and Prejudice: 200 years of Jane Austen's Darling Child (with Hazel Jones)

GROWING OLDER WITH *Jane Austen*

MAGGIE LANE

ROBERT HALE • LONDON

First published in Great Britain 2014

ISBN 978-0-7198-0697-1

Robert Hale Limited
Clerkenwell House
Clerkenwell Green
London EC1R 0HT

www.halebooks.com

A catalogue record for this book is available from the British Library

2 4 6 8 10 9 7 5 3 1

Typeset in Minion Pro
Printed in Great Britain by Berforts Information Press Ltd

CONTENTS

Dedicated to the Memory of
David Selwyn
1951–2013
Chairman of the Jane Austen Society
author and friend

INTRODUCTION

Unlike her parents and six of her seven siblings, who all lived into their seventies, eighties or even, in one case, nineties, Jane Austen did not see old age. She was just forty-one when she died, in the very prime of her writing life. But she *did* share, with everyone who outlives youth itself, the experience of growing *older.* Jane Austen at forty was a different woman from Jane Austen at twenty.

Like any thinking person, she was aware of the changes in herself wrought by time. 'Seven years I suppose are enough to change every pore of one's skin, & every feeling of one's mind',[1] she mused in a letter to her sister Cassandra on happening to return to a place in Bath previously visited seven years earlier.

She was twenty-nine years old when she made that comment in April 1805: still relatively young, yet aware that extreme youth, with its sense of endless possibility, had slipped away. Her father had died just three months earlier, perhaps the first death that she really cared about, and certainly one which affected her own circumstances and sense of security. Her future way of life was uncertain; any youthful hopes and dreams that she may have entertained, whether of love and marriage or of literary success, no longer seemed quite so easily achievable. Coinciding with the domestic turmoil of bereavement, and following an unsatisfactory romance (or two) and her ongoing failure to find a publisher for the three novels already written, the chance episode in Bath seems to have set her thinking deeply – about the inevitability of the ageing process, and old age itself. Just two weeks later, now staying with friends in Hampshire, she remarked of an elderly and tiresome acquaintance: 'Poor Mrs Stent! it has been her lot to be always in the way; but we must be merciful, for perhaps in time we may come to be Mrs Stents ourselves, unequal to anything & unwelcome to everybody'.[2]

Three and a half years later, Austen expressed a similar idea about another annoying old person: 'At her age perhaps one may be as friendless oneself, & in similar circumstances quite as captious.'[3] She was writing of an acquaintance, Miss Murden, whom she had accused the day before of 'sitting very ungracious & very silent with us from 7 o'clock to half after 11'. On deeper reflection, Jane was ready to make allowances for an aged spinster so friendless and homeless that she was relieved to find lodgings with the widow of a Southampton chemist. Behind her remarks about both Mrs Stent and Miss Murden lay the endeavour to live according to the imperative that she was habitually urging on herself (including in three prayers she composed)[4] to be more charitable towards other people, especially foolish or tiresome ones. It was often a struggle.

When she made these remarks about Miss Murden, Jane Austen was in a different phase of her life from when she had written about Mrs Stent. Then she had been down in spirits, so much down that literary composition had been impossible; but now the equilibrium and zest for life so characteristic of her nature were returning. In 1805 she had been at the start of an unsettling sequence of changes of home – moving from one lodging to another first in Bath, then in Southampton, with her widowed mother and sister, managing on an uncertain income donated by four of her brothers. But the passage of years, while closing some doors, was bringing new kinds of happiness to her: the happiness of renewed confidence in her work, and the happiness that came from accepting the limitations and relishing the consolations of incipient middle-aged spinsterhood. In her own life, Jane Austen exemplifies the truth that growing older need by no means imply growing sadder, and that while physical ageing is inevitable, renewal of hope and purpose, unexpected reasons for optimism or unforeseen twists of fate may occur at any time.

In December 1808, though as yet Jane was still living in Southampton, a settled home was in prospect, in the Hampshire village of Chawton (the gift of her richest brother, Edward), and with it, determination to resume her creative life. In another letter of the same month (and in a strange echo of the Bath experience) she describes her reaction to a ball at Southampton's Dolphin Inn: 'It was the same room in which we danced 15 years ago! I thought it all over – and in spite of the shame of being so much older, felt with thankfulness that I was quite as happy now as then.'[5]

Five years later, in November 1813, when she was a month short of her thirty-eighth birthday, she touched more humorously on the subject of ageing. 1813 was a good year for Jane Austen. It had begun with the publication, at last, of her 'own darling child' *Pride and Prejudice*; and had seen the completion of a wholly new novel, *Mansfield Park*, begun some time after the move to Chawton and finished in the summer of 1813. Her early works were coming before the public, and her writer's block was overcome. It is fair to say that she was more contented, busy and fulfilled at thirty-eight than at twenty-nine. After a party in Kent that month, she wrote to Cassandra: 'By the bye, as I must leave off being young, I find many Douceurs in being a sort of Chaperon for I am put on the sofa near the Fire and can drink as much wine as I like.'[6]

Jane Austen making fun of herself: it is a happy picture, though a poignant one. She had less than four years left to live, but what she accomplished in her brief lifespan would bring pleasure to readers across continents and for centuries to come, and inspire an inexhaustible interest in every aspect of her life, times and work.

If the comparative brevity of Jane Austen's life is one reason why commentators and critics have, amid this welter of approaches, largely overlooked her attitudes to ageing and old age, another is the extreme youthfulness of the principal characters of her fiction. With one exception, her heroines range in age from seventeen to twenty-one. Even the exception, Anne Elliot of *Persuasion*, is only twenty-seven, though presented as considerably more mature – sadder and wiser – than the others. Heroes and anti-heroes, siblings, friends and rivals are likewise at the start of their adult lives. (Heroes tend to be in their mid-twenties, though it is true that Captain Wentworth has turned thirty, Colonel Brandon is thirty-five and Mr Knightley thirty-six – the latter two being regarded by most of their acquaintance as unlikely now to marry.)

The narrative of an Austen novel usually occupies about a year, during which time hero and heroine, and many of their cohort, fix their destinies for life. The main focus of the novelist's interest is youth, because it is in youth that the widest array of choice is still possible. This is why, even as she grew older herself, leaving the twenty-something age group behind, she continued to find in the courtship *genre* wherewithal to express her ideas about striving to identify and live a good life.

But Austen also created a gallery of supporting characters who (unless actual children) are invariably older than the main players in her dramas. Parents, uncles, aunts, neighbours and acquaintance, these characters not only take their place in any realistic portrayal of family and social life, but they exemplify and confront the successive phases of human existence. Not all are old, by any means. But all are *older* than the protagonists, all are having to accommodate to life choices made earlier, and to navigate the path that fate – or not infrequently their own foolishness – has mapped out for them. Some grow older with grace and an accumulation of wisdom; for many others, age intensifies their worst traits.

Like the young couples who end Shakespeare's dramas on a note of renewal and hope, Austen's heroes and heroines embark on their own married lives blest with the vigour and optimism of youth, but also equipped with enhanced understanding from having observed the mistakes and struggles of those further on in life's journey.

In seeking to explore Austen's attitude to age, I have drawn not only on the six complete novels, but on all the major literary fragments: that is, all those between *Catharine, or the Bower,* written around

1792, which I class as her first attempt at creating realistic fiction, and *Sanditon,* left uncompleted at her death in 1817. Catharine's maiden aunt and *Sanditon's* great lady have much in common – dislike of modern ways, for a start – but also much to distinguish one from the other, for one of the glories of Austen is that she never repeats a character. Across the whole body of her work, she is adept at suggesting the outlook and idiolect shared by the elderly, without compromising the individuality of each specimen. She is interested in how characters view their own advancing years and those of others.

To aid understanding and enrich contextualization, I have also drawn on her letters, mainly to her sister and confidante Cassandra; on reminiscences and other writings of the wider Austen family; and in some instances on accounts of contemporaries, whose lives may or may not have been known to Jane Austen, but which seem to me to illuminate and amplify the issues under discussion and the mores of the time in which she wrote.

In Chapter 1, The Loss of Youth and Beauty, as well as examining the correlation between physical attractiveness in women and their value in the marriage market, I investigate processes which prematurely age, such as sickness and suffering, childbirth and – for men – all the professional hazards so systematically enumerated by Penelope Clay in *Persuasion.* The second chapter, My Time of Life, explores the way Austen renders the various stages of existence reached by her characters, their awareness of the passage of time, their speech patterns and habits. Chapter 3, Parent Against Child, is concerned with the interplay of generations, whether in conflict, subjugation or mutual dependence.

The next three chapters investigate how growing older impacts differently on women and men. The great divide made by marriage is reflected in Old Wives and Old Maids, as older women make sometimes painful adjustments to the decisions made in youth or forced on them by circumstance; while Still A Very Fine Man focuses chiefly on men who have lost their life partners, some going on to make a second choice, some looking instead to their daughters for practical and emotional support in their declining years.

The fact of widowhood was perhaps the biggest determinant in a woman's destiny in later life, and one over which she had no control. A woman might choose to marry or remain single, but widowhood came unbidden, sometimes welcomed (Mrs Norris's reflecting on the loss of her husband that 'she could do very well without him') and sometimes very much the reverse. Some widows were well-provided for and found they had money under their own control for the first time in their lives; others were suddenly reduced to penury. Three chapters are required to explore widowhood in its varying manifestations. Merry Widows focuses on those who relish their new liberty and the opportunity for further romantic adventures. Four Dowager Despots looks at elderly women with the financial clout to dictate to their families and sometimes to whole communities. Noting the range of rich and poor widows converging on the city in *Persuasion,* Not the Only Widow in Bath explores the phenomenon of the once fashionable resort now inhabited by so many widows, on the make or on the watch against loss of gentility.

The tendency of ageing to intensify affluence or poverty and the role played by inheritance in the novels and family history form the focus of Chapter 10, Age and Money. In The Dangerous Indulgence of Illness, maladies are examined not so much from a medical point of view as psychologically: how sufferers and their associates react to real or imagined loss of health. It is a remarkable fact that as Jane Austen herself was approaching and then succumbing to mortal illness, she was having fun with varying degrees of hypochondria in *Emma, Persuasion* and *Sanditon.* Nothing to Do but to Die looks at the small but significant role of death in the novels; how death was regarded and dealt with in Austen's lifetime and her response to her own approaching demise and that of others.

A note about terminology: when referring to the author of the literary text I use the academically accepted 'Austen'; but when referring to the woman as a member of her family I prefer 'Jane'. This is in no way to patronize her for being female, still less to indulge in dear Aunt-Janeism, but to recognize that in this context, she is one particular Austen among many others. And sometimes, when the complete person, woman and writer, is intended, only the full form 'Jane Austen' will do.

All who write about the Austen family are indebted to the remarkable scholarship of Deirdre Le Faye, whose edition of *Jane Austen's Letters*, inclusion of family history documents in *Jane Austen: A Family Record* and collection of facts amassed during a lifetime's research presented in *A Chronology of Jane Austen* not only provide a fount of factual information but attest, by their very existence, to the fascination with every facet of Jane Austen's life entertained by large numbers of readers. My other debt is to the incomparable knowledge of fellow-writer Hazel Jones, co-author with me of *Celebrating Pride and Prejudice* and author of *Jane Austen and Marriage* and *Jane Austen's Journeys,* for almost daily emails and regular coffee-shop meetings to discuss our favourite topic. I am grateful to Hazel's husband, David Brandreth, for helping me with technology. My own husband, John Jameson, kindly read the typescript with fresh eyes. At Robert Hale, Gill Jackson and Nikki Edwards have been a pleasure to work with. Beyond these, I am privileged to share my passion with hundreds of friends and colleagues in the Jane Austen Societies of the UK, North America, and Australia. The conferences of these organizations offer a combination of good fellowship and intellectual stimulation that is hard to beat. To ponder and constantly to re-read Jane Austen are for many people among life's keenest and most enduring pleasures. In that other sense, then, we may all happily grow older with Jane Austen.

A note on setting: quotations are set in single quotation marks with double within. When characters' speech is quoted without surrounding matter, double quotation marks have been used.

1. THE LOSS OF YOUTH AND BEAUTY

"When a woman has five grown up daughters, she ought to give over thinking of her own beauty", says Mrs Bennet, in the first, highly comical chapter of *Pride and Prejudice.* To which her husband replies, with more wit than gallantry, "In such cases, a woman has not often much beauty to think of."

Beauty of the kind which nature designs in order to attract a mate and continue the species was not unnaturally regarded as the preserve of the very young: certainly that aspect of beauty which Austen terms 'bloom' and which we might characterize as a healthy, glowing skin free from blemishes and wrinkles. In an age with little medical understanding or treatment, health was a fragile commodity, so where it was abundantly present it was noticed and admired. Mrs Weston describes the essential intertwining of health and beauty in her praise of 21-year-old Emma: "There is health, not merely in her bloom, but in her air, her head, her glance. One hears sometimes of a child being 'the picture of health'; now Emma always gives me the idea of being the complete picture of grown-up health."[1]

In the labouring classes bloom must have been fleeting, soon lost through physical drudgery, insanitary living conditions and poor diet. But even in the leisured classes, premature loss of bloom might occur in women if they happened to be afflicted with sickness or suffering.

Two of Austen's heroines fall into that category, although as it happens, both recover their attractiveness when mental anguish is removed. One loses her bloom during the events of the story (Marianne Dashwood of *Sense and Sensibility*); one has already lost hers before the novel begins (Anne Elliot of *Persuasion*).

In the first chapter of that novel we read, 'A few years before, Anne Elliot had been a very pretty girl, but her bloom had vanished early.' Persuaded at nineteen to give up the man she loves, Anne is destined to spend her early twenties in a depressed state of mind. 'Her attachment and regrets had, for a long time, clouded every enjoyment of youth, and an early loss of bloom and spirits had been their lasting effect.' With her slender figure, delicate features and mild dark eyes, she has every beauty except bloom; but still this is not enough for her acquaintance generally to regard her, at twenty-seven, as among the marriageable contingent of any party (they accept that she plays the piano rather than joining the young people in dancing). Meeting her again after eight years, her ex-lover remarks to a third person that she is so changed, he would not have known her again. Anne seems to find it understandable that despite the fact that he too is eight years older, his romantic interest now focuses on a pair of sisters nineteen and twenty years old, the age she was when she first caught his eye.

The other heroine whose looks seem prematurely destroyed by suffering is Marianne Dashwood. She is only seventeen, and begins her story with a healthy brown skin and sparkling eyes. But after wilfully depriving herself of sleep and food for many weeks in her heartbreak over Willoughby, she is sadly altered. John Dashwood notices that "she looks very unwell, has lost her colour, and is grown quite thin". His thoughts turn immediately to how this will affect his sister's value on the marriage market, telling Elinor:

> "At her time of life, anything of an illness destroys the bloom for ever! Hers has been a very short one! She was as handsome a girl last September, as any I ever saw; and as likely to attract the men. There was something in her style of beauty, to please them particularly. I remember Fanny used to say that she would

> marry sooner and better than you did. . . . She will be mistaken, however. I question whether Marianne *now,* will marry a man worth more than five or six hundred a year, at the utmost, and I am very much deceived if *you* do not do better."

John confides in Colonel Brandon: "There is something very trying to a young woman who *has been* a beauty, in the loss of her personal attractions. You would not think it perhaps, but Marianne *was* remarkably handsome a few months ago; quite as handsome as Elinor – Now you see it is all gone." As it happens, Brandon is not put off by 'the hollow eye, the sickly skin, the posture of reclining weakness' in the invalid. In fact they seem to add to Marianne's attractions in his eyes, as he has seen them all before in his earlier love, his cousin Eliza who, as a divorced and seduced mother of an illegitimate daughter, is discovered by Brandon confined in a debtor's 'sponging-house'. Though this discovery (which was shortly followed by her death from consumption, or TB) happened fourteen years before the main action of *Sense and Sensibility,* Brandon vividly describes Eliza's appearance to Elinor: "So altered – so faded – worn down by acute suffering of every kind! Hardly could I believe the melancholy and sickly figure before me, to be the remains of the lovely, blooming, healthful girl, on whom I had once doted." Ill treatment by a sequence of men – her guardian, her husband, her seducers – and want of money, have destroyed her looks and health.

But unlike Eliza, Marianne is not a 'fallen woman' with the prospect of her death being Brandon's 'greatest comfort'. *Sense and Sensibility* is a comedy, with the stories of Eliza and her daughter kept firmly in the background. Marianne has not only 'youth [and] natural strength' to help her recover, but a reformed mental attitude which, the author insists, is as important as the love and support of her family and Colonel Brandon in restoring her to health. In other words her health, and therefore her beauty, are under her own control.

Anne Elliot too is blest with 'a second spring of youth and

beauty'. The sea breezes at Lyme restore bloom to her cheeks, a stranger on the beach looks at her with admiration, and Captain Wentworth's interest is piqued. (The sea has a contrary effect on others. Mary Crawford, who is no lover of nature, warns Fanny Price, "Do not stay at Portsmouth to lose your pretty looks. Those vile sea-breezes are the ruin of beauty and health."[2])

Secure again in the love of Captain Wentworth, Anne ends the book 'glowing and lovely in sensibility and happiness, and more generally admired than she thought about or cared for'. All she does care for are the declarations of Captain Wentworth, deceiving himself or forgetting his earlier comments, that he cannot see any alteration in her. Austen observes, 'It is something for a woman to be assured, in her eight-and-twentieth year, that she has not lost one charm of earlier youth.' Wentworth has not exactly said this, but his passionate as well as rational preference for Anne over every other woman is felt by the reader. They will go on loving each other even as they age. Anne has the wisdom to feel glad that Wentworth is charmed by her looks *because* he values her character rather than the other way round.

Jane Austen knew that men were too often bedazzled by the looks of extreme youth, and was correspondingly pleased to report to Cassandra, in a letter of 30 November 1800, that a young man of their acquaintance seemed to have chosen his future wife more wisely: 'She is now seven or eight & twenty, & tho' still handsome less handsome than she has been. – This promises better, than the bloom of seventeen.'

In Austen's novels as in life, men rely all too often on their eyes rather than their brains in choosing a wife. Mr Bennet is an example of a man who has found himself married to a shallow, self-centred, irritating woman, precisely because, twenty-three years earlier, he had been 'captivated by youth and beauty, and the appearance of good humour that youth and beauty generally give'. Mr Palmer, in *Sense and Sensibility,* soon finds 'like many others of his sex, that through some unaccountable bias in favour of beauty, he was the husband of a very silly woman'; while surely it is only the possession of beauty which enables Miss Maria Ward of Huntingdon to captivate Sir Thomas Bertram of Mansfield Park, since her social status, fortune, intellect and character are all inferior to his. It is hard to imagine that Sir Thomas derives much comfort from his marriage, though certainly his wife is less contemptible than Mrs Bennet, and a shade less silly than Mrs Palmer. But as Elinor Dashwood reflects of the Palmers' match, 'this kind of blunder was too common for any sensible man to be lastingly hurt by it'.

Though loss of youth could comprise other losses – health, strength, innocence, hopefulness and the sense of boundless opportunity perhaps – it was the loss of beauty which made such a difference to women's destiny, because it was the key to obtaining a husband, a home, a family and a role in life. Although it is true that 'there certainly are not so many men of large fortune in the world as there are pretty women to deserve them',[3] a beautiful woman in Jane Austen's world will have more choice over her destiny than a plain one, and much more than an old one. Destiny comprises worldly as well as personal circumstances. A man cannot choose his financial and social level – he must inherit them by chance, or earn them by his own effort. But as Edmund Bertram says to the lady herself, "Miss Crawford may choose her degree of wealth. She has only to fix on her number of thousands a year, and there can be no doubt of their coming." He means that she is pretty enough to have a choice of husbands.

As Emma declares to Mr Knightley, "till it appears that men are much more philosophic on the subject of beauty than they are generally supposed, till they do fall in love with well-informed minds instead of handsome faces", a girl with such loveliness as plump, fair-haired little Harriet will be admired and sought after, and need not accept the first proposal that comes her way. She can pick and choose. Would she rather be the wife of a farmer, or the wife of a clergyman – or of any other gentleman who comes her way? Emma thinks she has the choice. Mr Knightley begs to differ. He considers that no man of sense or family will choose Harriet, and that once she has lost her looks, there will be nothing left to recommend her. She will find herself growing older and, because she is the sort of girl who will marry somebody or other, will, in his vivid word-picture, be "glad to catch at the old writing-master's son".

The Years of Danger

An almost exact contemporary of Jane Austen whose looks were affected by long-term ill health was Marianne Bridges, sister-in-law of Jane's brother Edward. On a visit to Kent in 1805, Jane was taken upstairs to see the 31-year-old Marianne, who had partially recovered from a long illness but was not well enough to dine with the family. In one of the letters which the Austen sisters regularly exchanged when apart, Jane reported to Cassandra:

> She is, of course, altered since we saw her in October, 1794. Eleven years could not pass away even in health without making some change, but in her case it is wonderful that the change should be so little. I have not seen her to advantage, as I understand she has frequently a nice colour, and her complexion has not yet recovered from the effects of her late illness. Her face is grown longer and thinner, and her features more marked.[4]

Suffering had not made her querulous: 'She is very pleasant, cheerful, and interested in everything about her, and at the same time shows a thoughtful, considerate, and decided turn of mind', added Jane. Marianne Bridges was to live only another six years.

Even when nothing occurred to cause a woman to lose her bloom prematurely, eventually every woman, however fortunate and pampered, must begin to show the passage of years and the effect of the weather on unprotected skin. Without effective creams and cosmetics, it happened earlier then than now and was much less easy to conceal. It was something that every woman, the plain and the beautiful alike, had to come to terms with after a brief enough youth.

In April 1811 Cassandra Austen told Jane that she had heard her described by an acquaintance as 'a pleasing looking young woman'. Jane was thirty-five. She wrote back wryly, '"A pleasing looking young woman" – that must do; one cannot pretend to anything better now – thankful to have it continued a few years longer!'[5]

In this same year was published a book entitled *The Mirror of the Graces*, by 'A Lady of Distinction'. It is not known whether Austen read it, but she did read widely among conduct literature, and the subject was one that could hardly fail to interest any woman, whether they looked for instruction or (unintentional) humour. The book is chiefly concerned with how young women should conduct themselves in all matters of appearance, such as deportment, fashion, dress, health and beauty. But it does have something to say about later life – albeit in high-flown language that would surely have made Jane Austen laugh.

At the age of thirty, the writer suggests, a woman 'lays aside the flowers of youth, and arrays herself in the majesty of sobriety, or in the grandeur of simple magnificence'. This period may last until she is fifty:

> But at that period, when she has numbered half a century, then it becomes her to throw aside [ornament] and gracefully acknowledging her entrance into the vale of years, to wrap herself in her mantle of grey, and move gently down till she passes through its extremest bourn to the mansions of immortality. . . .
>
> It has been most wisely said (and it would be well if the waning queens of beauty would adopt the reflection), that there is a *time for everything!* We may add, that there is a time to be young, a time to be old; a time to be loved, a time to be revered; a time to seek life, a time to be ready to lay it down.
>
> She who best knows how to fashion herself to these

> inevitable changes is the only truly, lastingly fair. Her beauty is in the mind, and shown in action; and when men cease to admire the woman, they do better, they revere the saint.[6]

Jane Austen herself was fortunate perhaps in that, though slender of figure, she had plump, round cheeks with a high colour (giving, as many remarked, a doll-like appearance) which aged comparatively well. 'Lady B. found me handsomer than she expected, so you see I am not so very bad as you might think for', she remarked humorously to Cassandra in November 1813.[7] Caroline Austen, who was not born until her aunt Jane was thirty, recalled that hers was the first face she remembered thinking pretty: 'Her face was rather round than long – she had a bright, but not a pink colour – a clear brown complexion and very good hazle [sic] eyes.'[8] Another woman, Charlotte Maria Beckford, who, as a child, had known Jane Austen in her thirties, wrote long afterwards: 'I remember her as a tall thin *spare* person, with very high cheek bones great colour – sparkling Eyes not large but joyous and intelligent.'[9]

Besides the complexion being subject to the ravages of time, dulling, greying hair showed a woman's loss of youth. When it no longer formed an attractive feature, hair was hidden away in a cap. Jane and Cassandra Austen themselves were thought to have adopted this custom earlier than they needed to do – signalling, perhaps, a mutually agreed and entirely comfortable withdrawal from the marriage market. Caroline Austen remembered:

> Her hair, a darkish brown, curled naturally – it was in short curls round her face. . . . She always wore a cap. Such was the custom with ladies who were not quite young – at least of a morning, but I never saw her without one, to the best of my remembrance, either morning or evening. I believe my two Aunts were not accounted very good dressers, and were thought to have taken to the garb of middle age unnecessarily soon – but they were particularly neat, and held all untidy ways in great disesteem.[10]

In September 1813, however, approaching the age of thirty-eight, staying with her brother Henry in London, Jane was persuaded to abandon her cap for an evening at the theatre. A hairdresser, Mr Hall, came to arrange the hair of all the ladies in residence: 'Mr Hall was very punctual yesterday & curled me out at a great rate. I thought it looked hideous, and longed for a snug cap instead, but my companions silenced me by their admiration. I had only a bit of velvet round my head.'[11] In fact Jane seems to have kept her hair colour to the end; a lock of hair taken from her after death is brown. In this she took after her mother, whose hair, in the recollection of a granddaughter, 'was dark, & to a very late period of her life, retained its colour'.[12]

The earlier fashion for hair powder had at least made grey hair acceptable, and most older women had cause to regret when it went out in favour of natural, glossy tresses. Not only that, but the Empire-line dresses and flimsy muslins of the Regency were far better suited to the slender forms of youth than to mature curves, which had benefited from the stiff, elaborate gowns of the eighteenth century. The sophisticated older woman, with her recourse to powder and paint, had done very well in modish London and Paris, but her day was over, seen off by the revolutionary ideas sweeping Europe. Clothes, hair and complexion had now to be as natural-looking as possible. Artifice was out. Austen was an adult at a time when the fashionable look favoured the young, which made growing older even more problematical.

Elizabeth Elliot, in *Persuasion,* keeps her looks longer than most, but even she feels concerned as she approaches the age of thirty. 'It sometimes happens,' writes Austen, 'that a woman is handsomer at twenty-nine than she was ten years before; and generally speaking, if there has been neither ill-health nor anxiety, it is a time of life at which scarcely any charm is lost. It was so with Elizabeth, still the same handsome Miss Elliot that she had begun to be thirteen years before.'

Elizabeth has enjoyed all the social deference and domestic power she could desire, but her youth has slipped away and she is uncomfortably, albeit unreflectively, aware of the fact. 'She had the consciousness of being nine-and-twenty to give her some regrets and some apprehensions; she was fully satisfied of being still quite as handsome as ever, but she felt her approach to the years of danger, and would have rejoiced to be certain of being properly solicited by baronet-blood within the next twelvemonth or two.'

The word 'handsome' is used three times in the two paragraphs describing Elizabeth's state at twenty-nine. It suits someone who is poised and privileged, someone expensively dressed and accustomed to leading the way, better than the more girlish, more feminine 'pretty'. *Pride and Prejudice's* Lady Catherine de Bourgh, the sort of woman Elizabeth Elliot may well grow into, has 'features which might once have been handsome'. 'Handsome' is also the first adjective applied to another socially confident young woman, the eponymous heroine of *Emma*. Like Elizabeth Elliot, Emma Woodhouse is a snob, but one capable of reforming herself. Perhaps the altogether wider capacities of Emma's personality are signalled by the fact that at various points in the narrative she is described as 'handsome' by the narrator, "beautiful" by Mrs Weston and "pretty" by Mr Knightley.

We are told in *Persuasion* that no woman could think more about her looks than Elizabeth's father, Sir Walter Elliot thought about his: 'He had been remarkably handsome in his youth; and at fifty-four, was still a very fine man.' Not only self-satisfied with regard to his own looks, he judges all around him in terms of their appearance, and specifically on how well they are ageing. Of his three daughters, he admires the looks only of Elizabeth, in whom he sees a reflection of himself. Observing that Elizabeth is still a handsome woman:

> Sir Walter might be excused, therefore, in forgetting her age, or, at least, be deemed only half a fool, for thinking himself and Elizabeth as blooming as ever, amidst the wreck of the good looks of everybody else; for he could plainly see how old all the rest of his family and acquaintance were growing.

> Anne haggard, Mary coarse, every face in the neighbourhood worsting, and the rapid increase of the crow's foot about Lady Russell's temples had long been a distress to him.

Lady Russell has the distinction of being the only woman in any Austen novel whose wrinkles are noticed, though they must have been possessed by many. Much later in the novel, when they are all living in Bath, Sir Walter remarks that "morning visits are never fair by women at her time of life, who make themselves up so little. If she would only wear rouge, she would not be afraid of being seen" in broad daylight. Lady Russell's age is unspecified, but as she was a friend of Lady Elliot, she is very likely in her fifties – and she has far too much sense to fret about what is not important. In the same novel, Mrs Croft, wife of Admiral Croft, is another older woman too comfortable in herself and in her marriage to bother about what cannot be helped: 'She had bright dark eyes, good teeth, and altogether an agreeable face; though her reddened and weather-beaten complexion, the consequence of her having been almost as much at sea as her husband, made her seem to have lived some years longer in the world than her real eight-and-thirty.' Her husband fondly recollects that even before he met her, he had heard her spoken of as "a very pretty girl", but Mrs Croft wastes no time mourning her youthful prettiness. Her complexion has been sacrificed to the enjoyment of being in her husband's company.

In *Emma,* Mrs Weston is another married woman of about the same age, and pleasing appearance, but we are left to guess what she might look like. She has attracted a good offer of marriage despite her age (she has been Emma's governess for sixteen years, so must be in her late thirties, though not much older, as she is able to bear a child) and she is the subject of this exchange between her new stepson and Emma:

> "Elegant, agreeable manners, I was prepared for," said he; "but I confess that, considering everything, I had not expected more

than a very tolerably well-looking woman of a certain age; I did not know that I was to find a pretty young woman in Mrs Weston."

"You cannot see too much perfection in Mrs Weston for my feelings," said Emma; "were you to guess her to be *eighteen,* I should listen with pleasure; but *she* would be ready to quarrel with you for using such words. Don't let her imagine that you have spoken of her as a pretty young woman."

Even modest Mrs Weston would surely be secretly gratified by such praise, but Emma's point is that she is too sensible a woman to wish to be judged by her looks, and also that she would find discussion of them improper. Mrs Weston's sense of self-worth is not dependent on her appearance, or on male reaction to it.

Mrs Croft and Mrs Weston, then, are two women of similar age to their author at the time of writing, who are both pleasing to look at, but both unconcerned with their looks – unlike Mrs Bennet, or indeed Lady Bertram, who cannot forget that they have once been beauties. When Mr Bennet teases his wife by saying, "as you are as handsome as any of them [their daughters] Mr Bingley might like you the best of the party", she takes him seriously, and fishes for more compliments, replying "My dear, you flatter me. I certainly *have* had my share of beauty, but I do not pretend to be anything extraordinary now."[13]

There is a tinge of insecurity in this but Lady Bertram, whose husband never teases and never criticizes, is left with her self-satisfaction intact. Aware that the status and domestic comforts she enjoys are a reward for having been beautiful, one of the few emotions she shows in the novel is feeling aggrieved that any plainer woman should prosper: 'she felt all the injuries of beauty in Mrs Grant's being so well settled in life without being handsome'. When Henry Crawford makes his proposals to Fanny, it raises the eighteen-year-old in her aunt's estimation, by 'convincing her that Fanny *was* very pretty, which she had been doubting about before . . . it made her feel a sort of credit in calling her niece'.[14]

Some mothers might feel wistful or even pained when their daughters grow up to usurp their own claims to beauty, as the rising generation usually must. Not Lady Bertram. When her daughters are first established 'among the belles of the neighbourhood' she fails to accompany them to the season's parties and balls even though she might have enjoyed 'a mother's gratification in witnessing their success'. But her refusal is the result not of jealousy, but of indolence. Either pleased to see her beauty replicated or, more likely, unable to perceive any alteration in herself, she remarks "Humph! We certainly are a handsome family."

The Business of Mothering

Since her marriage, Lady Bertram has been indulged and coddled, never having to lift a finger for herself. It is true (though hard to imagine) that she has conceived, carried and given birth to four children (before, in all probability, calling a halt to all fatiguing nonsense of that kind) but for the last twenty years she has had nothing to do but to sit on a sofa with a piece of needlework in her hands, while her sister, husband, niece and servants do everything else. Every comfort that money can buy is hers to command. Such sloth and luxury are a great preservative of beauty, especially in an era when any resultant plumpness would be admired as an indicator of status and wealth.

Lady Bertram is in complete contrast to her sister, Mrs Price, who has 'such a superfluity of children, and such a want of almost everything else', and whose Portsmouth home is 'the scene of mismanagement and discomfort from beginning to end'. When Fanny first sees her mother again after eight years, she is pleased to notice her resemblance to Lady Bertram: 'features which Fanny loved the more because they brought her aunt Bertram's before her'. This first impression does not last, and as she observes more, Fanny develops a mixture of pity and contempt for her mother, who has no aptitude for managing a very large family on a very small income. Only on a Sunday, when the whole family walk out in 'their cleanest skins and best attire', can Fanny take any comfort in her mother's appearance:

> Her poor mother now did not look so very unworthy of being Lady Bertram's sister as she was but too apt to look. It often grieved her to the heart to think of the contrast between them – to think that where nature had made so little difference, circumstance should have made so much, and that her mother, as handsome as Lady Bertram and some years her junior, should have an appearance so much more worn and faded, so comfortless, so slatternly, so shabby.

Mary Musgrove, of *Persuasion,* is a young mother whose looks are deteriorating fast. Though the youngest of the three Elliot sisters, she is the only one with children – so far, just two, though a large family might reasonably be predicted for her, however ill-suited to motherhood she may be. Neither her health nor her spirits are particularly good (though many of her complaints are imaginary) and she has never been a beauty: 'In person, she was inferior to both sisters and had, even in her bloom, only reached the dignity of being "a fine girl"'. So Mary's bloom is something of the past, yet she is only twenty-three. Twice her father refers to Mary's appearance as "coarse". The now 'faded sofa' and 'shabby' condition of the elegant furniture with which she embarked on married life four years ago are emblematic of her own loss of youth, and pick up on the same adjectives used of the much older Mrs Price. Unlike her sister Anne, there is no chance of her being blest with a second spring of youth and beauty. She lacks the emotional intelligence and generosity of spirit which give radiance to Anne's face.

During the last three years of her life, Jane Austen corresponded with her motherless niece, Fanny Knight, who sought her advice on her various suitors. Having wavered and discouraged at least two young men Fanny, at the age of twenty-four, felt some anxiety and regret, especially as she saw friends marry and start their families. Responding to the expression of these feelings on 13 March 1817, her aunt assures her that the right man will come along within the next two or three years, 'And then, by not beginning the business of Mothering quite so early in life, you will be young in Constitution, spirits, figure & countenance, while Mrs Wm Hammond [friend and contemporary of Fanny] is growing old by confinements & nursing.'

Another young woman whom Jane Austen feared would be worn out by constant childbirth and breastfeeding was Anna Austen, Fanny's cousin and exact contemporary, now Mrs Lefroy and already mother of two little girls. In the same letter to Fanny, Austen writes, 'Anna has a bad cold, looks pale, & we fear something else. She has just weaned Julia.' In her next letter she elaborates, with some impatience, 'Poor Animal, she will be worn out before she is thirty. – I am very sorry for her. – Mrs Clement too is in that way again. I am quite tired of so many children. – Mrs Benn has a 13th.' On this occasion her fears for Anna were unfounded, though she did go on to have seven children, at eighteen-month intervals, before the early death of her husband. Fanny herself married a widower with six children and, after five years of childless marriage (and who can know whether this was by contrivance or chance, whether the delayed appearance of a second brood was welcome or lamented) proceeded to give birth to seven children of her own between the ages of thirty-two and forty-four.

Jane's mother, Mrs Austen, had, rather shockingly, lost several front teeth by the time she was fifty which, according to her niece Philadelphia, 'makes her look old'[15]. This too might have been one of the tolls which the continuous alternation of pregnancy and nursing took on the female body, as calcium was directed to the foetus and infant; or it may have been a symptom of vitamin C deficiency, in an age when fresh fruit and vegetables were confined to such short seasons, and before potatoes became a staple of the British diet. One of the symptoms of mild scurvy is diseased gums and therefore loosened teeth. Whatever the cause – and it is unlikely to have been a surfeit of that expensive commodity, sugar – the effect was tremendously ageing. In later life Cassandra too lost some of her teeth, despite having borne no child. Her very elderly aunt Mrs Leigh Perrot complained that a combination of her own deafness and Cassandra's poor articulation as a consequence of missing teeth, made it too difficult to converse with her.[16] (By dying young, Jane escaped this particular horror.) Austen mentions the daughters of her most wealthy brother visiting a dentist when in London but, for the majority of not very rich country dwellers, competent dentistry, another of our modern beautifiers, was unknown.

Among the gentry classes, adding any kind of colour to the face was regarded as immoral, and it is another mark against Sir Walter Elliot that he thinks older women should hide behind rouge, rather than appearing as God made them. The white lead complexion paint, the rouge, black patches and powdered hair of the Georgian age had, as we have seen, given way to the natural look, which was to prevail until the end of the Victorian era. But 'painting' had in any case been confined to the fashionable upper classes, together with prostitutes and actresses (for so long, almost the same thing). In Fanny Burney's 1778 novel *Evelina*, the hero admires the heroine for her unpainted face: "The difference of natural and artificial colour, seems to me very easily discerned; that of Nature, is mottled, and varying; that of art, set and too smooth". It hardly needs to be said that eighteenth-century cosmetics were made of noxious materials, and hastened many a vain and foolish young woman's demise.

In her letters, Austen's only remark on the subject is, as we might expect, a joke – at the expense of a woman who was both aristocratic and vulgar. The Austens' Southampton lodgings were rented from Lord Lansdowne, whose home was the nearby Castle, and who had two years earlier married his middle-aged mistress, a widow with several daughters. The Austens received permission to make some alterations to the furniture, as Jane informed Cassandra, from 'Mr Husket Lord Lansdowne's Painter – domestic painter I sh^{d} call him, for he lives in the Castle – Domestic

Chaplains have given way to this more necessary office, & I suppose whenever the Walls want no touching up, he is employed about my Lady's face'.[17] (What a joy her letters must have been to receive!)

Four years later, the Marchioness was described by Lady Bessborough as a 'fat vulgar Irish woman near fifty'.[18] Jane must often have seen her in the neighbourhood, with her train of daughters, or driving ostentatiously in her phaeton, and known that her joke was all too apt. Lady Lansdowne was a relic of an earlier age.

This is not to say that respectable country gentlewomen, who would not have dreamt of 'painting', did not concoct their own home aids to beauty as best they could. Some turned to books such as *The Mirror of the Graces* which contained suggestions for 'A Paste for the Skin . . . recommended in cases when the skin seems to get too loosely attached to the muscles' (or in other words, as it ages) made of boiled egg whites and alum (hydrated double sulphate of aluminium and potassium); and 'A Wash to give Lustre to the Face' consisting this time of egg *yolks*, mixed with wheat bran and white wine vinegar. Women might collect recipes from friends and neighbours and write them down in a book. Martha Lloyd, who lived with the Austen women at Chawton, did exactly that. Her book combines cookery, home remedies for ailments and beauty improvements, including a recipe for Cold Cream, which had been contributed by Lady Bridges, mother-in-law to Edward Knight:

> 45 grains of white wax, 1½ drams of Spermacety, 2 ozs of oil of Sweet Almonds, mix't well together and beat up with rose water to a fine cream.

To make a salve for the hands, Martha has a recipe calling for:

> one lb of beef suet, ½ lb mutton ditto; ½ lb of wax. Melt them repeatedly, put them together when nearly cold, with an oz of essence (sweet smelling), pour into four moulds when almost

cold. The suet when melted must be laid in cold water for a week, changing it every day.

And finally for the teeth: '1 oz each of prepared coral powder'd and cuttle fish bone powder'd, three drachms Rose Pink and 2 drachms Cassia Bark, put all together in a mortar'.[19]

Martha's own sister Mary, who had married James Austen as his second wife, had her complexion marred irrevocably by smallpox, but nothing in Martha's collection could help with that. 'Was it not for the smallpox which has scarred and seamed her face dreadfully, her countenance would be pleasing',[20] wrote a neighbour on meeting Mary on her round of bridal visits (and what a daunting custom that was, to be inspected by the neighbours of one's new husband). Mary was twenty-six when she accepted James Austen, a widower with one child (whom Mary resented) and with her disfigurement she must have been as glad and perhaps as surprised as Charlotte Lucas to secure a comfortable home and a husband, even one who she knew had been in love with several women before herself – not only his first wife, but other women both before and after his first marriage (hankered after, it must be said, mainly at a distance: James was no philanderer, but he *was* a sentimental lover). James's cousin Eliza, who had refused his offer of marriage before he turned to Mary, described her rather patronizingly as, 'not either rich or handsome, but very sensible & good humoured'.[21] For her part, Mary could never bear to be near pretty, charming Eliza. If Mary could be difficult and demanding to live with, as Jane's letters and other sources suggest, insecurity about her looks may well account for it.

Even Dr Gowland did not claim to eradicate pockmarks; his lotion, the only commercially produced beautifier mentioned in the novels, was advertised to cure 'Pimples, Tetters, Ringworms, Freckles, Tan, Redness of the Nose, etc.'[22] This gives some idea of the blemishes which a woman might have to contend with, which the patches and paint of the past – and make-up of the future – were so useful in concealing, but which the women of Jane Austen's class and time had to manage without. Gowland's lotion was said to open the pores of the skin and extract 'acrid humours' when applied with a towel once a day for several weeks. In fact it contained mercuric chloride, powerful enough to remove the top layer of skin. It had the reputation of being used to mask the depredations of venereal disease. Its recommendation by the vain snob Sir Walter Elliot is sufficient to mark the author's disapproval. On Anne's return to her father's roof – now a Bath roof – from her invigorating experiences at Lyme and in the country:

> [H]e began to compliment her on her improved looks; he thought her "less thin in her person, in her cheeks; her skin, her complexion, greatly improved – clearer, fresher. Had she been using anything in particular?" "No, nothing." "Merely Gowland", he supposed. "No, nothing at all." "Ha! he was surprised at that"; and added, "certainly you cannot do better than to continue as you are; you cannot be better than well; or I should recommend Gowland, the constant use of Gowland, during the spring months. Mrs Clay has been using it at my recommendation, and you see what it has done for her. You see how it has carried away her freckles."[23]

Anne can see no difference in Mrs Clay's freckles, and takes this as evidence of her father's increasing susceptibility to the scheming widow's wiles.

Such Scarecrows

Persuasion is the only one of the six novels which concerns itself with male loss of beauty, Sir Walter Elliot, in his vanity, being fixated on the subject. Indeed he is more vain of his looks than any of the young women in Austen's novels, a character weakness that both his age and his gender make more risible. That he should still be 'a very fine man' himself is plausibly accounted for by the insinuating Mrs Clay who, describing the effect of the various professions on a man's looks, says:

> "It is only the lot of those who are not obliged to follow any, who can live in a regular way, in the country, choosing their own hours, following their own pursuits, and living on their own property, without the torment of trying for more; it is only *their* lot, I say, to hold the blessings of health and a good appearance to the utmost: I know of no other set of men but what lose something of their personableness when they cease to be quite young."

They are so much more to be envied than those who have to work: "the lawyer plods, quite careworn; the physician is up at all hours, and travelling in all weather; the clergyman . . . is obliged to go into infected rooms, and expose his health and looks to all the injury of a poisonous atmosphere". Sailors "soon lose the look of youth" and "soldiers, on active service, are not at all better off". This speech, pandering to the vanity of Sir Walter, is the longest she makes, her designs on Sir Walter later appearing to stall.

In the city of Bath, Sir Walter finds the looks of both sexes deplorable, possibly because it had become the chosen home of so many widows, shabby-genteel spinsters and retired professional men of modest means. These are not likely to be people particularly concerned with their appearance, or able to do much about it if they were. From a shop window Sir Walter counts eighty-seven women go by "without there being a tolerable face among them".

> There certainly were a multitude of ugly women in Bath; and as for the men! they were infinitely worse. Such scarecrows as the streets were full of! It was evidence how little the women were used to the sight of anything tolerable, by the effect which a man of decent appearance produced. He had never walked anywhere arm in arm with Colonel Wallis (who was a fine military figure, though sandy-haired) without observing that every

> woman's eye was upon him; every woman's eye was sure to be upon Colonel Wallis.

'Modest Sir Walter!' remarks Austen. 'He was not allowed to escape, however. His daughter and Mrs Clay united in hinting that Colonel Wallis's companion might have as good a figure as Colonel Wallis, and certainly was not sandy-haired.'

Sir Walter has two objections to the navy; that it raises men to honours unknown to their fathers, and that exposure to the elements destroys a man's youth and vigour and makes him grow old sooner than any other man. He describes meeting an Admiral Baldwin:

> "the most deplorable looking personage you can imagine, his face the colour of mahogany, rough and rugged to the last degree, all lines and wrinkles, nine grey hairs of a side, and nothing but a dab of powder at top. 'In the name of heaven, who is that old fellow?' said I to a friend of mine who was standing near (Sir Basil Morley). 'Old fellow!' cried Sir Basil, 'it is Admiral Baldwin. What do you take his age to be?' 'Sixty,' said I, 'or perhaps sixty-two.' 'Forty,' replied Sir Basil, 'forty and no more.' Picture to yourselves my amazement; I shall not easily forget Admiral Baldwin. I never saw quite so wretched an example of what a seafaring life can do; but to a degree, I know it is the same with them all: they are all knocked about, and exposed to every climate, and every weather, till they are not fit to be seen. It is a pity they are not knocked on the head at once, before they reach Admiral Baldwin's age."

Captain Wentworth, though some years younger than Admiral Baldwin, has spent many years at sea, but *his* personal attractions, in Anne's view, have by no means lessened: 'the years which had destroyed her youth and bloom had only given him a more glowing, manly, open look'. Nor is Anne the only one who loves to look at him: the two young Miss Musgroves feel an instant 'fever of admiration' for him, their female cousins are admitted to the honour of being in love with him – at a distance – and even Elizabeth Elliot allows that he has presence, and moves around well in her drawing room.

Spending most of his years at sea certainly did not destroy the good looks of Jane Austen's sailor brother Charles. His niece Anna Lefroy remembered him at seventy, a 'tall, erect figure' with 'bright eye & animated countenance', which would have given the impression of a much younger man had it not been for the hair which 'had become of a snowy white'.[24] Uprightness of posture as a man ages is much valued in the novels. In *Northanger Abbey* General Tilney, father of two handsome grown-up sons in Frederick and Henry, is himself still a fine figure of a man, despite being at least in his fifties. As with Colonel Wallis in *Persuasion*, his military training and bearing serve him well.

Austen seldom describes her older male characters because their appearance is not of much significance to anybody. When she does hint at description, it is with a purpose. In *Mansfield Park*, Tom Bertram's observation that Dr Grant is 'a short-neck'd, apoplectic sort of fellow,' likely to eat himself into an early death, not only alleviates Tom's own conscience for the present, but foreshadows events to come. Elizabeth Bennet's 'broad-faced, stuffy uncle Philips, breathing port wine'[25] serves to warn her of what a self-indulgent man may become in older age. Her revulsion is palpable. Likewise, as Emma Woodhouse observes, the stooping shoulders and bulky forms of the middle-aged men in the ballroom of the Crown Inn serve to set off the firm and upright figure of Mr Knightley, aged thirty-six, and to convince her with what grace he would dance if he would only take the trouble (as he soon does, becoming first Harriet's partner and then – at her own request – hers). In both these instances, the heroine is engaged in assessing and admiring a younger man (in Elizabeth's case, George Wickham) by comparing his manly attractions with those around him who are past their prime.

For of course, in men as well as in women, youth and beauty

work their magic and perform nature's function in attracting the opposite sex and continuing the species. "Girls nowadays will always give a handsome young man the preference before any other," laments Mrs Percival in Austen's juvenile fragment *Catharine, or the Bower;* "tho' for why, I never could discover, for what after all is Youth and Beauty? It is but a poor substitute for real worth and Merit." The endeavour of heroines and other young people to navigate between these pairings, to give each their due, is an important driver of the plot in most Austen novels, though the advice of their elders on such points is rarely wanted.

2. MY TIME OF LIFE

The Reverend George Austen always referred to his daughters Cassandra and Jane as 'the girls', even when they were grown women.[1] But to their nieces and nephews, as Jane herself once joked, they could seem 'the formidables'.[2] It was all relative. Long after Jane's death, Cassandra at the age of about seventy made an impression on a great-niece who recalled her as 'a pale, dark-eyed lady with a high arched nose and kind smile, dressed in a long cloak and a large drawn bonnet, both made of black satin. She looked to me quite different from anybody I had ever seen.'[3] In fact with that nose, those clothes and – as we have seen – some loss of teeth, the elderly Cassandra might have appeared quite witchlike, had it not been for the kind smile.

Over the years, other members of the Austen family reflected on their own ageing process. 'I suppose as I grow old, I grow dull & stupid', was how lifelong poet James Austen, already an ailing man at fifty-three, chose to account for his failure to write 'a long Poem, or any Poem upon Autumn' in 1818.[4] His aunt Mrs Leigh Perrot, who lived to be ninety-two, wrote slightly threateningly during the year before her death of not changing her will 'unless in my dotage', which she evidently did not think was yet upon her.[5]

Jane Austen of course did not 'live to be an old woman', to quote from one of her last letters, but on 30 November 1814, a fortnight before her thirty-ninth birthday, she wrote in connection with some social arrangements, 'tho' I like Miss H.M. as much as one can at my time of Life after a day's acquaintance, it is uphill work to be talking to those whom one knows so little'. In using the phrase 'my time of Life' Austen signals an awareness of the ageing process within herself, in this case less inclination to bother with new people. Her novels are replete with references to her characters' perceptions of age in themselves and in others, their awareness of the passage of time, of memory and change.

Age plays a large part in how we perceive ourselves and others, even today. We are younger or older than other people; we marvel at our own advancing years, incredulous that we can no longer lay claim to the youth that once seemed ours by right; we practise denial, or in some cases reach an age where we begin to boast of it, rather than feel ashamed of or resigned to it. In a fictional world such as that created by Jane Austen, every character belongs to an age group, which becomes part of what defines them, as we rarely see them as their other selves. They are created in their prime, or middle-aged, or elderly, and that is how we experience and remember them. The action of an Austen novel typically occupies about a year, giving scope for little outward change (though minds can and do develop). However, *Persuasion* has its famous retrospective of eight years earlier, and both *Mansfield Park* and *Emma* take slight backward and forward glances into other periods of their characters' lives. That these three novels belong to Austen's second period of writing is telling, her sensitivity to the passage of time increasing as she aged.

'Evening of life' and 'November of life' are rather similar expressions taken from two of the novels where they are used to prefigure the old age of women who are presently very young, but from whom – as from everybody – youth must depart. In *Emma,* Harriet Smith's collection of riddles is said to be 'the only mental provision she was making for the evening of life'. In *Persuasion,* Anne Elliot overhears Captain Wentworth, with 'serious warmth', addressing his companion on a country walk: 'If Louisa Musgrove would be beautiful and happy in her November of life, she will cherish all her present powers of mind.'

The last hours of the day and the last months of the year are of course common metaphors for the last stage of human life. These are references to the future, made (in one case ironically by the narrator and in the other with misplaced fervour by a man who fancies himself in love) about intellectually limited young women whose future lives, in fact, are unlikely to provide much mental solace to counteract physical decline. In both instances what is shown is an awareness of passing time, an acknowledgement that to live a satisfying full lifespan, the charm and freshness of youth need to be supplemented and then succeeded by something deeper. That a faulty hero understands this as well as the narrator marks him as profoundly thoughtful even while misunderstanding his own feelings of the moment.

Two characters anticipate and plan for their own later years, though in both cases life turns out very differently. Emma Woodhouse smugly looks forward to being 'forty or fifty', still living in her childhood home, unmarried, a fond aunt, and varying her life from what it is now only by taking to carpet-work and giving up music, drawing less and reading more. With greater energy and unselfishness, William Price foresees distributing among his family the prize money he hopes to gain in his career at sea, 'with only the reservation of enough to make the little cottage comfortable in which he and Fanny were to pass all their middle and later life together'.[6] This will be unnecessary, as life takes a different turn. William will have to look for a wife to share his cottage, as Fanny becomes the mistress of Mansfield Parsonage. As the narrator remarks drily, Sir Thomas's pleasure in this turn of affairs 'formed just such a contrast with his early opinion on the subject . . . as time is forever producing between the plans and decisions of mortals for their own instruction and their neighbours' entertainment'.

Many other characters have already reached or are approaching their evening of life, and to them, as to Austen herself, it is now referred to as 'my time of life'. When Lady Russell is indulging in daydreams of an alliance between the heir to Kellynch, Mr Elliot, and her god-daughter Anne, in the fullness of her heart she exclaims that, were such a union to come to pass, "My dearest

Anne, it would give me more delight than is often felt at my time of life!"[7] The exclamation mark itself is uncharacteristic of the speech of this woman 'of steady age and character' who is, as she herself says, "steady and matter of fact" in her general pronouncements and who boasts, even as she projects this match, of being no matchmaker.

As a middle-aged woman, Lady Russell is fixed in her world view, not expecting to be ambushed by any great change, either of opinion or of circumstance. She has her life organized to her liking, and feels qualified by considerable experience of the world to judge for herself, and to give others the benefit of her judgement. The middle-agedness of Lady Russell is conveyed not only by 'the rapid increase of the crow's foot' about her temples, so distressing to Sir Walter and, seemingly, of so little concern to herself, but by the rigidity of her opinions and deliberation of her speech. At the same time, her active social life, her financial acumen and her mobility – she has her own carriage, and travels to Bath for part of every year – mark her out as not yet elderly. She is in fact in the prime of her life and, while she continues to relish life's pleasures, will remain so, despite Elizabeth Elliot's scorn for the way she sits so upright at a concert, looks so formal and has, to the fashionable younger woman, a hideous taste in dress – all external indications of her belonging to the older generation.

'The father and mother were in the old English style, and the young people in the new.' This description of the Musgrove family comes from the same novel, and is reflected in changes wrought in their home, the Great House at Uppercross, with its 'old-fashioned square parlour, with a small carpet and shining floor, to which the present daughters of the house were gradually giving the proper air of confusion by a grand piano-forte and a harp, flower-stands and little tables placed in every direction.' Formality of every kind is the hallmark of the old. In the next novel that Austen began, the unfinished *Sanditon,* the heroine closely observes the conduct of Lady Denham towards her dependent young companion Clara Brereton, but 'could see nothing worse in Lady Denham than the sort of old-fashioned formality of always calling her *Miss Clara*'.

With the lightest of touches, Jane Austen grounds her characters in the age range they inhabit. Small details of clothes, hair or deportment, or more frequently and consistently of speech, outlook and habit, help us perceive her older characters to be middle-aged or elderly. We experience them as older people, acting and speaking in ways that distinguish them – yet without exaggerated effect – from the youthful cohort whose foils they are. In fact, from infancy to senescence, her characters act in age, while not sacrificing individuality.

Beyond the marriageable characters, whose ages are usually known to us, only rarely is a specific age ascribed to an individual. When Austen gives a precise age to a character, she does so not just for the better information of her readers. There is always some good narrative reason. Mrs Dashwood is "hardly forty"[8] according to her step-daughter-in-law, who is reluctant to allow her an annuity in case she should live another fifteen years or more, in which case she and her husband will be worse off than parting with a lump sum. (In the end they give her neither.) Mrs Dashwood herself mentions her age when Marianne is expostulating about Colonel Brandon – who is 'the wrong side of thirty-five' – suffering from rheumatism, which Marianne considers "the commonest infirmity of declining life". Mrs Dashwood 'could not think a man five years younger than herself, so exceedingly ancient as he appeared to the youthful fancy of her daughter'. The absurdity of Marianne's ideas about age are gently mocked: '"My dearest child," said her mother, laughing, "at this rate you must be in continual terror of *my* decay; and it must seem to you a miracle that my life has been extended to the advanced age of forty."' Nevertheless, at the end of the novel when Mrs Dashwood is contemplating, with happiness, the possible marriage of Marianne with Colonel Brandon, she too uses Lady Russell's terminology. After discussing with Elinor the excellence of his character, she adds, "His fortune too! – for at my time of life you know, everybody cares about *that*."

Mrs Dashwood is one of only two heroine-parents whose

age is known to us. Sir Walter Elliot is the other. He is fifty-four, and prides himself on looking as handsome and upright as ever. As these two examples indicate, parents in Austen are likely to be younger in years than we are apt to imagine when given no specific information. We picture them as middle-aged; but the mothers are probably only in their forties. Even Lady Catherine de Bourgh, who is cast in TV and film as an old woman, is probably barely fifty, for her daughter is twenty-eight; and the same goes for Mrs Ferrars. One older woman's age *is* known to us, that of Lady Denham of *Sanditon*. She is precisely seventy, and prides herself on being exceptionally shrewd and active for her age. She has reached not only a milestone number, but the biblical lifespan, and she is inclined to marvel at her own age.

Mrs Gardiner in *Pride and Prejudice* and Mrs Weston in *Emma* are older (but not elderly) women admired and to some extent taken as role models by the respective motherless heroines of those novels; we would guess their age to be somewhere in their thirties, ten years or so older than the heroines. As befits the specificity of *Persuasion,* the novel containing more information about age than any other, we know that the person with an equivalent relationship to the heroine, Mrs Croft, is thirty-eight. Among other considerations it is, perhaps, important that Sophia Croft is known to be older than her brother, and thus licensed to advise and even upbraid him, when she thinks he is acting or speaking foolishly.

'Her manners were open, easy and decided'; such manners would not be right in a young woman or a bride like *Emma's* Mrs Elton, but they are admirable in a woman in the prime of her active life. Though without children to raise, Mrs Croft has taken her rightful place in the world as her husband's equal and helpmeet. The experiences that life has thrown at her have helped her grow into a sage, useful and unafraid member of society. She is as well acquainted with the ways of business as her husband and, without the slightest tinge of bossiness, even helps him to drive their curricle (which Anne, amused, takes for an emblem of how they conduct their married life generally). During the course of the narrative Anne does not turn for advice to the woman who will, as it happens, one day be her sister-in-law, for she is too much used to keeping her own counsel; but she is interested to observe her in the role of wife and older woman playing her full part in the naval and social communities to which she belongs. This will be Anne's destiny too, and therefore Mrs Croft (and to a lesser extent, Mrs Harville, another naval wife) provide more useful role models than a woman twenty years their senior, Lady Russell.

Mrs Gardiner gives advice naturally and pleasantly to her niece Elizabeth, by virtue of being older and having more experience of the world: and though Mrs Weston is too gentle to exercise much influence over her ex-pupil Emma, her judgement is valued by the younger woman (as long as it does not go against her own) and her motherly, protective feelings for Emma are well portrayed. Picking up on Emma's absence of mind she asks "Are you well, my Emma?" and then writes, "I did not quite like your looks on Tuesday, but it was an ungenial morning; and though you will never own being affected by weather, I think everybody feels a north-east wind." A contemporary is unlikely to observe, speak or write like this: we feel Mrs Weston's seniority to Emma.

Older in Ways than in Years

Mr Woodhouse may not be the oldest character in Austen's fiction, or even in *Emma* itself – that honour must go to Mrs Bates, 'a very old lady, almost past everything but tea and quadrille' or to old John Abdy, the former clerk to the Reverend Mr Bates and now "bedridden and very poorly". But John Abdy does not have a speaking part, and Mrs Bates says very little, though she does have the distinction of being the only character whose age has rendered her slightly deaf, and unable to read without spectacles. But Mr Woodhouse is certainly the most fully developed psychological portrait of any elderly person in the novels. His hatred of change of any kind, and his extreme nervousness and timidity, are the characteristics of an elderly man – but of a *specific* elderly man, for probably these traits were always with him and have merely intensified with the ageing process. In terms of his being a fit companion for his twenty-year-old daughter Emma, we read: 'The evil of the actual disparity in their ages (and Mr Woodhouse had not married early) was much increased by his constitution and habits; for having been a valetudinarian all his life, without activity of mind or body, he was a much older man in ways than in years . . .'.

His fearful approach to life ranges from fear of leaving his own house, especially in the evening, to fear of being burgled; despite having a full complement of staff in his household, by the end of the book he is unwilling to live in his own house unless one of the Mr Knightleys is in residence. He is fearful for other people, not only himself: afraid that anyone attending a ball will catch cold, and afraid that in crossing a road Frank Churchill may step in a puddle. He thinks it never safe to sit out of doors, even on a warm day in summer. Not only must he coddle himself by the fire while his neighbours are picking strawberries at Donwell, but an imaginary portrait of Harriet Smith sitting under a tree with only a little shawl round her shoulders distresses him.

He shares this trait with another old – in ways if not in years – character, Mrs Percival, in Austen's unfinished 1792 fragment, *Catharine, or The Bower.* Catharine is usually safe from her aunt's intrusion in her garden bower, because it is a strict rule with Mrs Percival never to sit down out of doors – but when she does so inadvertently one day in May, in her anxiety to lecture her niece about her behaviour with a young man, she becomes convinced that she will never have a day's health all winter, and will probably be dead before the next summer comes round.

Mrs Percival is a highly comic portrait, but is only a little more exaggerated than Mr Woodhouse. For him to leave his own property is a rarity; he gets his exercise by walking round his own shrubbery. (He is not so infirm that he needs someone to lean on, since he is prepared to do this walk alone.) As Emma understands so well, it is often not an action itself, but the suddenness of it, that spooks him; to prepare him by speaking of an event many times before it happens is the best way to win him round.

> In the hope of diverting her father's thoughts from the disagreeableness of Mr Knightley's going to London, and going so suddenly, and going on horseback, which she knew would be all very bad, Emma communicated her news of Jane Fairfax, and her dependence on the effect was justified; it supplied a very useful check – interested, without disturbing him. He had long made up his mind to Jane Fairfax's going out as governess, and could talk of it cheerfully, but Mr Knightley's going to London had been an unexpected blow.

Similarly, he is very willing to send out his horses, coach and coachman to convey his old neighbours to his fireside of an evening, because it is a ritual he is used to: 'Had it taken place only once a year, it would have been a grievance.'

In entertaining these ladies, after a few rounds of cards, Mr Woodhouse shows his inability to think himself into anybody else's position. Emma, as hostess, provides delicacies that form part of the pleasure of the evening for them – better fare than they are used to at home – but Mr Woodhouse does his best to dissuade them from eating most of it: 'His own stomach could bear nothing rich, and he could never believe other people to be different from himself.' A basin of gruel, thin but not too thin, is his favourite foodstuff. He is totally miserable while Mrs Weston's wedding cake is being shared among his neighbours and until it is eaten up his nerves know no rest. All this is very amusing, but also trying. His guests are put in a difficult position, since their desire to be deferential is at war with their desire to eat the good things they see before them. But everyone makes allowances for Mr Woodhouse's idiosyncrasies because they know him to be fundamentally good-natured, and to have their welfare at heart.

As well as being unable to enter into the point of view of others, Mr Woodhouse is slow on the uptake: slow to the point of paralysis, since he almost never *does* take up a new idea. His thought patterns run along familiar lines and can never be stimulated to do otherwise. He is unable to converse on equal terms with Emma, either rationally or playfully. It would be useless to seek his advice on anything serious; luckily Emma never feels in want of advice. If she indulges in a gentle tease, he becomes fretful, and she has to desist. Both physically and mentally, Mr Woodhouse has the attributes of an old man. His memory is poor: "my memory is very bad" he confesses to Emma when trying to remember the contents of Frank Churchill's letter (all he can recall is the date and the signing-off) and, on another occasion, "your dear mother was so clever . . . if I had but her memory. But I can remember nothing." To Mr Woodhouse time flies by so fast: he still thinks of Frank Churchill as the boy of two who lost his mother, and can hardly believe that he is now twenty-three.

Another attribute of old age is adherence to the habits of youth. We read that Mr Woodhouse 'loved to have the cloth laid [at suppertime] because it had been the fashion of his youth' even though to eat anything except gruel for supper is in his present opinion highly dangerous. Substantial suppers had been part of the eating pattern of the day a generation before, but as dinner became a later and later meal – migrating gradually from mid-afternoon to early evening – so hot suppers taken round the dining table (as opposed to a few elegant cold items on a tray) became unnecessary and unfashionable. Mrs Bennet likewise is attached to the habit of supper. We must remember that though much younger in years than Mr Woodhouse when she appears in the narrative of *Pride and Prejudice*, that book was drafted twenty years earlier, so in one sense they belong to the same generation. When *Pride and Prejudice* was published, Austen realized that among all her revisions, she had not updated this detail. 'There might as well have been no suppers at Longbourn,' she wrote ruefully to Cassandra on 4 February 1813, 'but I suppose it was the remains of Mrs Bennet's old Meryton habits.'

Mr Woodhouse is similarly attached to the furniture of his

youth, and only because Emma has such influence over him is she able to introduce a 'large modern circular table' in place of the smaller Pembroke, with drawers, on which his meals had formerly been taken; just as the young ladies of Uppercross have prevailed upon their 'not much educated, and not at all elegant' parents to update their interior decor.

In creating her older characters, Austen may have called on a memory of her youth. She was twelve and a half when taken to see her great-uncle Francis Austen, perhaps the only person she ever met who had been born in the seventeenth century. He lived in Tonbridge, where he had accumulated a fortune by practising law and marrying two wealthy widows. Jane's father, orphaned from an early age, owed to his uncle Francis both his education and benefice, and on the old man's death in 1791, he was left a legacy of £500, so it was politic as well as dutiful of him to take his young family to visit from time to time. Jane's brother Henry, looking back from his own old age, wrote of Francis, 'I think he was born in Anne's reign [actually William III's], and was of course a smart young man of George I's'.[9] A portrait of Francis painted in about 1750 hung over his mantelpiece, and Henry noted that his present suit of clothes 'retained a perfect identity of colour, texture and make' to those of nearly half a century earlier, except that he had discarded the narrow gold lace edging on his grey coat and vest. The fact that great-uncle Francis 'wore a wig like a Bishop', a long-discarded fashion among the other men of their acquaintance, struck Henry, and almost certainly Jane. As Henry wrote, 'It is a sort of privilege to have seen and conversed with such a model of a hundred years since.'

The Idiolect of Age

His conservatism, dull-wittedness, nervousness and bad memory all mark Mr Woodhouse as an old man. But these characteristics would not be so effective did he not also *speak* as an old man. In a society where all conversation tends to the fairly formal, Mr Woodhouse's is ceremonious and courteous in the extreme. Welcoming Miss Fairfax to his dinner party – youthful, humble and familiar as she is, of hardly any social standing at all – he addresses her, "You do us a great deal of honour today, I am sure. My daughter and I are both highly sensible of your goodness, and have the greatest satisfaction in seeing you at Hartfield."[10] Even self-obsessed Mrs Elton can see that he is different from other men: "I admire all that quaint, old-fashioned politeness; it is much more to my taste than modern ease; modern ease often disgusts me."

'Pretty' is a favourite word of approbation in Mr Woodhouse's vocabulary. Used as an indicator of generalized approval, it is an old-fashioned term employed only by the elderly in Jane Austen. He calls the servant Hannah "a civil, pretty-spoken girl" and says that "she always curtseys and asks me how I do, in a very pretty manner". In the same chapter, he describes Mr Elton as "a very pretty young man, to be sure, and a very good young man". Emma's sketch of Harriet is "so prettily done! Just as your drawings always are, my dear." His daughter Isabella's naming her eldest son Henry (Mr Woodhouse's name) rather than John, after his own father, "I thought very pretty of her." His grandsons "have so many pretty ways". Mr Elton's rhyme is "such a pretty charade" and Frank Churchill's letter to his new stepmother is "an exceeding good, pretty letter" – even though its contents cannot be remembered.

Another old person who uses the word 'pretty' in a similar nothing-meaning way is Mrs Jennings, in *Sense and Sensibility.* She is probably not as old in years as Mr Woodhouse – with a daughter of not much more than twenty ("several years younger" than her 27-year-old sister) Mrs Jennings is not likely to be over sixty, and is probably considerably younger – but the novel itself was written twenty years earlier, so her youth, like Mrs Bennet's, lies further back in time than Mr Woodhouse's. She also belongs to a lower class, so was brought up hearing idioms that her social superiors would have begun to regard as *passé.* When given the sight of Lucy's letter, Mrs Jennings 'read it aloud with many comments of satisfaction and praise'. "How prettily she writes!" she exclaims, and "That sentence is very prettily turned. . . . It is as pretty a letter as ever I saw and does Lucy's head and heart great credit."

In describing Delaford (Colonel Brandon's home) to Elinor, Mrs Jennings again uses the word 'prettier' as a general indicator of satisfaction and praise rather than aesthetically, as is clear from the association with butchers and neighbours: "Oh! 'tis a nice place! A butcher hard by in the village, and the parsonage-house within a stone's throw. To my fancy, a thousand times prettier than Barton Park, where they are forced to send three miles for their meat, and have not a neighbour nearer than your mother."

Earlier in the passage, preceding the obsolescent "'tis", Mrs Jennings exclaims: "Such a great mulberry tree in one corner! Lord! How Charlotte and I did stuff the only time we were there!" The ejaculation "Lord!" and the idioms "stone's throw" and "stuff" all characterize her speech as that of an older and coarser woman than, for example, her daughters. Earthy and uninhibited, she is thoroughly Georgian; the next generation, though not yet Victorian, were becoming more refined in speech and habit. When Mrs Jennings tells everybody that her younger daughter "expects to be confined in February" her other daughter, Lady Middleton, 'could no longer endure such a conversation' and tries to change the subject.

Mrs Jennings is one of only a handful of characters in Jane Austen who reminisce. "Well! I was young once, but I never was very handsome – worse luck for me. However, I got a very good husband, and I don't know what the greatest beauty can do more. Ah! poor man! He has been dead these eight years and better." She speaks indulgently of his "cholicky gout" and fondness for Constantia wine. When Willoughby engages himself to a Miss Grey, Mrs Jennings is able to place her: "I remember her aunt well, Biddy Henshawe; she married a very wealthy man." Biddy – a diminutive for Bridget – is one of those names (like Betty, Patty, Molly, Nancy and Sally) denoting both an earlier period and a lower class background; in Austen they are most frequently, though not invariably, given to servants. Biddy Henshawe and Mrs Jennings were probably young women together.

Mrs Jennings shares with Mrs Percival of *Catharine, or the Bower* the very common tendency in the elderly to decry the lax morality of the younger generation. Discovering her niece sitting in conversation with Edward Stanley in the arbour (the young man running off with a kiss of Catharine's hand as her aunt approaches), Mrs Percival declares, "Oh! Catharine, you are an abandoned Creature, and I do not know what will become of you. . . . But I plainly see that everything is going to sixes and sevens and all order will soon be at an end throughout the Kingdom." Jolly Mrs Jennings entertains no such gloomy prognostications in general, but when it is discovered that the extravagant Willoughby has abandoned Marianne for a wealthy bride, the honest old woman exclaims indignantly:

> "He has no business to fly off from his word only because he grows poor, and a richer girl is ready to have him. Why don't he, in such a case, sell his horses, let his house, turn off his servants, and make a thorough reform at once? . . . But that won't do, nowadays; nothing in the way of pleasure can ever be given up by the young men of this age."

Another old person whose memories go back a long way is Mrs Bates, in *Emma*. Speaking of Mr Knightley's generosity with apples, Miss Bates remarks, "My mother says the orchard was always famous in her younger days." *Emma* is a portrait of a community with roots stretching back the length of living memory. The older members recall the days when the village was in 'a more populous, dancing state' and balls were regularly held at the Crown. When Miss Bates speaks of old John Abdy having been clerk to her father for twenty-seven years, she is actually taking us back half a century, as we know Mr Bates has been dead over twenty years (he must have died before Jane Fairfax was orphaned). In no other of Austen's novels is such a long period painted in.

Reminiscences are not, of course, the preserve of the very elderly. Everybody has a past, and is witness to change. Two women who are far from *old*, yet are *twelve years older* than when they last saw each other, are Anne Elliot and her former schoolfriend Miss Hamilton. When they encounter one another again after twelve years' separation they have the pleasure of indulging in 'the interesting charm of remembering former partialities and talking over old times'. The passage of time has had effect not only on their looks and their health, which might be expected, but because of the vagaries of life, on their social relationship to one another, as they cannot help but be aware themselves:

> Twelve years were gone since they had parted, and each presented a somewhat different person from what the other had imagined. Twelve years had changed Anne from the blooming, silent, unformed girl of fifteen, to the elegant little woman of seven and twenty, with every beauty except bloom, and with manners as consciously right as they were invariably gentle; and twelve years had transformed the fine-looking, well-grown Miss Hamilton, in all the glow of health and confidence of superiority, into a poor, infirm, helpless widow, receiving the visit of her former protégée as a favour.[11]

The other young characters who have reason to muse on the passage of time are the Price siblings in *Mansfield Park*. When Fanny and William are reunited after seven years' separation she is at first disappointed by 'the alteration of person' which she sees in William – whom the years and his experiences at sea have changed from the boy she remembers to a young man. But this little shock (which she might have anticipated) is soon overcome, and she finds him the same affectionate brother underneath. In the course of his visit they indulge in reminiscing, and 'all the evil and good of their earliest years could be gone over again, and every former united pain and pleasure retraced with the fondest recollection'. Though it is not the case with all siblings, the narrator tells us, in William and

Fanny their fraternal love is not diminished but increased by 'the influence of time and absence'.

One specific memory of William's is how "we used to jump about together many a time, did not we, when the hand organ was in the street?" It is an incongruous picture to be conjured up amid the almost stultifying calm and luxury of Mansfield Park, where streets, jumping and itinerant organ-grinders are all alien concepts. Later, when Fanny returns to Portsmouth, she is assailed by many other recollections of her early family life, including those of a sister who died, another sister whom she did not like much, and a mother who failed to give her all the love and attention she craved. These memories come flooding back. No other heroine has a back story as colourful and in such contrast to her present life as Fanny's; no other heroine has been known to us since she was a child.

And it is Fanny, of course, who muses on the changes wrought by time and on the wonders of the human memory:

> "How wonderful, how very wonderful the operations of time, and the changes of the human mind! . . . If any one faculty of our nature may be called more wonderful than the rest, I do think it is memory. There seems something more speakingly incomprehensible in the powers, the failures, the inequalities of memory, than in any other of our intelligences. The memory is sometimes so retentive, so serviceable, so obedient – at others, so bewildered and so weak – and at others again, so tyrannic, so beyond control! We are to be sure a miracle every way – but our powers of recollecting and of forgetting do seem peculiarly past finding out."

Fanny Price is as young as either Harriet Smith or Louisa Musgrove when she makes these reflections, but if her mind is capable of such thoughts now, we can be sure that her evening or autumn of life will be fuller and richer than theirs, to her own benefit and that of her husband and children. There is a sense, of course, in which Fanny's personality has always been middle-aged: a very clever portrayal by Austen of a character who is at the same time and in so many of her ways convincingly youthful. This would seem a paradox and yet, in Fanny (more than in any other heroine) we observe the truth that the child is mother to the woman: that the one is always present in the other.

3. PARENT AGAINST CHILD

In *Sense and Sensibility,* Austen suggests that however deplorable, 'the old, well-established grievance of duty against will, parent against child', is only too common between the generations. Sometimes (as here with Mrs Ferrars) it is the fault of the old, sometimes of the young – differing outlooks, agendas and experience make conflict likely. For some of the young men of the novels, the older generation certainly stands in the way of their pleasures. This is very much the case with Willoughby, who tries to shield his misdemeanours from the notice of his elderly relation Mrs Smith, whose money he hopes to inherit, and whose notions of correct behaviour are unbending. Tom Bertram, whose future title and fortune are assured, lives only for enjoyment and privilege, and while early in *Mansfield Park* his father's lecture on extravagance is the cause of some passing shame, on escaping Sir Thomas's presence he reflects that he is not half as much in debt as some of his friends, and moreover 'that his father had made a most tiresome piece of work of it'.

Frederick Tilney keeps out of the way of *his* father as much as possible, while the young William Walter Elliot is one who would rather go his own way and seek his fortune in a mercenary marriage than be controlled and patronized by the head of his family. All these examples are young men, because young women hardly expect to have their own way or control their own destiny. Like Jane Austen herself, Anne Elliot, also in her mid-twenties, is forced to live in Bath when her father moves there, though it is very much against her inclination. Maria Bertram goes so far as to marry (a man for whom she feels only contempt) in order to escape her father's control and her father's house.

That same father, Sir Thomas Bertram, but now acting *in loco parentis* to his niece Fanny, is the only older figure in the course of an Austen narrative to put grave and considered pressure on a young person to marry somebody against her inclination – though even he does not force the issue. (Mrs Bennet's attempt to pressurize Elizabeth is more absurd than serious.) Part of the back story of *Sense and Sensibility* is the account of the ward of Mr Brandon, who is actually forced into a marriage with his son – her cousin – out of avarice, for her fortune is required to pay off the debts of the Brandons. This is a melodramatic history which harks back to the common narratives of late eighteenth-century novels, the sort which Austen had burlesqued in her juvenilia. Not only her own literary taste, but the customs of the country, had moved on. From arranging marriages for their children, parents now merely authorized the young people's own choices. As Lawrence Stone explains in his book *The Family, Sex and Marriage in England 1500–1800*,[1] in the eighteenth century it was increasingly believed that the way to promote fidelity in marriage was to allow couples to follow their hearts, rather than forcing them into the dynastic arrangements of the past. It was this move towards personal choice, together with the older generation's reluctance to yield authority, which novelists found so fruitful for their stories.

Jane Austen's brothers James and Henry tapped into this scope for conflict in their 1789–90 Oxford periodical *The Loiterer*, much of which takes the form of letters to the editor. One such, purporting to come from a young lady called Cecilia, reads:

> Sir, While you have been exerting the united powers of reason and ridicule, to correct the foibles of the Young, I cannot but think it extraordinary that you have never attempted to expose the prejudices of the Old; since they are not perhaps less numerous or less extensive than the former, and are certainly

> more prejudicial to society; for the giddy or foolish actions of Youth can seldom affect any but themselves, whereas the obstinate opinions of Age, when confirmed by power, and exerted with Authority, will naturally extend their influence to all their immediate connections. – Of the prejudices which are the subject of my present complaint, the most striking and mischievous is the eagerness with which, in the most important actions of their lives, they endeavour to promote the *Interest* of their Children at the expense of their Sensibility, and the pains which they consequently take to extinguish or suppress, what they are pleased to call *Romantic Ideas.*[2]

The juvenile pieces which their sister Jane was writing at about the same time often exaggerated the same ideas for comic effect, for example in 'Love and Freindship' [sic] where Edward accounts for his turning up on a stranger's doorstep by telling them that his father "insisted on my giving my hand to Lady Dorothea. No never exclaimed I. Lady Dorothea is lovely and Engaging; I prefer no woman to her; but know Sir that I scorn to marry her in compliance with your Wishes. No! Never shall it be said that I obliged my Father" and his listeners not only 'all admired the Manliness of his reply' but one of them immediately marries him.[3]

While, in the mature fiction, Austen shows young couples consistently making their own choice of matrimonial partner, they are still obliged upon entering into their engagements to seek parental consent. The novels are full of such instances. Even Emma Woodhouse, who can coax her father into doing what she wants, does not announce her marriage plans as the done deal they really are, but introduces the subject to him with the courteous proviso 'if his consent and approbation could be obtained'.[4] When Anne Elliot enters into her first engagement with Frederick Wentworth, her father 'without saying it could not be, gave it all the negative of great coldness' – he does not forbid the match.[5] In the same novel, when Henrietta Musgrove and her young clergyman cousin Charles Hayter wish to marry, 'on the strength of his present income, with almost a certainty of something more permanent [before long] the two families had consented to the young people's wishes'. With her own very different experience in mind, Anne speaks her pleasure to Henrietta's brother Charles: "What a blessing to young people to be in such hands! Your father and mother seem so totally free from all those ambitious feelings which have led to so much misconduct and misery, both in young and old."

Another sensible and unambitious set of parents, Mr and Mrs Morland, while they have no objections to their daughter marrying Henry Tilney, will not 'sanction the engagement' until assured of 'the decent appearance of consent' on General Tilney's side, which Austen ascribes to the steadiness of their principles.[6] Mr Bennet, turning everything to a joke, tells Elizabeth that Darcy is the sort of man to whom he could never dare refuse anything, and gives his consent to the marriage "if you are determined to have him".[7] He is troubled, however, that his most intelligent daughter is temporarily blinded by Darcy's wealth, and does not know what she is doing. After a few minutes' serious conversation in which she convinces him of her real love and Mr Darcy's real worth, and with Bingley's recent application for Jane also in mind, he reverts to comic mode by 'saying, as she quitted the room, "If any young men come for Mary or Kitty, send them in, for I am quite at leisure"'.

In accordance with the rules of propriety, the general pattern is of deference by the younger to the older generation. This is the default setting of social and family relationships, and any deviation from it is liable to censure by the author. Fanny Price is shocked and distressed by her sister Susan's habit of contending with their mother. Fanny's ineradicable feelings of 'duty, honour and tenderness' are all violated by her sister's argumentative approach and although she can see that on the subject of managing the house and family Susan is usually right and Mrs Price invariably wrong, Fanny finds Susan's 'looks and language very often indefensible'.[8]

Anne Elliot, too, has a code of conduct regarding the older generation which no provocation will permit her to violate. 'With a great deal of quiet observation, and a knowledge, which she often wished less, of her father's character',[9] she sees him clearly in all his vanity and shallowness; but when Sir Walter pours scorn on her friendship with Mrs Smith, to the point of being downright rude about a woman he does not know, 'her sense of personal respect to her father' prevents Anne from making a rational retort. 'She made no reply.' On the whole, Jane Austen's characters are exquisitely polite to their elders, even when those elders are fools, and many a tongue is bitten rather than allowed to utter a disrespectful word. When Emma Woodhouse slips up from her usual gracious persona and makes a rather cruel joke at Miss Bates's expense, Mr Knightley's rebuke focuses on the equal claims of the older woman's age and poverty:

> "How could you be so insolent in your wit to a woman of her character, age and situation? . . . You, whom she had known from an infant, whom she had seen grow up from a period when her notice was an honour – to have you now, in thoughtless spirits, and the pride of the moment, laugh at her, humble her – and before her niece too."[10]

Only when dealing with someone very tyrannical and rude themselves, or perhaps with someone who is trying to exert an authority over them that is not justified, are the young admired for lack of deference. We love (and are intended by the author to love) Elizabeth Bennet for standing up to Lady Catherine de Bourgh, both at Rosings, her Ladyship's home, and at Longbourn, which her ladyship visits expressly to enforce her very unreasonable will. On their first evening together at Rosings, after Elizabeth has 'very composedly' answered a series of impertinent questions about her family, she takes a stand on the custom of holding back younger sisters until the older are married, saying:

> "I think it would not be very likely to promote sisterly affection or delicacy of mind."
>
> "Upon my word," said her Ladyship, "you give your opinion

very decidedly for so young a person. Pray, what is your age?"

"With three younger sisters grown up," replied Elizabeth smiling, "your Ladyship can hardly expect me to own it."

Lady Catherine seemed quite astonished at not receiving a direct answer; and Elizabeth suspected herself to be the first creature who had ever dared to trifle with so much dignified impertinence. [11]

When assailed on something much more important – the possibility of marriage with Darcy – in their extraordinary interview at Longbourn, Elizabeth asserts her own right to act "in that manner which will, in my own opinion, constitute my happiness, without reference to *you,* or to any person so wholly unconnected with me." When Lady Catherine cites her right to know her nephew's nearest concerns, Elizabeth retorts, "But you are not entitled to know mine" and "You have certainly no right to concern yourself in mine."

But it is notable that even the spirited Elizabeth does not contend with her mother, to whom she owes a different duty: the duty of being forbearing in the interests of family harmony, and the religious imperative of honouring mother and father. This is why Mr Bennet is so wrong to expose his wife to the ridicule of her children by his own contemptuous remarks and jokes at her expense. Elizabeth does occasionally try to reason with her mother – calling her "dear ma'am" – but usually she behaves as quietly as she can until the storm is over. When Mrs Bennet says, "Lizzy, I *insist* upon your staying and hearing Mr Collins", 'Elizabeth would not oppose such an injunction'. And when, much later in the novel, Mrs Bennet calls Elizabeth out of the room on purpose to leave Mr Bingley with Jane, Elizabeth is forced to go, but then returns quietly.

The attitude of the young to the old is frequently one of irritation: Catharine Percival finds her aunt's conversation 'tedious'; Emma Woodhouse, though patience itself with her father, can hardly bear to listen to the inconsequential talk of Miss Bates, and regards the matrons of Highbury generally as "tiresome wretches". Marianne Dashwood has no patience or politeness for Mrs Jennings or indeed for any of the older people of her acquaintance, finding their company irksome or boring. Having already, with her younger sister, written off Colonel Brandon as 'an absolute old bachelor', she unites with Willoughby in 'prejudice[d] against him for being neither lively nor young'.[12] As we have seen, Elizabeth Elliot deplores the old-fashioned appearance of Lady Russell and preserves only an outward show of respect for her. Julia Bertram finds it 'a penance' to be civil, though only for an hour, to Mr Rushworth's "horrible mother" when they are thrown into each other's company.[13]

Some of the young men in Austen – those of more questionable morals, it has to be said – manage their elders by the exercise of charm and verbal fluency. Thus Frank Churchill often gets his own way with his uncle and aunt; Henry Crawford works on *his* uncle's indolence to get him to do what he wants; and Edward Stanley, in *Catharine, or the Bower* can talk his father into overlooking any transgression.

Pleasure-seeking young men whose fathers are *not* so malleable include Tom Bertram and Frederick Tilney; they can get away with nothing, their best expedient being to get away from *home* as much as they can. As these examples suggest, the attitude of the old to the young is mainly dictatorial or controlling, to a greater or lesser degree. There are dozens of such people in Austen, male and female, some of whom will be encountered in later chapters: their motivations vary, from a love of manipulation to a heavy sense of responsibility. Sir Thomas is perhaps the parent who feels this responsibility most keenly, and acts on it most conscientiously. The result is often to alienate his own children, to 'repress their spirits in his presence' and to make a casual young acquaintance like John Yates reflect that 'he had known many disagreeable fathers before, and often been struck with the inconveniences they occasioned, but never in the whole course of his life had he seen one of that class, so unintelligibly moral, so infamously tyrannical as Sir Thomas'.[14]

Mansfield Park is unusual in that it is an older character, not a hero or heroine, who learns most lessons during the course of the narrative, and who at the end of the novel reflects most deeply on his own errors: 'Wretchedly did he feel that with all the cost and care of an anxious and expensive education, he had brought up his daughters without their understanding their first duties, or his being acquainted with their character and temper.' It is true that Lady Russell has to 'admit that she had been pretty completely wrong, and to take up a new set of opinions and hopes'[15] in learning to accept Captain Wentworth as a worthy husband for her beloved god-daughter Anne; but though her earlier error has resulted in pain for Anne, it has not been detrimental to her character. Mr Bennet, too, has a moment of self-reproach over the laxity of upbringing that facilitated Lydia's transgression: "Let me once in my life feel how much I have been to blame",[16] but he knows that the impression will pass away soon enough and he will return to his detached mode of parenting; and Mrs Dashwood suddenly realizes that she has rather neglected Elinor in concentrating on Marianne; but these are momentary flashes of thought compared with Sir Thomas's lengthy self-examination.

While these are parents or parent-substitutes who are at least trying to do their best for their children, others are so selfish as to put their own ambitions or feelings first. Mrs Churchill, though she operates offstage in *Emma,* seems motivated wholly by selfishness. Likewise Mrs Ferrars, whose tyranny over her son Edward in *Sense and Sensibility* operates regardless of his welfare. In this relationship, neither parent nor child derives any pleasure from the other.

Happily there are other older people, especially those who do not stand in relation as a parent, who can take delight in the younger generation. Much of the savour of Mrs Jennings's existence comes from the way she treats all her unmarried acquaintance and their romances as the butt of her good-natured humour. *They* may find her jokes embarrassing, but to her, this entering into the concerns of the young keeps her young herself. Dr Grant likes to have the pretty, talkative younger half-sister of his wife under his roof. Mr and Mrs Allen find that in taking their young neighbour, Catherine Morland, to Bath, their own enjoyment is much enhanced by the freshness and innocence of hers.

The Joy of Grandchildren

And then there is the joy of grandchildren, one of the consolations of advancing years. In *Sense and Sensibility* there are two grandmothers, who at one point get into competition with each other. The occasion is a dinner party given by Mr and Mrs John Dashwood in their Harley Street home. When the females of the party retire to the drawing-room after dinner only one subject of conversation engages them until coffee comes in, the comparative heights of Harry Dashwood and Lady Middleton's second son William, who are nearly of the same age. As only Harry is present, it has to be conjecture. 'The two mothers, though each really convinced that her own son was the tallest, politely decided in favour of the other. The two grandmothers, with not less partiality, but more sincerity, were equally earnest in support of their own descendant.' It is amusing that the rules of politeness allow grandmothers (at one remove) but not mothers to speak in praise of their offspring.

One of these grandmothers is Mrs Ferrars, whose observed interaction with her only grandchild, Harry Dashwood, is limited to this boast. The other is the much more warm-hearted Mrs Jennings. Though she makes a lengthy visit to Barton Park, presumably to enjoy the company of her elder daughter and her three Middleton grandchildren, John, William and the atrociously spoilt Annamaria, we see Mrs Jennings in action as a grandmother chiefly when her second daughter, Charlotte Palmer, gives birth during the course of the novel. This event is 'highly important to Mrs Jennings's happiness' and, spending the next two weeks largely at her daughter's bedside, she is 'full of delight and importance, attributing Charlotte's well doing to her own care'. As for her new grandson, Mrs Jennings can 'plainly perceive, at different times, the most striking resemblance between this baby and every one of his relations on both sides'. She is a besotted grandmother, but also a practical and experienced one, not easily panicked. About two and a half weeks after the birth, she has this to narrate to the sisters (strangely using the impersonal pronoun for her grandson):

> "When I got to Mr Palmer's, I found Charlotte quite in a fuss about the child. She was sure it was very ill – it cried, and fretted, and was all over pimples. So I looked at it directly, and 'Lord! My dear,' says I, 'it is nothing in the world but the red-gum,' and nurse said just the same. But Charlotte, she would not be satisfied, so Mr Donovan was sent for; and luckily he happened to be just come in from Harley Street, so he stepped over directly, and as soon as ever he saw the child, he said just as we did, that it was nothing in the world but the red-gum, and then Charlotte was easy."

Jane Austen herself did not know any of her grandparents. Her father, George Austen, was orphaned at an early age. Her mother, Cassandra Leigh, lost her own father shortly before her marriage to George, and her mother a few years afterwards, seven years before the birth of Jane, who was given her name.

Perhaps for this reason, there are very few three-generational families in Austen's fiction. None of the heroes or heroines has a living grandparent, though it would be entirely feasible, from the point of view of age, for them to do so. A person in their twenties, whose parents are in their forties or fifties, could very well – even in the eighteenth century – have a grandparent alive in their seventies or eighties. One such family grouping, briefly glimpsed on the streets of Bath, is that of old Sir Archibald Drew and his grown-up grandson, naval acquaintance of Admiral Croft. But Jane Fairfax, in *Emma,* is the only major character to possess a living grandparent. The middle generation, her own parents, are both dead.

Although *life expectancy,* at birth, was so much lower at that period than now, once the perils of infancy and childhood – and in the case of women, childbearing – had been survived, *lifespan* was not so very different. As we know, most of Jane's own siblings lived into their eighties, one until ninety. Her own parents became grandparents many times over during their lifetimes. Mrs Austen, who reached the age of eighty-seven, had thirty-one grandchildren living at the time of her death and a remarkable nineteen great-grandchildren. Jane Austen lived to see her mother become a great-grandmother to Anna Lefroy's first two little girls. But she certainly has no *four*-generational families in her fiction.

In her *three*-generational families, with the exception of Jane Fairfax, the third generation consists of young children. A good example is the Musgrove family. Mr and Mrs Musgrove are parents of an unspecified number of children, of whom Charles is the eldest at about the age of twenty-seven, and 'the much-petted Master Harry' is the youngest, still at school.[17] Charles has been married five years, and has two boys of four and two. So there is very little gap between the last of their own brood of children and the first of their grandchildren. They pass seamlessly from parenting young children to being grandparents.

With so much experience, no wonder Mrs Musgrove feels that she knows better than her daughter-in-law how to bring up children. The criticisms and counter-criticisms of the two Musgrove mothers, young and old, funnelled through the reluctant, peacemaking Anne, are among the comic passages of the novel. Even more memorable, the jolly, noisy Christmas scene in which an unspecified number of children from both generations, augmented by small Harvilles, cluster round laden tables and a roaring fire under the indulgent gaze of the elder Musgroves, anticipates the Dickensian cult of Christmas. Jane Austen herself, while terming it 'a fine family piece' seems ambivalent about such pleasures, and they are certainly not to the taste of the more intellectual Lady Russell. But Lady Russell is not related to the Musgroves, and cannot be expected to share their fondness. Little Charles's and Walter's other grandparent – Sir Walter Elliot – takes no interest in his grandchildren during the whole course of the novel, not even including them in his enquiries when he asks after their mother, Mary. Besides his habitual self-centredness, perhaps he'd rather forget that he's of grandfatherly age by ignoring their existence.

Unlike Sir Walter, Mr Woodhouse is a fond grandfather of his small grandsons. He is so pleased and flattered that the eldest was named after himself that he continues to talk about it six years on. In a charming illustration of the pleasure grandparents can derive from their grandchildren, and of grandparents' tendency to think no grandchildren were ever so clever as their own, he tells Harriet Smith:

> "Henry is a fine boy, but John is very like his mamma. Henry is the eldest; he was named after me, not after his father. John, the second, is named after his father. Some people are surprised, I believe, that the eldest was not, but Isabella would have him called Henry, which I thought very pretty of her. And he is a very clever boy indeed. They are all remarkably clever; and they have so many pretty ways. They will come and stand by my chair and say, 'Grandpapa, can you give me a bit of string?' and once Henry asked me for a knife, but I told him knives were only made for grandpapas."[18]

Emma is the only Jane Austen novel in which the affectionate names *grandpapa* and *grandmamma* appear. *Grandpapa* occurs four times, with the more formal *grandfather* not at all. The word *grandmother* occurs nine times, always in relation to Mrs Bates, but this is exceeded by the occurrence of *grandmamma* thirteen times. Only two of these are actually spoken by Jane Fairfax. She uses the term once when she insists to the interfering Mrs Elton that her grandmamma's servant can fetch their letters (and she is quite correct in assigning the servant to *Mrs* Bates, even though it seems to be *Miss* Bates who runs the household); and once in a snatch of reported speech, relayed by Miss Bates, in which Jane marvels at her grandmamma's eyesight. But the vast majority of the instances of *grandmamma* are heard from Miss Bates's mouth, in speaking of her mother to Jane: "I ran home, as I said I should, to help grandmamma to bed", for example, or "the evening is closing in, and grandmamma will be looking for us". Miss Bates's affection for both her mother and her niece are reflected in this terminology – affection which Jane might experience sometimes as a bath of warm security, at other times as infantilization and stultification. As for Mrs Bates in the role of grandmother, she is, by the time the novel starts, the gentlest of presences in Jane Fairfax's life. Dozing in the corner without the use of her broken spectacles, and hard of hearing, she is no hindrance at all to Frank's courtship of Jane.

Austen gives us a small number of grandparents but, whether loving or indifferent, they are all convincing in their individual ways. They add depth and texture to her portrayals of family life; and if her heroes and heroines are without this supportive relationship, it may be because their parents (where they have any) often themselves have lessons to learn, character errors to correct. An even older, wiser generation would dilute the difficulties that the heroes and heroines have to overcome on their own merits, without much guidance from those whose experience of life is so much greater.

The Importance of Aunts

Jane Austen herself became an aunt at the age of seventeen to two nieces born very close together; Edward's daughter Fanny and James's daughter Anna. Though her tally of nephews and nieces went on growing through the rest of her life – she had twenty-five at the time of her death, and two great-nieces – she was always particularly fond of Fanny and Anna, who both lost their mothers. Fanny turned to Aunt Jane for advice with her love life, Anna for criticism of the novel she was writing. Fanny, who had to mother her ten younger siblings, was dutiful, while Anna, who had to contend with a difficult stepmother from an early age, was wayward. Jane even referred to Fanny as 'almost another sister',[19] a great accolade considering how much pleasure and comfort she drew from her relationship with her real sister, Cassandra.

When Anna's own eldest child was born her half-sister Caroline, at the age of only ten, became an aunt herself. Jane Austen wrote to Caroline, 'Now that you are become an Aunt, you are a person of some consequence & must excite great Interest whatever You do. I have always maintained the importance of Aunts as much as possible, & am sure of your doing the same now.'[20] It was not only her nieces whom Jane Austen loved; she was particularly close to Caroline's brother James Edward (who was to become his aunt's first biographer), writing of him in July 1816, when he was seventeen, 'He has not lost one good quality or good Look, & is only altered in being improved by being some months older when we saw him last. He is getting very near our own age, for we do not grow old of course.'[21] Her tender but practical concern for two younger nephews, Edward and George, who were at boarding-school at the time of their mother's death, and who went to stay for a few days with Mrs Austen and Jane, show what a good mother she would have made.

The same is true of certain heroines. Anne Elliot is more consistent, more capable and much less selfish in her management of her nephews than their own mother. Emma Woodhouse avoids her sister Isabella's tendency to overprotect her children and dose them with unnecessary medicine; Emma enjoys playing alphabet games and telling stories to the two eldest boys and delights in dancing the eight-month baby, 'little Emma', about in her arms. Mr Knightley, uncle to the same brood, observes that he and she never disagree where the children are concerned; he praises Emma's behaviour as an aunt as being "guided by nature". This promises well for their own future family life. He is probably not aware that he is assessing Emma as a mother for his children, but subconsciously it must be adding to his reasons for wanting her as his wife.

Both Emma and Anne belong to the late phase of Austen's creativity, when she had accumulated much experience of being an aunt herself. That her many nephews and nieces provided Austen with the best of both worlds – the enjoyment of watching young people grow up without full-time responsibility for them, let alone the risky business of giving birth to them – is echoed in Emma's words when she is smugly expressing to Harriet her intention of never marrying:

> "As for objects of interest, objects for the affections, which is, in truth, the great evil to be avoided in *not* marrying, I shall be very well off, with all the children of a sister I love so much to care about. There will be enough of them, in all probability, to supply every sort of sensation that declining life can need. There will be enough for every hope and every fear; and though my attachment to none can equal that of a parent, it suits my ideas of comfort better than what is warmer and blinder. My nephews and nieces: I shall often have a niece with me."

This ushers in discussion of Jane Fairfax, niece of a doting aunt. 'Heaven forbid . . . that I should ever bore people half so much about all the Knightleys together as she does about Jane Fairfax.' Miss Bates (discussed more fully in Chapter 5) must be the aunt to end all aunts in English literature. Jane Fairfax (who addresses her aunt as "ma'am", just as Miss Bates herself addresses her mother) requires all her powers of forbearance to live with so talkative and fussily attentive an aunt in so small a domestic space, and sometimes the stress shows; though Miss Bates, happily unaware, is able to say "We never had a quarrel in our life". In one of her more sympathetic moments towards Jane, Emma reflects "Such a home, indeed! Such an aunt! . . . I do pity you." (Maybe she would find her own father more irritating than she does if she were confined within such a small space with him, day in, day out.)

A maiden aunt of an orphaned niece is a particularly potent combination, calculated to focus the aunt's attention, sometimes to a suffocating extent, on the niece. Another such aunt appears in the early fragment *Catharine, or the Bower* under the title Mrs Percival, Mrs being a courtesy style for a maiden lady who is head of her household; but she is definitely a 'maiden aunt'. Whereas Miss Bates's love for Jane is only too overwhelming, Mrs Percival takes her responsibilities so seriously, and watches over Catharine's conduct 'with so scrutinizing a severity, as to make it very doubtful to many people, and to Catharine amongst the rest, whether she loved her or not'.

In *Emma,* Jane Fairfax's affectionate but impoverished aunt is in full contrast to Frank Churchill's rich and capricious one, who exercises almost complete control over his movements, indulging him one moment and reining him in the next, so that he never knows where he stands – an aunt, it is thought, who would never have given permission for him to marry Jane. According to Mr Weston, "Mr Churchill has pride; but his pride is nothing to his wife's; his is a quiet, indolent, gentlemanlike sort of pride, that would harm nobody, and only make himself a little helpless and tiresome; but her pride is arrogance and insolence." Frank himself speaks neither disrespectfully nor fondly of her, but bears with her caprice extraordinarily patiently, though whether this shows the fundamental sweetness of his nature, or mercenary calculation and indolence, is open to interpretation.

Another person brought up by an aunt is Mary Crawford. Fanny Price suggests to Edmund that Mary's late aunt was at fault in bringing her up without due respect for their uncle; Mary herself shows a pleasing loyalty, always defending her aunt, while Henry Crawford takes the part of the Admiral. When Mary asserts that Mrs Crawford's "knowledge of the world made her judgement very generally and deservedly looked up to by all the young people of her acquaintance"[22] she is speaking from the heart, not with her usual semi-ironic playfulness. Mary is one of the few young people to acknowledge the benefit of having the wisdom of the older generation to call on in this way.

Catherine Morland is the only heroine with a *great-aunt,* whose role in Catherine's history is to lecture her on the frivolity of dress during a Christmas visit to Fullerton Rectory. *Mansfield Park* and *Pride and Prejudice* both offer pairings of memorable aunts. In *Mansfield Park,* during all the years she is growing up after her adoption, Fanny spends every day of her life in the company of her two aunts, the sisters Lady Bertram and Mrs Norris, one unthinkingly selfish, the other officious, oppressive and mentally abusive. There is no getting away. The house and grounds are large, but Fanny rarely goes beyond them. She is always under observation. While Lady Bertram, thinking always of herself and not of Fanny's good, gives her only one piece of advice in the whole eight years (which is that it is every young woman's duty to accept an advantageous offer of marriage), Mrs Norris is constantly haranguing her. Fanny's tender-heartedness turns most naturally to her other aunt, though Lady Bertram does little enough to deserve or reward it, but their interdependence grows organically; as Fanny becomes less needy, Lady Bertram becomes more so, and Fanny responds to this not with impatience but with real love. It is telling that when Fanny is reunited with her own mother after so many years of separation, the first thing she notices about her are 'features which Fanny loved the more because they brought her aunt Bertram's before her'.

In *Pride and Prejudice* the obnoxiously interfering aunt of the hero is contrasted with the amiable aunt of the heroine, and both sit down to write letters to their respective aunts when the engagement is formed. Lady Catherine, despite her rank, has less perfect manners than Mrs Gardiner, wife of a businessman, making the novel in part a treatise against snobbery. Mr and Mrs Gardiner fulfil several functions in the novel, from showing Darcy that Elizabeth has some relations she need not be ashamed of, to facilitating her journey into Derbyshire, and providing her with role models for a good marriage; but perhaps the most important is in demonstrating an aspect of Elizabeth's character that would not otherwise be perceived by the reader. Elizabeth is so scornful of most of the older people about her, including her other aunt and uncle, Mr and Mrs Philips, that we need to know that she can love where love is merited, as it is by Mr and Mrs Gardiner. The scene where Mrs Gardiner gives Elizabeth some good advice about being on her guard against falling in love with a man who cannot afford to marry, and Elizabeth thanks her for the kindness of her hints, is offered as 'a wonderful instance of advice being given on such a point, without being resented'. Mrs Gardiner's own children still being small, she takes real pleasure from her grown-up nieces Jane and Elizabeth. When the Gardiners and Elizabeth set off for their holiday in the north, 'One enjoyment was certain – that of suitableness as companions; a suitableness that comprehended health and temper to bear inconveniences, cheerfulness to enhance every pleasure, and affection and intelligence, which might supply it among themselves if there were disappointments abroad.'

There are no reservations, no nasty undercurrents in this relationship; all is open and mutually rewarding. As an aunt, therefore, Mrs Gardiner has the satisfaction of feeling she is useful to two deserving nieces whose parents, she is aware, leave something wanting; and of knowing herself respected and beloved by two well-judging members of the younger generation. It is a model of how an aunt/niece relationship, or indeed any relationship between the generations, should be.

4. OLD WIVES

By old wives in this context I mean not women who were necessarily old in our terms, but those who had been married long enough to come to some accommodation with the choices they had made in youth and to learn to live with whatever idiosyncrasies they may have discovered in their husbands. Austen shows us every kind of marriage: shows her heroines, rather, for it is they who need to learn by example. There are particularly well-matched couples, like the Crofts and the Gardiners and the Westons; there are the run-of-the-mill couples to whose interior lives we are not privy, but who seem to rub along together well enough; and there are the ill-matched couples, of whom the Bennets are the prime example. But we see the Bennets' marriage only from the point of view of the disappointed husband and the observing daughter, both of whom have a clear perception of Mrs Bennet's faults. She herself hardly seems to realize that her husband despises her. There can never be a *rapprochement* between these two, they are chained together for life, and it is Mr Bennet who has the best of the bargain, for he not only has physical escape into his own space – his beloved library, his grounds in which to go shooting – but he has the pleasure of getting the better of his wife in every exchange, which polishes up his ego. In his book *Jane Austen and the Body*, John Wiltshire points out that the most violent of Mrs Bennet's nervous outbreaks occur when she has been especially thwarted and humiliated by her husband, such as in the aftermath of Mr Collins's proposal to Elizabeth, when Mr Bennet is especially witty at his wife's expense

– and in front of a daughter who fully understands his triumph.[1]

Self-pity, one of Mrs Bennet's principal faults, is a severe failing in Austen's estimation, because it is something that could and should be remedied. She particularly admires wives who do not repine but exert themselves to find happiness where they can. The two supreme examples of this are Charlotte Collins and Mrs Grant. Charlotte's husband is the worse, because at least Dr Grant is intelligent and sensible; Mr Collins is anything but. Charlotte uses her own intelligence to manage him, encouraging him to be out in the garden as much as possible, and choosing for herself a morning sitting room without a view of the road which might tempt him to join her. A woman married to a clergyman – as both these wives are – has him at home all the time, without the relief of space and grounds and distant outdoor occupations of the sportsman or the landowner. The clerical wife is at the other extreme from the naval wife who – unless she accompany her husband to sea, as occasionally happened – may be parted from him for months or even years at a time, which certainly happened to some of Jane Austen's own sisters-in-law.

Mrs Collins finds her pleasure in 'her home and her housekeeping, her parish and her poultry'.[2] As she shows Elizabeth round her house, 'When Mr Collins could be forgotten, there was really a great air of comfort throughout, and by Charlotte's evident enjoyment of it, Elizabeth supposed he must often be forgotten.' Marital relations with a man whose 'society is irksome to her' is the price she has to pay for these pleasures, but the resulting children (provided there are not too many – and Charlotte Collins surely has the strength of mind to persuade her husband into separate rooms when she has her 'heir and spare' to save her from the Longbourn entail) will be further recompense. Mrs Grant does not have this consolation and source of interest, but she too takes pleasure in her home, her garden and her poultry; though being longer married than Charlotte, and having everything now as she likes it, she is looking for something else to fill up her heart and her time. Tom Bertram thinks Mrs Grant needs a lover: 'a desperate dull life hers must be with the doctor',[3] but the company of a beloved half-sister is enough for her.

Mrs Weston keeps poultry too – for Austen it seems to be a marker for contented domesticity in married women. Even the foolish Charlotte Palmer enjoys visiting her poultry yard when she has been away from her country home for some while. And for all her warnings about marrying for the wrong motives, Austen *is* broadly sympathetic to the innocent pleasure taken by newly married women in a home of their own. From Elinor Ferrars choosing her wallpapers to Catherine Tilney learning by experience how to transform herself from a girl with no responsibilities into a reasonably competent housekeeper, Austen accepts that this progression from girlhood to wifehood is the right and natural course for most women in her society. Marriage and a home to run bring not just financial security but a sense of purpose and usefulness to daily pursuits. Without them, a woman as she grows older is in danger of having nothing to do or to occupy her thoughts beyond continuing that search for a mate which becomes unseemly and self-obsessed with the passage of time. Even Mrs Elton, ghastly though she is as a married woman, would become less endurable as time progresses without a home and a husband to absorb her energies. So would Lucy Steele.

Mrs Grant's philosophy is that "there will be little rubs and disappointments everywhere, and we are all apt to expect too much; but then, if one scheme of happiness fails, human nature turns to another; if the first calculation is wrong, we make a second better; we find comfort somewhere".[4] She puts up with her husband's ill humour and demanding palate without allowing his frequent moans to drag her down; after Mary Crawford has observed the marriage for some months, she declares that Mrs Grant is her standard of perfection in a wife. However, her mildness could be said to obviate the need in her husband to reform his ways; a few reproaches might do him good. Charlotte Palmer, too, by laughing off her husband's rude remarks, makes it unnecessary for him to reform.

Another husband whose behaviour goes unchallenged by a doting and slightly dense wife is John Knightley, whose 'temper was not his great perfection; and indeed, with such a worshipping wife, it was hardly possible that any natural defects in it should not be increased. The extreme sweetness of her temper must hurt his.'[5] The emotional knocks administered by her impatient husband are internalized by Isabella Knightley, who cannot bear to admit to herself that he is less than perfect. But such repression takes its toll, emerging as the physical symptoms of "those little nervous headaches and palpitations which I am never entirely free from anywhere".

There are two wives at least who do repine and lament over the bargains into which they have entered freely: Mrs Price, who has brought all her hardships on herself by marrying without thought of the financial consequences; and Mary Musgrove, whose husband Charles is far from a bad husband – in fact he puts up with her moods very admirably, but does not always do what she wants. She feels neglected while he spends his days in field sports, and other disagreements occur, during which Anne usually thinks it is Mary who is in the wrong. Sometimes Mary is disobliging to him, sometimes he is deliberately stubborn with her, either to punish her or simply to assert his rights to do what he likes. In fact, were he not to show his strength sometimes, he would become quite henpecked, because Mary would be sure to take advantage. 'Husbands and wives generally know when opposition will be in vain'[6] says the narrator wisely, and shows Mary submitting, though self-pityingly, on those occasions when Charles is determined to prevail. Mary is the only wife who calls her husband by his Christian name, which makes their marriage, which has faults on both sides, and which is not conducted with the perfect courtesy observed, for example, in the Bertram marriage, seem the most modern in any of the novels. Like many another husband and wife they are not really essential to one another's happiness (in a phrase Austen uses elsewhere in the book) but through time and habit they are conjoined in a way that enables them to 'pass for a happy couple'.

Some wives do gain the upper hand over their husbands: such a one is Fanny Dashwood, whose skill in manipulating her husband is so brilliantly illustrated in their conversation about what he should do for his sisters. Another is probably Mrs Norris, though she is widowed before we really get to know her. Mr Norris seems a supine fellow who takes to the role of invalid, in all likelihood, to avoid confrontation with his domineering wife. Mrs Elton is set to be the dominant one too, despite much wit on her side about being under the control of her lord and master. It is noticeable that after his marriage, Mr Elton scarcely says a word for himself. Having been so ready to talk in the first volume of *Emma*, he has only two or three brief passages of speech in the following two, which are full of his wife's verbal incontinence – her 'sparkling vivacity' as she likes to think of it herself.

As wives cease to be brides and grow into matrons, they may be viewed collectively as a kind of local chorus, passing judgement and commentary on the communities to which they belong – gossiping, reinforcing one another's opinions, deciding on acceptable behaviour. Highbury is the supreme example of this in Jane Austen's work. Nothing happens in the village without its being discussed *ad nauseam* by the female part of the population. On the marriage of Mr Weston and Miss Taylor, Highbury decides that it would be proper for his son Frank to visit the couple: 'there was not a dissentient voice on the subject, either when Mrs Perry drank tea with Mrs and Miss Bates, or when Mrs and Miss Bates returned the visit'.[7] When Frank writes with congratulations on the marriage, 'For a few days, every morning visit in Highbury included some mention of the handsome letter Mrs Weston had received. "I suppose you have heard of the handsome letter Mr Frank Churchill has written to Mrs Weston? I understand it was a very handsome letter indeed."'

"Highbury gossips" and "tiresome wretches" Emma calls them, and shudders at the thought that she might be 'classed with the Mrs Eltons, the Mrs Perrys, and the Mrs Coles' of the place. Towards the end of the novel, when Mr Weston tells Jane Fairfax, now regarded as 'his eldest daughter', of the engagement of Emma and Mr Knightley, 'Miss Bates being present, it passed, of course, to Mrs Cole, Mrs Perry and Mrs Elton immediately afterwards.' Anticipating 'that it would soon be over Highbury' the engaged couple are amused to think of themselves as 'the evening wonder in many a family circle' as their neighbours discuss which of the two is more fortunate, and where they should make their home.

To a lesser extent, so it is in the other communities that Austen writes about. In *Mansfield Park* Mrs Price has neighbours with whom to discuss the badness of the Portsmouth servants, thus relieving her feelings, in which probably her husband takes no share. In *Pride and Prejudice* the solace of Mrs Bennet's existence is 'visiting and news'. Between Longbourn and Meryton, a mile apart, a group of old wives consisting of Mrs Bennet, her sister Mrs Philips, Mrs Long and Lady Lucas, plus others unnamed, circulate all the local news. When Jane Bennet becomes engaged, 'Mrs Bennet was privileged to whisper it to Mrs Philips, and *she* ventured, without any permission, to do the same by all her neighbours in Meryton.' If the news happens to be shocking, that only adds relish to the tittle-tattle. The 'spiteful old ladies of Meryton' positively gloat over Lydia's disgrace. Having first foretold that she would 'come upon the town' – that is, be forced into prostitution – they next prophesy that her situation will be very little less wretched as the wife of Wickham, a gambler and seducer. Meryton is viewed by Austen less indulgently than Highbury, where Mrs Elton, though an insufferable busybody, is not actually malicious, and where everybody else is either harmless or benign. In *Pride and Prejudice,* Mrs Philips's home in the heart of the town, and her habit of taking much of the information which she spreads from the tradespeople around her, contributes to authorial disapproval of her vulgarity. But as Austen admits in *Persuasion,* where at Uppercross 'the females were fully occupied in all the other common subjects of housekeeping, neighbours, dress, dancing and music', it is 'very fitting, that every little social commonwealth should dictate its own matters of discourse'.

Not that women have a monopoly on gossip. Men have the advantage of being able to bring back news from their wider range outside the home. Mr Weston is happy to be principal talker when a day in London gives him fresh matter of discourse; Mr Perry and Mr Cole often spread news as they go about their professional duties, though perhaps without the embellishments of what Mr Knightley terms 'all the minute particulars which only women's language can make interesting'.[8] In *The Watsons,* Mr Edwards, another town inhabitant, is actually chattier than his rather severe wife: on his return home for dinner, 'Mr Edwards proceeded to relate every other little article of news which his morning's lounge had supplied him with.'

Clerical Wives

The sub-category of the clerical wife, to which many of Jane Austen's acquaintance and family belonged, was especially subject to shifting fortunes. While her husband lived, such a woman had a defined role in the community, her status inferior only to that of the wife of the local squire. She would almost certainly have a comfortable home. This was a period when country rectories were being upgraded into gracious dwellings fit for the younger sons of the gentry, such as Edmund Bertram. In *Mansfield Park,* talk of improvements is not reserved for the great property of Sotherton Court. The kitchen garden and shrubbery have been improved by the two most recent incumbents of Mansfield Parsonage, and the parsonage at Thornton Lacey is to be altered before Edmund Bertram takes up residence. While rejecting Henry Crawford's more grandiose ideas, even Edmund plans to move the farmyard which has been allowed to spoil the approach, and create for himself a home that is not only "comfortable" but which has "the air of a gentleman's residence".[9] Elinor and Edward Ferrars, for all their modest tastes and moderate wishes, spend the first month of their marriage staying with Colonel Brandon 'at the mansion house, from whence they could superintend the progress of the parsonage, and direct everything as they liked on the spot – could choose papers, project shrubberies, and invent a sweep'. Catherine Morland, one of Austen's three heroines to marry a clergyman, thinks there is no home so delightful as 'a well-connected parsonage house'.[10] The Reverend Mr Collins reckons his 'humble abode'[11] to be one of the attractions in his power to offer a young lady; and the Reverend Mr Elton, with much the same aggrandizing ideas in view, has made what he can of his vicarage. All the young wives who slot into these homes take pleasure in their new roles as somebody of significance in their parishes, though Mrs Elton's parading exultation is of a different texture from the quiet satisfaction of the others.

But, trust in Providence though these wives and others like them undoubtedly did, at the back of their minds had to be the worry of what would happen if their husbands predeceased them, particularly if there were young children. At the very moment of a clergyman's death, his widow lost not only her life companion, but her home and income in one stroke. Of course, such women were given a few weeks' grace to accommodate themselves elsewhere, but such a sudden and complete change could be traumatic in families who had nothing to fall back on. From being an important person in the local community, a clerical widow could find herself not only homeless and penniless, but without a public role or social standing. As an appendage to her husband, everything depended on him.

Many clerical wives connected to Jane Austen found themselves in dire circumstances when their husbands died. Her eldest brother James's widow Mary (née Lloyd) was one. Marriage to James had proved a good move for Mary, who enjoyed not only increasing prosperity – Jane's letters often mention (with some bitterness and envy) some undeserved accession of wealth to the couple, some stroke of luck or extra luxury afforded – but the devotion of her husband, attested in poems he wrote on her birthday and wedding anniversary. But all that ended when James died on 13 December 1819, aged fifty-four (the only one of Jane's seven siblings to die before the age of seventy). The wheel of fortune completely turned for Mary. Her daughter Caroline, who had been born in 1805, the same year James had succeeded his father as Rector of Steventon, recorded in her *Reminiscences* how 'we were out by the end of January'. The living was in the gift of James's brother Edward Knight who, with six sons of his own to provide for, designed it for one of them, William, then a student at Oxford, rather than for James's own son James Edward. Until William was old enough to be ordained, 'Uncle Henry' was to hold the living in trust. Although a widower, Henry did not invite his sister-in-law to remain and keep house for him; he had his own second marriage in view, now that he had a home to offer. Mary Austen and 14-year-old Caroline had to shift as they could:

> We left Uncle Henry in possession. He was always very affectionate in manner to us, and paid my mother every due attention, but his own spirits he could not repress, and it is not pleasant to witness the elation of your successor in gaining what you have lost; and altogether tho' we left our home with sad hearts, we did not desire to linger in it any longer. My mother's old friend, Mrs Hulbert, received us at Bath. She had just lost her only sister, for whom she very sincerely mourned, and she offered us a quiet retreat for a little while.[12]

They were with Mrs Hulbert for eighteen months. Not until her own son was old enough to be ordained and to earn a small income did Mary Austen have a home of her own again, albeit a very modest one, and even then the little family was constantly shifting lodgings. Her sense of belonging to a community and having a role to play was gone forever. Some years later an almost identical fate befell Caroline's half-sister, Anna, child of her father's first marriage. Anna married Ben Lefroy in 1814 and went on to have six daughters and one son in quick succession. Ben was Rector of Ashe at the time of his premature death, aged thirty-eight, on 27 August 1829. Anna wrote in her pocket-book of 'My irreparable loss in my dear husband, who died at Ashe after months of slow decay.'[13] She had to hurry out of her home while her grief was still fresh, and her responsibilities so acute. On 13 November, Anna and her little children (the eldest fourteen, the youngest two) left Ashe Rectory and found a temporary home with her unmarried brother-in-law Christopher Edward Lefroy, thereafter living in a succession of rented houses. Anna was even worse off in widowhood than her stepmother Mary, in that her children were more numerous and, crucially, so much younger. Three years into her widowhood her aunt Cassandra wrote of her, 'She is left, poor thing! with a large family, a narrow income and indifferent health'.[14] The indifferent health was not surprising considering what she had had to cope with before and after her husband's death, but must have caused her additional anxiety on her little children's account: how would they fare as orphans?

The possession or otherwise of male relations able and willing to help out was what made all the difference to such clerical widows. In *Mansfield Park*, when the Reverend Mr Norris dies, his widow is provided with an alternative home in the village by her brother-in-law Sir Thomas Bertram. But Mrs Bates, widow of a former vicar of Highbury, has no male relations to assist her, and for a quarter of a century has been renting a modest apartment above a shop in Highbury's main street, with just one female domestic. Mr Weston describes Mrs Bates as "a poor old grandmother, who has barely enough to live on."[15] As Mr Knightley points out, her middle-aged daughter Hetty, one of two sisters growing up in Highbury Vicarage, "has sunk from the comforts she was born to".

Charlotte Collins is an interesting case in point. If Mr Collins predeceases Mr Bennet, leaving Charlotte a widow, she will suffer the usual fate of clerical wives in losing her home at once. If, however, Mr Collins has already come into his inheritance by the death of Mr Bennet, Charlotte will be mistress of Longbourn at the time of her widowhood (presuming she survives her husband) and then her fate will be entirely dependent on whether she has a son. If she does, he will inherit Longbourn and be able to provide for his mother. If not, the entail will come into play yet again, and Mrs Collins will be in the same position as her predecessor Mrs Bennet, being rendered homeless, together with any daughters she may have. Though in worldly terms everyone in *Pride and Prejudice* agrees that, in marrying Mr Collins, Charlotte has done very well for herself, in fact her long-term prosperity in life depends entirely on the birth and survival of at least one son. At the end of the novel she is expecting a 'little olive-branch' but more than that Austen does not divulge.

Although Jane's mother, Mrs Austen, did not lose a home on the death of her husband (they had already left Steventon Rectory for Bath), she did lose his income, and was reliant on the contributions of her sons for a reasonable standard of living. Even so, the widow and daughters could not afford to renew their lease in Bath and moved to a succession of ever-cheaper rented accommodation, finding respite from their quarters in less salubrious parts of the city by parcelling themselves out for long stretches at a time among their relations. Tracing their movements, Hazel Jones concludes that Jane and Cassandra 'spent most of 1805 living an unsatisfactory, nomadic life in other people's houses'.[16] It was no wonder that Austen wrote little or nothing in that period. For all her woes, however, and for all her impatience with large families, Jane might well have considered that it was only because her own mother had faced the perils of childbirth eight times that the Austen women had so many men to share the burden of their upkeep. Mr Austen's brother-in-law Tysoe Saul Hancock had, in the 1770s, tutted over the 'violently rapid increase of their family', and expressed the fear that 'George will find it easier to get a family than to provide for one',[17] but in fact the large number of sons proved a good investment and certainly saved Jane and Cassandra from having to hire themselves out to work. Of the eight Austen siblings, one was wealthy through inheritance and four were economically active, thus able between them to support their mother, the two sisters and the disabled brother. Less kindly, less reliable or fewer brothers, or more selfish, more resentful sisters-in-law (easily imagined when one considers, say, Fanny Dashwood's attitude in *Sense and Sensibility*) would have left the Miss Austens in as dire straits as spinsters they knew like Miss Murden and Miss Benn. And after all, when money was in short supply, to spare any for female hangers-on was not easy, even for the most angelic of wives and mothers of their own families, especially if it were felt that a maiden sister had turned down an opportunity to marry well, as had Jane. Such wives might well feel 'displeased at seeing the property of *her* children lavished on a helpless sister' – helpless, that is, to earn her own living – as Mary Wollstonecraft warned in *A Vindication of the Rights of Women* of 1792. Maiden or married, life was financially precarious for the majority of women, even in the more genteel reaches of society in which Jane Austen lived and grounded all her fiction.

Late Marriage

There is one other category of 'old wives', and that is those women who marry for the first time when no longer young. In the novels, Mrs Weston probably comes closest to this, though she is still young enough to bear a child. Nevertheless, it is said of her that 'she felt herself a most fortunate woman; and she had *lived long enough* to know how fortunate she might well be thought'[18] in her marriage (my italics).

In Jane Austen's circle there were several examples of late marriage. Her brother James's first wife, Anne Mathew, married him when she was thirty-two and he twenty-seven. The grand-daughter of a duke, she was much better born than he, but having reached her fourth decade without marrying she was induced to settle for a lowly (though highly educated) country curate. In worldly terms it was a very big step down, and without an allowance from her own father, the young couple would not have had enough to live on. Jane's friend Catherine Bigg, who had been living comfortably in her father's large house, was thirty-three when she married (as his first wife) the Reverend Herbert Hill, uncle to the poet Robert Southey, and twenty-six years her senior. It was rather an imprudent step for Catherine to take as the couple did nothing to prevent their family increasing almost as rapidly as the Prices in *Mansfield Park*. It is hard to believe that Jane Austen approved such lack of thought for the consequences. Six children – five of them boys – were born in seven years, and in visiting them, Jane remarked on the 'melancholy' age difference between the father and the little children.[19] He was sixty-eight when the youngest was born – in a period of history when sixty-eight was old. Not surprisingly, he died before any of them had reached adulthood. (This highly procreative marriage makes one wonder what Herbert Hill had done for sex until he was fifty-nine.)

Marrying in their thirties, Anne Mathew and Catherine Bigg had been beyond the usual marriageable age in the terms of the time, but not really old. However, there were two more marriages in Jane Austen's family in which the first-time bride really was advanced in years. Jane's cousin Philadelphia Walter, born in 1761, seemed set to remain a spinster, reaching the age of fifty without marrying, and having besides (if one judges from letters written in her youth to Eliza de Feuillide) a prim outlook that fitted her for the appellation old maid. Yet in 1811 she married George Whitaker, a farmer. He was probably looking for someone to run his home, and she for the status and security of marriage. Her mother had died recently, and perhaps she was desperate for a home; though the more romantic possibilities of a love match put on hold while the lady devoted herself to an ailing mother, or even of an imperious old woman who disapproved of her daughter's marriage to a farmer, cannot absolutely be ruled out. It is tantalizing not to know more of Philadelphia's story, and what Jane Austen made of it. Jane and Cassandra, so much younger than Philadelphia yet apparently fully reconciled to their single status, must have been somewhat startled by the news; and moreover, her letter announcing her engagement evidently contained some complaints, for in replying on behalf of the Austen women with their best wishes on the occasion, Cassandra wrote in terms somewhat extraordinary for a congratulatory letter:

> From what you have already said I am sure it [Philadelphia's new home] must be comfortable and tho' there may be some things you wish otherwise, for where is the situation on earth exempt from evils? you are too wise and too good to dwell on the wrong side of the Picture. Use will reconcile you to some things which appear evils at first and others you will bear as the necessary attendants of humanity, so you see I am determined you shall be happy whether you will or no.[20]

Jane did not live to know of one other even more extraordinary example of late marriage in her circle, but Cassandra did. One year after the death of Mrs Austen in 1827, Cassandra found herself the sole inhabitant of Chawton Cottage when their friend and housemate Martha Lloyd, who had lived with them since 1805 on the death of her mother, was sought in marriage at the age of sixty-three by their brother Captain Francis Austen, fifty-four. When Frank's first wife died in giving birth to their eleventh child in 1823, his eldest daughter Mary Jane had assumed running of the home. It was her marriage to a naval officer in June 1828 that motivated Frank to look for a replacement housekeeper. Writing stiffly of himself in the third person, he anticipated that as he would find

> his situation very lonely after his daughter's marriage, he selected as his second wife a lady he had long and intimately known and considered almost a sister, Miss Martha Lloyd, the elder sister of his eldest brother's second wife, and who being several years older than himself made it improbable there would be any child of such a union, which considering the number he had had by his first marriage seems to have been much wished.[21]

This begs the question of whether Frank intended to consummate his second marriage – it would seem that he did – and what Martha thought of conjugal relations after a lifetime of celibacy. An alternative interpretation is that Frank chose an unattractively ageing woman to prevent his being tempted into sex. Jane had once described Martha as 'elegant', but the daguerreotype of her in later life looks grim. The marriage was resented by Frank's younger daughters, who disliked having an old lady, set in her ways, foisted on them. Martha was of an older generation even than their own mother, who had been born in 1785, twenty years later than Martha. The choice of Martha also brought down the wrath of Frank's wealthy and capricious aunt Mrs Leigh Perrot, who had meditated making him her heir. 'This is a year of marriages – but not all have been so hard of digestion as the Gosport arrangements'[22] she wrote to another relation: one very old lady disapproving of the elevation into matrimony of one whom at best could be called middle-aged. Exactly why Mrs Leigh Perrot disapproved so strongly of the match is hard to fathom. But what both Philadelphia's and Martha's marriages show is that, remote as was the possibility, it was never too late to be rescued by some needy man from the disgrace of being an old maid.

5. OLD MAIDS

On 26 August 1813 Jane and Cassandra Austen and their niece Fanny Knight walked after dinner from Chawton to the nearby village of Farringdon to call upon the Reverend John Benn and his wife Elizabeth. The couple had then eleven children to show for their twenty-three years of marriage, and had not yet stopped breeding. There was evidently no room in Farringdon Rectory for – or any money left over to help support – Mr Benn's unmarried sister, Mary, who occupied a dismal cottage in Chawton and lived in a very small way.

The high-point of Mary Benn's existence, the moment for which she is famed, had come just seven months before, when she happened to be dining with Mrs Austen and Jane on the day that the newly published *Pride and Prejudice* arrived from London. Cassandra was away, and Jane reported:

> In the eve[nin]g we set fairly at it & read half the 1st vol. to her – prefacing that having intelligence from Henry that such a work w[oul]d soon appear we had desired him to send it whenever it came out – & I believe it passed with her unsuspected. – She was amused, poor soul! *that* she c[oul]d not help you know, with two such people to lead the way; but she really does seem to admire Elizabeth.[1]

Miss Benn was invited back the next evening – and other evenings thereafter – to continue listening, and it is to be hoped that although she could have no idea what an extraordinary privilege was being extended to her, it nevertheless sweetened her existence for a little while. As Claire Tomalin has said: 'the thought of meek Miss Benn sitting in Chawton Cottage while Jane Austen and her mother performed *Pride and Prejudice* for her – something many of us would give a great deal to have experienced – makes one surprising and glowing episode in that sad little life, provided by her friend Jane Austen.'[2]

And it *was* a sad little life; the life of an impoverished spinster of gentle birth but scanty means. For all our envy of those amazing evenings, few of us would really exchange our own lives for that of Miss Benn. She was by no means as comfortably circumstanced as the Austen ladies, but then they had more brothers to augment their income. The sympathy with which Jane Austen writes of Mary Benn's predicament suggests that she was well aware of this: there but for the Grace of God went Cassandra and she. Instead of having a kindly brother for a landlord, Miss Benn had to rent as she could. The property she was inhabiting when the Austens first knew her had been divided in two, her landlord John Philimore occupying the other part. Less than a month after the *Pride and Prejudice* readings, she was given notice to quit her home to make way for the son of old Philimore. Jane wrote to Cassandra:

> Poor Creature! – You may imagine how full of cares she must be, & how anxious all Chawton will feel to get her decently settled somewhere. – She will have 3 months before her – & if anything else can be met with, she will be glad enough to be driven from her present wretched abode; – it has been terrible for her during the late storms of wind & rain.[3]

In fact it seems that Miss Benn accepted (how willingly we cannot tell) the dwelling, again probably little better than a hovel, vacated by Philimore's son Edward, effectively 'swapping' homes with him for his convenience rather than her own.[4] So while the note of panic in Jane's letter may have been unwarranted, it remains true not only that, in something as fundamental as her home, Miss Benn was at the mercy of other people's decisions, but that despite belonging to the genteel classes, her domestic circumstances were on a par with the village labourers. The Philimores were respectable carpenters and Overseers of the Poor, but not of a class to mix socially with the Austens and Knights.

That the Austen sisters never referred to Miss Benn as Mary, though she was just two years older than Cassandra, suggests they regarded her as elderly: 'poor soul!' and 'poor creature!' as Jane had exclaimed; and that she was a recipient of their kindness and charity rather than someone who could be regarded as a real friend, or whose conversation could give instruction or pleasure. Years of struggle seem to have ground her down and made her both physically weak and pathetically thankful for any small addition to her comforts. Before the *Pride and Prejudice* readings, Jane had written to Martha Lloyd on 30 November 1812:

> You have sometimes expressed a wish of making Miss Benn some present; Cassandra and I think that something of the Shawl kind to wear over her Shoulders within doors in very cold weather might be useful, but it must not be very handsome or she would not use it. Her long Fur tippet is almost worn out.

On 24 January she reported, 'Miss Benn wore her new shawl last night, sat in it the whole even[g] & seemed to enjoy it very much.' Mary Benn died in January 1816, at the age of forty-six.

Which of the Benn ladies was more to be pitied, the wife or the old maid? The wife might seem in a better position, with husband and status and (while he lived) a secure home; but then, there was all that childbearing to endure, with a real risk of death every time (about one in forty births resulted in maternal death), with each addition to the family threatening to leave those already born motherless, and certainly diminishing their parents' ability to provide for them. Elizabeth Benn went on to have at least two more children. 'I am quite tired of so many children – Mrs Benn has a 13th' reported Jane with some asperity in 1817.[5] She probably regarded Elizabeth with less pity than Mary, considering that the number of offspring might have been limited, if only by 'the simple regimen of separate rooms'[6] which she advocated for another couple over-endowed with children. Mrs Benn's reward for all that childbearing was that she had plenty of adult children to take her in when her husband died, though that did not happen until he was ninety-one – she died four years later, aged eighty-seven. She must have had a remarkable constitution.

Two other single women whose acquaintance Jane Austen made in Kent and whose destinies interested her were Anne Sharp, one-time governess to her brother Edward's children and, a generation older, Molly Milles, who lived with her widowed mother in Canterbury. Anne Sharp was something of a kindred spirit and became a lifelong friend of Jane's. She seems to have been a restless soul, as we hear of her over the years residing in various places and taking up various posts – governess, companion, schoolteacher – and of Jane always longing for something better for her; even wishing the bachelor brother of one of her employers would fall in love with her.

A glimpse of Anne Sharp while still in Edward Knight's employment is intriguing. During a family visit, twelve-year-old Fanny Knight described in her diary a day of play-acting with Aunt Cassandra as Mrs Teachum, Aunt Jane as Miss Popham (another teacher), Grandmama Austen as Betty Jones the Pie Woman, Mama playing the Bathing Woman and Miss Sharp taking sundry male parts as 'The Dancing Master, the Apothecary & the Serjeant [sic]'.[7] Fanny wrote, 'They dressed in Character & we had a most delightful day.' Was this an example of the lowly governess being obliged to take the parts real ladies did not want? Or – more pleasingly – did Miss Sharp relish the chance to stride about in breeches and play the male, and was Jane even a little envious and admiring of her boldness?

It was perhaps her sense of humour that attracted Jane, as in

1820 James Edward Austen was to find her 'horridly affected but rather amusing'.[8] Affectation was not a characteristic usually tolerated by Jane, and neither was being over-concerned with one's own health, which emerges in several of Jane Austen's letters with reference to Miss Sharp. As David Selwyn remarks in *Jane Austen and Children*, it is not easy to come to an assessment of Anne Sharp's character.[9] Whatever her shortcomings, Jane must have been willing to make allowances for a clever woman in difficult circumstances. Maybe Anne Sharp's cleverness and sense of humour were so exceptional among Austen's acquaintance that her true worth was appreciated and her faults excused. Most of Jane's female friendships had been formed in girlhood; she was thirty when she met Anne, making her the principal new friend of her maturity. Anne was invited to pay several visits to Chawton Cottage, and it was to her that Jane Austen wrote her very last letter from the place, addressing her as 'my dearest Anne', and referring to herself as 'your friend Jane'.[10]

Miss Milles had no such intellectual parity with Jane Austen but she has another claim on our attention. As someone 'foolishly minute' in her conversation, who undertook to tell a story in three words and then rambled on for half an hour, she may well have been the inspiration for Miss Bates.[11] Or perhaps Miss Bates was a compound of mother and daughter. *Mrs* Milles was one of the few very old people to draw Austen's praise: 'I like the Mother,' she wrote in 1813, 'because she is chearful [sic] & grateful for what she is at the age of 90 & upwards.'[12] Cheerfulness and gratitude for one's blessings were attitudes of mind always urged and commended by Austen, and form the endearing part of *Miss* Bates's sometimes trying character. Mrs Milles in fact lived for another three years, dying only four months before Austen herself, though she was more than fifty years older. Jane wrote to Kent niece Fanny:

> Poor Mrs C. Milles, that she should die on the wrong day at last, after being about it so long! It was unlucky that the Goodnestone Party could not meet you, & I hope her friendly,

> obliging, social spirit, which delighted in drawing People together, was not conscious of the division & disappointment she was occasioning.[13]

Miss Milles was sixty-nine when her mother died. For a clerical widow, Mrs Milles had seemed in relatively comfortable circumstances, renting a succession of houses in the Cathedral precincts from absent prebendaries; her husband, who had died as long ago as 1749, came from a wealthy local family, which is why the Godmersham and Goodnestone families knew her socially. Jane continued to Fanny:

> I am sorry & surprised that you speak of her as having little to leave & must feel for Miss Milles. . . . if a material loss of Income is to attend her other loss. Single Women have a dreadful propensity for being poor – which is one very strong argument in favour of Matrimony.

To Grow Old and Be Laughed At

William Hayley's *Essay on Old Maids* of 1785, which Austen may have known – she certainly read other works by him, and was familiar with most of the polemical literature of her day – begins with an attempt to define the crossing point between unmarried girl and old maid. After consulting his acquaintance Hayley writes:

> The misses of twenty considered all their unmarried friends, who had passed their thirtieth year, as absolute Old Maids; those of thirty supposed the aera to commence at about forty-five; and some ladies of fifty convinced me how differently they thought upon the subject, by calling others, about three or four years younger than themselves, by the infantine appellation of girls; from whence I presumed they would advance the aera I speak of to the age of sixty at least. [However] the world in

> general . . .never fail to give the unwelcome title of Old Maid to unmarried ladies of forty.

Charlotte Lucas is twenty-seven when she becomes engaged to Mr Collins and her brothers are deeply relieved that she will not die an old maid. It is as if the label 'old maid' is worse than anything more material that the brothers might fear: having to contribute to her maintenance, for example, or having her always at home. When Harriet Smith hears that Emma Woodhouse has no intention of marrying, she exclaims, "But then, to be an old maid at last!" adding "and that's so dreadful!"[14] Though a moment's thought would show Harriet that Emma will be rich and comfortable whether she is married or unmarried (as Emma goes on to explain), once again, it is the label itself that strikes such horror into Harriet's breast. Sixteen-year-old Lydia Bennet warns her sister Jane, who seems to have lost Bingley, that she is in danger of becoming "quite an old maid" at twenty-three.[15]

William Hayley notwithstanding, it has often been noticed that one age seems to signify the loss not only of youth but eligibility in marriage for Jane Austen. "A woman of seven and twenty," declares Marianne Dashwood in *Sense and Sensibility,* "can never hope to feel or inspire affection again, and if her home be uncomfortable, or her fortune small . . . might bring herself to submit to the offices of a nurse, for the sake of the provision and security of a wife." The extreme views of Marianne, a girl of seventeen, are not those of the author. But twenty-seven does seem to be the age which in Jane Austen's imagination marks the end of the first youthful period of life – at least in women. Twenty-seven occurs in this context whether she is writing from the vantage point of twenty or forty. Marianne's scenario is almost exactly the deal which twenty-seven-year-old Charlotte Lucas grasps with eyes wide open in *Pride and Prejudice,* though her foolish husband requires humouring and guiding rather than actual nursing:

> Mr Collins to be sure was neither sensible nor agreeable; his

> society was irksome, and his attachment to her must be imaginary. But still he would be her husband. Without thinking highly either of men or matrimony, marriage had always been her object; it was the only honourable provision for well-educated young women of small fortune, and however uncertain of giving happiness, must be their pleasantest preservative from want. This preservative she had now obtained; and at the age of twenty-seven, without having ever been handsome, she felt all the good luck of it.

Both these novels are the creation of a very young woman, to whom the age of twenty-seven might indeed have seemed old. But *Persuasion,* with its 27-year-old heroine who has lost her 'remarkably pretty' youthful looks to become 'faded and thin', regarded by her acquaintance as unlikely now to marry, was begun in the months leading up to the author's fortieth birthday.

It is probably just a coincidence that Jane Austen's own two last chances of romance occurred when she herself was approaching twenty-seven. In the summer of 1802, during a family jaunt to the seaside, she may have met and fallen in love with a man whom even her sister thought worthy of her – but he died. (The details are unverifiable and scanty, based on what Cassandra is said to have told a niece many years after Jane's death, and not written down until many years after that.) Better documented is the fact that Jane received her only known proposal of marriage in December of that year: an unanticipated proposal which in the first shock she accepted, for her suitor, Harris Bigg Wither (himself only twenty-one) was the brother of friends and heir to a good estate – it would have been a good match for her. After a sleepless night, and in considerable distress for the pain she was causing, she withdrew her acceptance, almost certainly acknowledging to herself that she was not, and could not imagine herself ever being, in love with the young man.

She appears to have had no regrets and thereafter to have regarded herself, as far as we can tell, as past the likelihood of marriage and motherhood, finding plenty to enjoy in her extended family, her settled home at Chawton, her closeness to her sister, and of course, in her imaginative life and increasing success as a published author. It is possible to infer from her letters a certain amount of relief that she had escaped the various toils of childbearing, housekeeping (at Chawton, Cassandra took on most of the responsibility for that) and – possibly – managing a difficult husband.

By assuming the badge of middle age (indoor caps to hide their hair) long before they had to, the sisters had seemed to signal their cessation of interest in attracting marriage offers. Certainly this was the case with Cassandra, who had been engaged to marry but who, on the death of her fiancé, behaved as if she had been widowed and, at the age of twenty-three, resolutely turned her back on any further thoughts of romance; perhaps she was the model for Anne Elliot, for whom 'no second attachment . . . had been possible to the nice tone of her mind, the fastidiousness of her taste'.[16] In her own slightly different trajectory to the same place, Jane had not set out intending to remain single; as a child she had imagined husbands for herself in spoof entries in her father's marriage register; later she had flirted and danced like any other young lady, and shown herself susceptible to male charms. Her mother had certainly expected her to marry and to be whisked away 'the Lord knows where'.[17] It did not happen, and Jane Austen's growing experience of life showed her that married women were not always to be envied, and that her own chance lot in life carried many consolations.

In her fiction, however, as critics have remarked, every woman seeks to be married. Emma's defence of the unmarried state is the only partial exception, and that is presented as one of her youthful delusions and is undermined by her eventual eagerness to marry Mr Knightley. Emma's word portrait of what she will be 'at forty or fifty' is a rare example in any of the novels of a character imagining her life decades hence – but then Emma has a more powerful imagination than most. Yet as she acknowledges, it is the possession of money that makes the single life for women viable: "a single woman of good fortune is always respectable, and may be as sensible and pleasant as anybody else!"[18] She concedes, however, and without its seeming to distress her, that "a single woman with a very narrow income must be a ridiculous, disagreeable old maid! the proper sport of boys and girls".

"It is very bad to grow old & be poor & laughed at" says Elizabeth, the eldest of the Watson sisters, in contemplating the future if, as is likely, she fails to marry.[19] Her tone is darker than Emma Woodhouse's because she has real and well-justified fears that she will experience what she speaks of. That society seemed to licence the open ridicule of unmarried women is, to us, the most shocking aspect of their situation. A widow could be poor, but not laughed at: a man had once liked her well enough to choose her, and thus had validated her existence. Neither was an unmarried man the subject of mockery; his single state was deemed to be his choice. If a woman had turned him down she must never make this public knowledge (Mr Knightley knows that Emma is too correct to confirm his guess about Mr Elton) and a rejected suitor could, and usually did, make another choice. Mr Collins, Mr Elton and Jane Austen's own suitor Harris Bigg Wither all did exactly that, and without much lapse of time.

The accepted truths that Emma Woodhouse and Elizabeth Watson in their different ways express are endorsed in the words of a real-life governess of the period, a Miss Weeton: 'An old maid is a stock for everyone to laugh at. Every article of dress, every word, every movement is satirized. Boys play tricks on them and are applauded. Girls sneer at them and are unreproved.'[20]

There was only one defence against public mockery that a single woman without fortune might muster, one that Jane Austen knew herself to possess (and perhaps recognized in Anne Sharp) but which she denied to her creation Miss Bates: an acute intelligence. In the sentence that first introduces Miss Bates, long before we hear her speak, we learn that 'she had no intellectual superiority to make atonement to herself, or frighten those who might hate her into outward respect'. Austen's mental powers fulfilled both these functions: in every joyous, critical or impish sentence, her letters testify to the atonement her mind brought her, while the fear and outward respect of casual acquaintance are captured in a letter of 1815 which is quoted in almost every Austen biography:

> I have discovered that our great favourite, Miss Austen, is my countrywoman; that mamma knew all her family intimately; and that she herself is an old maid (I beg her pardon, I mean a young lady) . . . and a friend of mine, who visits her now, says that she has stiffened into the most perpendicular, precise, taciturn piece of 'single blessedness' that ever existed, and that, till *Pride and Prejudice* showed what a precious gem was hidden in that unbending case, she was no more regarded in society than a poker or a firescreen, or any other thin upright piece of wood or iron that fills its corner in peace and quietness. The case is very different now: she is still a poker – but a poker of whom everyone is afraid.[21]

Whatever inaccuracies or hidden agendas may be at work here, there is no gainsaying the ingrained assumptions that spinsters had to contend with (the writer of the letter, Mary Russell Mitford, was a spinster herself) or failing to appreciate that an involuntary impulse of deference superimposed over a grounding of dislike – itself based on a sense of inferiority – must have been evoked in some at least of Austen's common acquaintance.

Neither Charlotte Lucas nor Elizabeth Watson wants a husband for reasons of sex, romance or companionship. Charlotte accepts her only offer of marriage 'for the pure and disinterested motive of gaining a home',[22] while Elizabeth tells her sister that she could do very well single "if one could be young for ever".[23] But as one cannot, and as their clergyman father is unable to provide for four daughters, she, like all of them, must pursue any leads that offer. She tells Emma that their sister Penelope is chasing "a rich old Dr Harding, uncle to the friend she goes to see – and she has taken a vast deal of trouble about him and given up a great deal of time to no purpose as yet."

Emma is shocked:

> "To be so bent on marriage – to pursue a man merely for the sake of situation – is the sort of thing that shocks me; I cannot understand it. Poverty is a great evil, but to a woman of education and feeling it ought not, it cannot be the greatest. I would rather be teacher at a school (and I can think of nothing worse) than marry a man I did not like."
>
> "I would rather do anything than be teacher at a school", said her sister. "*I* have been at school, Emma, and know what a life they lead; *you* never have. I should not like marrying a disagreeable man any more than yourself – but I do not think there *are* many very disagreeable men – I think I could like any good-humoured man with a comfortable income."

To be a teacher at a school is, of course, the fate of three of the old maids in *Emma*. Miss Richardson, Miss Nash and Miss Prince are treated well by their employer, Mrs Goddard, and no doubt they are better off than some; Mrs Goddard shares with them the gift of a goose, from the farming mother of one of her pupils, having it cooked on a Sunday when all can enjoy it. But the lives of these three women are narrower even than that of Miss Bates. The latter is included in the social life of Highbury, but the three teachers are never invited anywhere, not even to the ball at the Crown. Emma never thinks of befriending them – they are as much beneath her notice as the farmer Robert Martin. All they can do is press their faces to the school windows to watch any handsome man go by. For company they have each other and the girls of the school, some of whom may be polite like Harriet, but others who are likely to mock. "I . . . know what a life they lead", as Elizabeth Watson says. No wonder if they became sour, narrow-minded and bad-tempered.

Gentlewomen who had to find employment had the choice between being governess in a family or teacher in a school – both had their privations and humiliations, as Mary Wollstonecraft wrote in her chapter 'The Unfortunate Situation of Females

Fashionably Educated and Left without a Fortune' in her 1787 book *Thoughts on the Education of Daughters*: 'A teacher at a school is only a kind of upper servant, who has more work than the menial ones. A governess to young ladies is equally disagreeable.' For such women, after spending their youth and strength on such work, what was the prospect in old age? Wollstonecraft continues, 'Life glides away, and the spirits with it; and when youth and genial years are flown, they have nothing to subsist on; or perhaps, on some extraordinary occasion, some small allowance may be made for them, which is thought a great charity'.

Jane Fairfax, in *Emma*, likens hiring herself out as a governess to the slave trade, but dealing in human intellect rather than human flesh. Mrs Weston, who as Miss Taylor has been governess for sixteen years, has undoubtedly been fortunate in Mr Woodhouse's employment and his willingness to keep her on after his daughter is grown – but she is an exception. Jane Austen knew a succession of governesses employed by her wealthy brother Edward, not only Anne Sharp. Edward Knight, kind, humorous and relaxed, with no feelings of snobbery to be affronted when his sister befriended his governess, owner of a large and comfortable house and grounds, seems as good an employer as any working woman could hope for – yet for one reason or another governesses never stayed long at Godmersham; perhaps even the well brought-up little girls of that household were trying. 'By this time I suppose she is hard at it, governing away,' Jane wrote of the latest replacement in 1811; 'poor creature! I pity her, tho' they are my nieces.'[24]

Emma, then, has three teachers, two governesses and one unmarried middle-aged woman who, despite desperate poverty, has managed to cling on to her genteel status by *not* going out to work: Miss Bates. Emma herself muses on 'the destiny of women' when comparing the importance of Mrs Churchill with the insignificance of Jane Fairfax (who will, however, unsuspected by anybody, turn out to be the next Mrs Churchill). It is the novel which has the most to say about old maids, and the most developed portrait of such a one in her middle years.

Two other older unmarried women in Austen's fiction are only fleetingly portrayed. Both Mrs Percival in *Catharine, or the Bower,* and Mrs Smith in *Sense and Sensibility,* who does not even have a speaking part, are comfortably off, with their own homes, resembling Emma Woodhouse's projections for herself. Both take the title 'Mrs' because they are the heads of their own households. Being rich, they are not subject to anyone's mockery or abuse. They are rather respected and feared. The old maidenhood of these two women shows itself in their strict notions and disapproval of the easy morals (as they see it) of the young.

Austen also has a clutch of what one might term incipient old maids: Elizabeth, Penelope and Margaret Watson; Elizabeth Elliot, Nancy Steele, Caroline Bingley and Mary Bennet have an air of desperation about them, but have not yet quite given up all hope. Though each is an individual, some more unpleasant than others, it is almost wholly for their husband-hunting proclivities that they take their places in the drama; they are mainly comically and unsympathetically depicted. As a body, a sort of background noise to the main action, they seem to stand for the fact that almost every young woman is in search of a husband.

That leaves Miss Bates as the only archetypal impoverished old maid old enough to have accepted spinsterhood as her way of life – and, as such, she has to carry a lot of modern-day expectations. While Miss Bates did very well to be laughed at among nineteenth- and twentieth-century critics and readers, feminist commentators have looked for a greater degree of empathy on Austen's part. Since she was an old maid herself, and apparently a very happy one, some recent critics have expressed disappointment that Austen did not vouchsafe a portrait of an older woman finding satisfaction in life without being married, and that despite (though perhaps it is because of) her own situation being so similar, she 'mildly disdains and distances herself from spinsters'.[25] It is true that Miss Bates is treated with a fair degree of authorial gentleness, and defended by the hero, but still, she is regarded patronizingly, as much *after* Emma's reformation as before. That she is one of the great comic characters in Austen's *oeuvre*, an individual rather than an example of a type, not to mention a marvellously contrived device for plot furtherance, should perhaps temper such criticism, which nevertheless demands to be taken seriously in any review of Austen's depiction of women approaching old age.

Austen was up against a convention that she had either no desire, or no courage, to break down completely. The eighteenth-century novel contained no model of unmarried female happiness and fulfilment in middle or older age. Fanny Burney, a role model for Austen, has none. Her novel *Cecilia* (1782) contains a typical specimen of the eighteenth-century literary old maid in the manipulative, mean-spirited, ill-educated man-hunting spinster Miss Larolles – the very character with whom Anne Elliot wryly compares herself during the Bath concert when she is trying to make it possible for Captain Wentworth to approach her:

> by some other removals, and a little scheming of her own, Anne was enabled to place herself much nearer the end of the bench than she had been before, much more within reach of a passer-by. She could not do so without comparing herself with Miss Larolles, the inimitable Miss Larolles, but still she did it, and not with much happier effect.[26]

This is the passage which springs into Anne Elliot's thoughts, a passage and a character which Austen expected her readers to be able to call to mind:

> "Do you know," continued Miss Larolles, "Mr Meadows has not spoke one word to me all the evening! Though I am sure he saw me, for I sat at the outside on purpose to speak to a person or two, that I knew would be strolling about; for if one sits on the inside, there's no speaking to a creature you know. . . . It's the shockingest thing you can conceive to be made to sit in the middle of those forms; one might as well be at home."

On the stage, too, old maids were often grossly ridiculed: Arthur Murphy's play *The Old Maid* of 1761 contains the line about an unwanted sister, 'an old maid in the house is a devil'. Whether in the novel or in drama, whether created by men or by women, fictional ageing spinsters tended to be either garrulous like Miss Bates, peevish like Margaret Watson or single-minded man-chasers like Penelope Watson and Nancy Steele. Nancy Steele of *Sense and Sensibility* speaks and acts very much like Miss Larolles. Indeed, perhaps the real reason why Austen abandoned *The Watsons* was that she foresaw the danger of falling into the various negative stereotypes surrounding old maids.

When she came to revisit the subject in *Emma,* a decade further on in her own life, it was with a happier touch and tone. Miss Bates *does* break the mould of fictional old maids in that she plays a full part in her community; though desperately poor she is not marginalized and, as far as it is within her power, she tries to give as well as to accept – if not food and material help, then gratitude, compliments and concern that make her neighbours of all classes feel better about themselves. Together with her remarkably good language (despite her many sentences broken off, she speaks with perfect politeness and exquisite grammar) this sense of obligation to others is the legacy of her being a clergyman's daughter, like Austen herself. Socially and linguistically, Miss Bates is above both Harriet Smith and Augusta Elton. Contemporary readers would have realized this, though it may elude us today. In *Emma,* Austen was able to combine a realistic view of the lot of old maids in the conditions and prospects of the group of teachers and Jane Fairfax, with a tenderly handled, nuanced portrait of one individual in Miss Bates.

Spinster Nieces

Among Jane Austen's many nieces, several remained unmarried, though she was not to know this at the time of her death. Their vicissitudes are instructive in contemplating the lot of genteel spinsters into the decades when Jane herself should have been growing old. The comfort, security and way of life of these women were completely at the mercy of fathers, brothers and nephews.

As we have seen, Caroline Austen was fourteen when her clergyman father died and his little family was forced to vacate Steventon Rectory. Here it is Caroline's subsequent life which concerns us. Until her mother's death in 1843, when Caroline was thirty-eight, the two women seem to have been completely bound up in one another and in their mutual love for the only son and brother Edward, who married and had a large family of his own. Until 1837 Caroline and her mother subsisted on little money, but in that year Edward inherited the property Scarlets from his capricious great-aunt Mrs Leigh Perrot. Thereafter he was able to make his mother a generous allowance, and to continue this for Caroline, so she did not have to fear for her old age; in fact, in 1851 she was able to buy her own house, Wargrave Lodge, for the sum of £1,200.[27] The experience of losing her home at the age of fourteen may have made her especially wish to be a property-owner, quite an unusual circumstance for a single woman of the time. For a while, she seems to have lived contentedly by herself. Almost the perfect single life: enough money, family nearby, a secure home. But in 1860, when Caroline was fifty-five, there was a call of duty which she felt obliged to answer. Two of Edward's unmarried adult sons required a female relative to keep house for them at Frog Firle, a 550-acre farm which they purchased together. Caroline left her own home to look after them, first letting out and then selling Wargrave Lodge in 1863 – relinquishing her independence. It is true that she had the satisfaction of being wanted and needed, and of repaying in the only way she was able her brother's lifelong kindness towards her. Yet one is left with the impression (perhaps anachronistically) that, having eluded marriage, housekeeping for two men had been thrust on her, and that she did not have much choice in the matter of how and with whom she passed the last decades of her life.

Jane's other unmarried nieces did not lose their fathers until their own middle age. Unmarried daughters of widower fathers were of course expected to keep the family house for them. Following the death of his second wife, Francis Austen looked to his two unmarried daughters, Cassandra and Fanny, to fulfil this role at his house Portsdown Lodge. Unexpectedly in 1845 he was appointed Admiral and Commander-in-Charge of the North American and West Indian Station – having not been to sea since 1814. He took Fanny and Cassandra with him on board HMS *Vindictive,* either because they could not be left alone in his house – which he let out – or to serve as his companions and hostesses at social functions over there; they did not return until June 1848. Perhaps they enjoyed the adventure – *Vindictive* sailed up and down the coast between Halifax and Bermuda, often putting into port; but it had an adverse effect on the health of Cassandra, who was seven years older than her sister. Possibly she was turning into a sour old maid already since one of the lieutenants on board expressed the opinion that she 'had every bad quality of head and heart' and that her father was under her thumb.[28] She died the year after their return to England, leaving Fanny the only surviving unmarried daughter.

When Francis Austen died in 1865, Fanny was forty-four. She was taken in by a clergyman brother, Edward, whose wife died two years later, leaving to her care three little girls and therefore a useful role in life. Fanny was just one year younger than her brother Edward, and she was fortunate indeed that he survived her by two years, so although she lived to be eighty-three, she never found herself homeless.[29]

This was to be the fate of her first cousin, Marianne Knight. It was all the more surprising in that Marianne belonged to the most affluent branch of the family – she was the third daughter of Jane's brother Edward, who in 1812 had changed his surname to Knight. Though her cousin James Edward Austen-Leigh had, as a young man, found her the most 'bewitching' and 'beautiful' of the five Knight sisters, it chanced that she never married.[30] After their own marriages had taken her two elder sisters from home,

Marianne assumed the role and duties of hostess and housekeeper for her father at Godmersham, for a period of about thirty years. It was a large estate, with a gracious and sociable style of living, as Jane's own letters when staying there attest. Certainly Marianne had never known anything different, and as the mistress of her father's home she had enjoyed similar comforts and status to Emma Woodhouse or Elizabeth Elliot in *Persuasion*. But this way of life came to an abrupt end when her father died. Kindly man though he was, he made no special provision for her, not questioning the conventions of primogeniture by which the eldest son inherited almost everything, and trusting to this son to do the right thing (shades of Dashwood father and son) by any of his siblings who needed help. This second Edward Knight, long settled at Chawton House with a very large number of children by two successive wives, decided to let out the old family home in Kent, to the sorrow of all his brothers and sisters but particularly distressing to Marianne, the only one of the eleven who had lived there all her life. At the age of fifty-one, she was left with no home, and just £200 a year of her own. This was not enough to afford her an independent establishment. As the author of a book about this branch of the family so pertinently remarks of Marianne, 'No longer Miss Woodhouse, she had suddenly become poor Miss Bates.'[31]

Marianne uprooted herself from Kent to Hampshire and found a role keeping house for her bachelor brother Charles, now Rector of Chawton: taking over where Jane and Cassandra had left off in the life of the village, and like her grandmother finding pleasure in working a Chawton garden in her late middle age. The gardening book in which she recorded her activities is preserved in the Hampshire Record Office.[32] This quiet, settled life, which had seemed to solve her problems, was to be hers for only fourteen years. The death of Charles aged sixty-three left her homeless once more. 'Charley has left me all he had – it is not much,' she told her sister Fanny.[33] For a second time, she was in effect turned out by her eldest brother, Edward, who held all the power over property and livings in the family, and had a son of his own waiting in the wings for Chawton Rectory. Next Marianne, was invited to share expenses with her youngest brother, John, and his wife Margaret, a childless and not very well-off couple. 'They like it and I can't live by myself,' she continued to Fanny. 'We don't know where – it will depend on Edward when he has made up his mind.' After ten years John too died. For the third time, the death of a male relation robbed Marianne of a home, and she was getting older all the time. Aged seventy-seven, this brave lady took herself off to Ireland to help her sister Louisa nurse her Irish husband, Lord George Hill; and, after a spell back in Kent in the home of Lizzy Rice, the sister closest to her in age, Marianne eventually returned to Ireland to join forces with the widowed Louisa. Marianne outlived all her siblings and died in 1895 at the age of ninety-four, and was buried in Ireland. She may have been a beloved 'Aunt May' to her extended family, and she may never have actually had to earn her living, for there were enough brothers and sisters, nephews and nieces to shuffle her about between them, but her life exemplifies the fact that for a whole century after Austen, even well-born women who remained single were as likely as not to suffer insecurity, dependence and lack of choice as they aged.

6. STILL A VERY FINE MAN

"Man is more robust than woman, but he is not longer lived", says Anne Elliot to Captain Harville towards the end of *Persuasion*. In Austen's fiction, men have their own issues with the ageing process. Sir Walter Elliot notwithstanding, they tend to be less troubled by the change in their looks. A good half of that 'foolish, spendthrift baronet's' self-esteem is founded on his appearance (the other half on his rank) so it is fortunate for him that he can continue to look in the mirror with self-satisfaction. The narrator tells us, with no irony to undercut the assertion, that 'He had been remarkably handsome in his youth; and, at fifty-four, was still a very fine man.' But that Sir Walter is to some extent deluding himself about his youthful appearance is likewise hinted at by the narrator, who says that he might be 'deemed only half a fool, for thinking himself and Elizabeth as blooming as ever, amidst the wreck of the good looks of everybody else'.

More pressing for the older man than fretting about his appearance seems to have been the need to be looked after. Whilst being widowed, for example, often makes a woman more autonomous, powerful and liberated in Austen's world, becoming a widower usually seems to increase the neediness of men. That is largely because the financial support which forms the usual male contribution to the marriage passes, if women are lucky, into their own hands on widowhood; whereas the housekeeping role of the wife has to be supplied by somebody else or the bereaved husband will have an uncomfortable old age. Very few of Austen's men live without a female relation in the household. Those who do live alone, with only a paid housekeeper to run the home, are either very young and expecting to marry, like Henry Tilney and Edmund Bertram, or they are relatively young, like Mr Knightley and Colonel Brandon, who though appearing confirmed bachelors have not in fact – as their stories prove – given up on the prospect of marriage. Old men, however, like the Dashwood sisters' great-uncle, a single man who 'lived to a very advanced age', cannot manage alone. When the sister who has looked after him all their lives dies, he invites into his house his nephew and family.

> In the society of his nephew and niece, and their children, the old gentleman's days were comfortably spent. His attachment to them all increased. The constant attention of Mr and Mrs Henry Dashwood to his wishes, which proceeded not merely from interest, but from goodness of heart, gave him every degree of solid comfort which his age could receive; and the cheerfulness of the children added a relish to his existence.[1]

Few men in Austen's world live to be 'retired' in the sense we know it, so few are affected by that major change of lifestyle. The Reverend George Austen, Jane's own father, who relinquished his rectory and farm in Hampshire at the age of seventy to live an easier life in Bath, was an exception to the norm. Despite her father's age, Jane herself was so little expecting any such change that she is said to have fainted away at the news. In her last completed novel, *Persuasion,* she has an elderly and increasingly frail clergyman, Dr Shirley, contemplate retirement to some seaside resort – or at least, his well-wishers (and those who would like to put a curate in the parish) contemplate it for him. Clergymen were inducted for life, the legal recipient of the tithes until their death, and had to come to some arrangement with a curate as to how much he would be paid to undertake the duties if the incumbent resided elsewhere; and the Bishop's agreement had to be sought. In the Reverend George Austen's case, his son James became the resident clergyman, but

Rector only after his father had died.

Other men retire from business in the sense that they have made enough to live on, but this may be at any age. Sir William Lucas of *Pride and Prejudice* and Mr Weston of *Emma* are in this category, both wishing to shift the tenor of their daily lives from business to social occupation. In the navy, a man was never too old to go to sea, as is proved by the case of Jane's own brothers. Both became Admirals in late middle age; Francis Austen was still commanding a ship at age seventy-five and Charles died at sea aged seventy-two. In *Persuasion,* Admiral Croft is one of many naval officers turned ashore by the peace of 1815 (on half pay) but he hopes to see another war. General Tilney and Colonel Brandon are no longer on active service, but again, this may be out of choice, having made their fortunes and turning their time and attention to the country estates they have inherited.

Older men have usually settled down into an accommodation with their wives, and Austen presents many portraits of ageing couples who seem well-knit together: the Shirleys, the senior Musgroves and the Morlands, for example. Even Sir Thomas Bertram and Mr Allen, two men who may reasonably feel disappointed in their wives, never fail in courtesy towards them. Widowers have to decide whether to attempt to marry again. Sir Walter Elliot has 'met with one or two private disappointments in very unreasonable applications'[2] – that is, he has proposed marriage to women who are not interested, probably because they regard him as too old. Susceptible to female beauty as he is – or it might be truer to say, scathing about *lack* of female beauty as he is – his eye has most likely fallen on beautiful young women who know they can do better for themselves. Certainly he has had no thought of pairing up with a woman of his own age, his wife's widowed friend Lady Russell, she of the crows' feet. As close neighbours they remain on friendly and even intimate terms, admitted to knowledge of one another's business (he is her landlord, among other things) but there is no undercurrent of romantic interest on either side in their friendship. And it seems doubtful whether he would have proposed to Mrs Clay, however long she had remained in his household. It might well massage his vanity to believe himself pursued and admired by her, but he would surely never demean himself by marriage to a woman labouring under the multiple disadvantages of low birth, a protruding tooth and freckles.

Second Attachments

Second marriages which do prosper include those of Mr Weston and Mr (Henry) Dashwood. There is a gap of almost twenty years between the death of Mr Weston's first wife and his second marriage, two decades which he fills enjoyably enough to himself in a mixture of social life and business. We might wonder what he does for sex all these years, since the moment he is married again he is making his wife pregnant. Does the new *Mrs* Weston ask herself the same question about her husband's past? Does Emma, when she embarks on marriage with a man of thirty-seven? Austen of course is silent on such points. We are apt to focus on the woman's need for marriage in Jane Austen's era, recognizing it as their best, often their only option for financial security and status: 'their pleasantest preservative from want'.[3] But despite their greater financial independence, men had almost equal need of marriage, in their case for a woman to run the home, give them legitimate offspring and provide conjugal rights on tap. While sex of some sort was probably always available to a man, there would have been many whose sense of decency, religious scruples or fear of infection would make marital sex the only sort with which they could be comfortable. We can imagine the respectable yet worldly wise Sir Thomas Bertram of Mansfield Park to be this kind of man, with his own unstated reasons for advocating early marriage in young men. Whether or not he gives in to temptation himself, he has experienced the deprivation of marital sex both in London, when his wife refuses to accompany him as he sits in Parliament, and in Antigua, during his two-year sojourn among the slaves. For just these reasons, there was no stigma attaching to a man's wish for a second wife, as there was for women; on the contrary, it was generally approved.

Mr Weston having been slightly taken in by his first marriage, which was 'an unsuitable connection' productive of not much happiness, leaving him a rather poorer man at its close, takes his time over his second choice:

> It was now some time since Miss Taylor had begun to influence his schemes, but as it was not the tyrannic influence of youth on youth, it had not shaken his determination of never settling till he could purchase Randalls, and the sale of Randalls was long looked forward to; but he had gone steadily on, with these objects in view, till they were accomplished. He had made his fortune, bought his house, and obtained his wife; and was beginning a new period of existence, with every probability of greater happiness than any yet passed through. He had never been an unhappy man; his own temper had secured him from that, even in his first marriage; but his second must show him how delightful a well-judging and truly amiable woman could be, and must give him the pleasantest proof of its being a great deal better to choose than to be chosen, to excite gratitude rather than to feel it.[4]

When we see Mr Weston at the end of the book with his wife and baby daughter, and a daughter-in-law introduced into the family by the son of his first marriage, we see him – probably a man of about fifty – surrounded by youth and hope and new beginnings; yet in rejoicing on his behalf that 'a Miss Weston' rather than a Master Weston has been born, Emma reasons, 'It would be a great comfort to Mr Weston, as he grew older – and even Mr Weston might be growing older ten years hence – to have his fireside enlivened by the sports and the nonsense, the freaks and the fancies of a child never banished from home.'

Mr Henry Dashwood likewise has two families: a son by his

first marriage and three daughters by his second. We know nothing of Mr Dashwood's first wife, except what we can deduce from the fact that the son she brought into the world turned out rather hard-hearted and selfish; and as these traits are not inherited from his father, who is 'cheerful and sanguine' with 'strong feelings' it may be supposed that they come from the first Mrs Henry Dashwood.[5] Perhaps the first marriage was made for prudential motives, or on the advice of parents, or out of youthful infatuation; whereas second time around Mr Dashwood marries a much less rich woman with whom, we may infer, he is properly in love. The couple bear a strong resemblance to one another, since the second Mrs Dashwood is cheerful, sanguine and of strong feelings likewise. The fact that Mr Dashwood is much mourned and regretted by his affectionate wife and three daughters certainly suggests that his second marriage was happier and more congenial than his first. When the middle daughter, Marianne, is expressing her fears (at sixteen) that she will never meet a man she can truly love, her newly widowed mother exclaims, "Why should you be less fortunate than your mother? In one circumstance only, my Marianne, may your destiny be different from hers!" True love, then; and on Marianne's repeated denial that a second attachment can ever be the result of genuine feeling, Elinor wonders how she can hold such views without reflecting on their own parents' marriage.

A relatively young widower who seeks to make a more congenial second choice is Mr Elliot of *Persuasion*. Rather like the Miss Churchill who marries Mr Weston, his first wife – also very rich, but from the opposite end of the social spectrum – chases and chooses him. It is considered by the Elliot family at large a very great extenuation of his first match that the lady was not only 'a very fine woman' but 'well educated, accomplished, rich and excessively in love with him'. Mr Elliot's second choice alights on his cousin Anne, but before he can go far down the road of courtship, retarded as he is by the need for a proper period of mourning to pass, his true nature is revealed to her – not, of course, that Anne could ever bring herself to accept any other man than her old love, Captain Wentworth. Before it becomes clear to Anne that she is the focus of Mr Elliot's admiration, and interesting herself in his welfare, she imagines he might be renewing his youthful but aborted pursuit of her sister Elizabeth:

> There might really have been a liking formerly, though convenience and accident had drawn him a different way; and now that he could afford to please himself, he might mean to pay his addresses to her. . . . How her temper and understanding might bear the investigation of his present keener time of life was another concern, and rather a fearful one. Most earnestly did she wish that he might not be too nice, or too observant, if Elizabeth were his object.

Messrs Weston, Dashwood and Elliot, different as they are, all bring a more mature judgment to their second choices, as well as enjoying easier circumstances that allow them to follow their hearts second time around. Austen's very reasonable view seems to be that age brings greater wisdom to the choice of marriage partner (and that money helps too) and she shows this not only in her remarrying widowers, but in those men who marry for the first time somewhat late in life, like Mr Knightley, whose opinion is that 'at three and twenty . . . if a man chooses a wife, he generally chooses ill';[6] and Captain Wentworth, who, as he tells his sister, has thought much on the subject and will be a fool indeed if he makes a mistake (as in fact he nearly does) but who, when he secures Anne's promises second time around, shares with her 'the advantage of maturity of mind'.[7]

Foiled in his wish to marry Anne, and unsatisfied with Elizabeth by comparison, Mr Elliot at least pleases himself in taking as a mistress Mrs Clay (who will pit her cunning against his in attempting to caress and wheedle her way into marriage). Similar is Admiral Crawford, who in introducing a mistress into his house after the death of his wife reconstructs his household with self-indulgence. Both mistresses will be abandoned if they fail to please, so endeavour to please they probably will, more than many a wife in her security.

Widowers with small children had special difficulties to contend with. All four of Jane's brothers who had children lost their first wives; James, still young, married again and started a second family, though he had only three children altogether, to whom he was a very fond and attentive father (at least he was to the children of his second marriage; he seems to have been relatively neglectful of his firstborn, perhaps to keep the peace if there was friction with her stepmother). Edward, with eleven children, did not marry again, perhaps fearful of having even more. Husbands like Edward whose wives died in actual childbirth could hardly have escaped experiencing a certain amount of guilt and remorse. As we have seen in a previous chapter, Frank chose a wife past the menopause deliberately to avoid more procreation. And Charles, in marrying his deceased wife's sister, who like many women in such a position had moved in to take care of her sister's little children, created for himself a different difficulty by falling foul of canon law. The Deceased Wife's Sister Act was not yet on the statute books to make such a marriage illegal, but it contravened the Table of Kindred and Affinity as set out in the *Book of Common Prayer*, and Charles and his Harriet were glad to escape to Cornwall, where he had a low-paid post patrolling the coast for smugglers, to be out of the way of disapproving tongues until the fuss about their marriage died down. As his mother wrote, 'I am *now* very glad that his residence is at such a distance, and by and bye wonder and censure will subside and in a year or two he may be willing to change his station for one nearer his family and friends'.[8] She added, 'Charles has certainly secured a careful and attentive mother to his children for such she has proved herself during the almost six years she has had the charge of them.' Poor Charles, always the most hard-up of Jane's brothers, now began a second family of four.

There were many reasons why a man might seek to marry his deceased wife's sister: because living under the same roof had made them fall in love (or fall into bed); because she had given up other chances to marry for the sake of *his* children; because few other women might consider taking on another woman's brood. Jane Austen certainly thought such responsibilities reduced a man's value on the marriage market. 'A Widower with 3 children has no right to look higher than his daughter's Governess', she wrote in 1807.[9]

Widowers with small children might agonize on their account over whether to seek a second wife. Jane Austen's niece Fanny Knight became second wife to a man who certainly had his doubts about the wisdom of remarriage. Edward – later Sir Edward – Knatchbull lost his beloved first wife in childbirth in 1814, leaving him with six little children. 'I hardly know how to manage them without their Mother's Assistance', he confided to his diary in 1816.[10] Two years later, he was still wrestling with the problem: 'Will it be better for me and My Children, that I should again marry, or that I should remain a Widower?' His uncertainty sprang from his own unhappy experience as a boy with two successive stepmothers. His mind was at last made up when in 1819 he inherited his father's title and large estate, becoming ninth baronet and Member of Parliament. Before leaving his old home he wrote, 'Here I think I should have remained a Widower – at Hatch [his inherited property] the Case must be otherwise – this for my Children & My Family's Sake – God grant that I may do what is best for My dear Children!' With this unromantic attitude, within four months he had proposed to Fanny Knight, at twenty-seven twelve years his junior but accustomed to running a household and looking after her ten siblings since their own mother's death twelve years before. She had once written that 'I am an inveterate enemy to second marriage in general, particularly where there is any family'[11] but that was now forgotten. That Fanny, with her 'queer little heart' and 'delicious play of mind' who had dithered about whether to encourage various suitors during her aunt Jane's lifetime, should have accepted such a man and such another set of family responsibilities suggests that the age of twenty-seven seemed to her quite as problematic as it had done to her aunt. She found too late that she had taken on a difficult, exacting man, certainly not fulfilling her aunt's 1817 prophesy that

> depend upon it, the right Man will come at last; you will in the course of the next two or three years, meet with somebody more generally unexceptionable than anyone you have yet known, who will love you as warmly as *He* ever did, & who will so completely attach you, that you will feel you never really loved before.[12]

Whatever good reasons Fanny thought she had for marrying Sir Edward Knatchbull, romantic love was not one of them, though undoubtedly she made him a good and dutiful wife.

My Father's Keeper

In the novels, men whose wives *don't* conveniently die to allow them a second bite at the cherry, whether of wife or live-in mistress, include Mr Bennet, perhaps the most unhappily married man in Austen's fiction. Most men accept their married lot, whatever they may think of it privately, and keep up a united front. Only Mr Bennet among Austen's older men chafes at being shackled for life to a woman he cannot like or respect, though it is possible that the fairly young Mr Palmer is moving towards the same slighting contempt, and even Mr John Knightley sometimes shows flashes of it. But Charlotte Palmer and Isabella Knightley fall short only in intelligence, not in good humour, as their husbands have wit enough to perceive; only Mrs Bennet fails her husband on every count. After his love of reading and country pursuits, Mr Bennet finds his greatest solace in his two eldest daughters, and especially in Elizabeth. Of none of the other married men in Austen's fiction could something similar be said – no other daughter usurps her living mother in her father's affections – but among the *widowers* are three who look to their daughters rather than to a second wife to provide emotional and practical support. Such demands can prove burdensome, in a variety of ways, to the young women concerned.

In *Northanger Abbey's* General Tilney, Austen gives us a portrait of a man whose sphere of influence has contracted and who, having been used to commanding others in his military life, now has only his family and servants to order about. As an only daughter, Eleanor bears the brunt of his temper and demands. Hours, days and weeks of her life are spent with only her father for company when her two brothers are away following their respective professions; *she* can never get away, and the full weight of his tyranny falls on her shoulders. Missing her mother dreadfully, she does not have even the consolation of responsibility and usefulness in the home. Though nominally mistress of Northanger Abbey, she appears to have little say in how it is run. General Tilney enjoys the exercise of power for its own sake, dictating times of meals, what he expects to see on the table, and how his kitchens and kitchen gardens should be organized, down to the smallest detail. No man could be more master of his own household. Though he is not positively cruel to Eleanor, he pays no attention to her feelings; his word is law.

Often, the General does not even allow his daughter to speak. In Bath, Eleanor is just about to invite Catherine to Northanger when General Tilney enters the room, asking "Well, Eleanor, may I congratulate you on being successful in your application to your fair friend?"

"I was just beginning to make the request, sir, as you came in."

"Well, proceed by all means. I know how much your heart is in it. My daughter, Miss Morland," he continued, without leaving his daughter time to speak, "has been forming a very bold wish." He then proceeds to give the invitation himself, in a long paragraph of high-flown language. Again at Northanger, when Catherine asks whether Woodston is a pretty place, the General responds, "What say you Eleanor? Speak your opinion, for ladies can best tell the taste of ladies in regard to places as well as men", but he proceeds to give his own opinion without allowing Eleanor the chance to utter a word. Worse, Catherine finds she has involved her friend in 'a lecture' for being a few minutes late for dinner on the first evening at Northanger, and to the offence of unpunctuality is added the offence of trying to avoid it as the General is soon 'scolding his daughter for hurrying her fair friend'; poor Eleanor cannot win. Yet she behaves impeccably to her father, neither contesting any point nor defending herself nor expressing any wishes contrary to his. Happy is the reader when, at the very end of the book, Eleanor escapes into marriage, but it is only at this point of release that a full indictment of the General in his role as father, which we have seen in action throughout, is made explicit by a narrator intruding herself into the narrative:

> The marriage of Eleanor Tilney, her removal from all the evils of such a home as Northanger had been made by Henry's banishment, to the home of her choice and the man of her choice, is an event which I expect to give general satisfaction among all her acquaintance. My own joy on the occasion is very sincere. I know no one more entitled, by unpretending merit, or better prepared by habitual suffering, to receive and enjoy felicity. Her partiality for this gentleman was not of recent origin; and he had been long withheld only by inferiority of situation from addressing her. His unexpected accession to title and fortune had removed all his difficulties; and never had the general loved his daughter so well in all her hours of companionship, utility and patient endurance as when he first hailed her "Your Ladyship!"

Some of General Tilney's domestic shortcomings and the severity with which he treats Eleanor may be put down to his retirement from active life in the army. It is hard for him to adjust to a less hierarchical arrangement. In contrast, neither of Austen's other two widowers who look to their daughters to fill the social and domestic roles of their dead mothers have ever done anything useful in their whole lives, both having enjoyed every luxury and comfort that money can buy without effort. The result of this idleness and sense of entitlement is that, once deprived of the support of their wives, they have an inclination to lean instead on their daughters. Both Elizabeth Elliot and Emma Woodhouse enjoy the enhanced social status that comes from being mistress of their fathers' homes. But whereas not many drawbacks attend Elizabeth's position, Emma's life is compromised by her father's fond dependency.

Sir Walter and his eldest daughter make a well-matched couple. 'Elizabeth had succeeded, at sixteen, to all that was possible of her mother's rights and consequence, and being very handsome, and very like himself, her influence had always been great, and they had gone on together most happily.'[13] Since his wife had been very different from himself in looks and character, it seems that he gets on better with Elizabeth, who moreover, despite her nominal power, and her actual power in small things, cannot rein in her father's spending (even if she had seen the need) as her mother had been wont to do. This must make him happier, even if it is a happiness based on increasing debt which eventually must be faced. 'Thirteen years had seen her mistress of Kellynch Hall, presiding and directing with . . . self-possession and decision. For thirteen years had she been doing the honours, and laying down the domestic law at home.' Where Sir Walter Elliot is at fault is that, though he has two daughters remaining at home, only one is allowed any influence in domestic matters. 'Anne, with an elegance of mind and sweetness of character, which must have placed her high with any people of real understanding, was nobody with either father or sister; her word had no weight, her convenience was always to give way – she was only Anne.' Her life at home is very little different from what it would have been as a child; and though she is aged twenty-seven at the time of the family's removal to Bath, there is no question but that she must eventually join them there, and make her home, perhaps forever, in a place to which she has a strong aversion. At fifty-four Sir Walter seems in excellent shape – he thinks so himself – and as long as he is alive, to reside under his roof is a duty from which Anne cannot easily escape (though she determines to find a home with Lady Russell if her father should marry Mrs Clay).

The fact of Sir Walter's widowhood is to elevate Elizabeth and suppress Anne, but it could be said that even Elizabeth is not well served by his domestic arrangements, since the prejudices and snobbery of the father are confirmed and hardened in the daughter to an extent that is unlikely to have happened without their close confederacy during all the years of her youth. Elizabeth, in fact, behaves like a much older woman than she is, spreading 'a general chill' over the company with the 'heartless elegance' which she shares with her father. As a consequence, she has inadvertently ruled herself out of the marriage market, and fails to attract any suitor. For all his partiality, her father has done her no favours.

Even more damaging in his way is Mr Woodhouse, with his complete dependence upon and confidence in his second daughter, Emma. She calls herself 'always first and always right in my father's eyes'.[14] She is always "dear Emma" to him, and he admires everything about her, from her handwriting to her memory. Mostly, Emma very much enjoys her role as mistress of the household, sometimes contravening her father's gentle directives, usually in favour of providing more or better food for their visitors and neighbours than his nervous care for their digestions prompts. Mr Woodhouse offloads almost all his responsibilities on Emma, retaining only the unfailing courtesy of a host. Virtually every decision is made for him, sometimes by Emma and sometimes, in the more public or community sphere, by Mr Knightley, whose social visit on one occasion begins 'as soon as Mr Woodhouse had been talked into what was necessary, told that he understood, and the papers swept away' and who, by the end of the novel, has become an indispensable inmate of Hartfield itself.

There is a price to pay for Emma's dominance in the home, and that is her corresponding duty, fully accepted by her, to keep her father happy and comfortable at all times, however much that might curtail her own freedoms. She can never be away from him for more than a short while, never make arrangements of her own without taking his welfare into account, never cease administrations that often make her a parent to her own parent. These constrictions are woven into the fabric of her life throughout the narrative, but are especially marked on two occasions. In Chapter One, following the marriage and departure of Miss Taylor, 'Emma spared no exertion . . . and hoped, by the help of backgammon, to get her father tolerably through the evening.' Nine months later, on a stormy July evening, 'The weather affected Mr Woodhouse; and he could only be kept tolerably comfortable by almost ceaseless attention on his daughter's side, and by exertions which had never cost her so much before.' Her consolation is that 'As a daughter, she hoped she was not without heart. She hoped no one could have said to her, "How could you be so unfeeling to your father?"' as she has been unfeeling to Miss Bates.

It is hard to know what Mr Woodhouse has ever done to deserve to live in such a pampered state, or whether his retreat from life, exemplified by his extreme fear of food, is something that *should* be humoured so selflessly by his daughter. She is even ready to defer her marriage indefinitely to the man she loves to avoid upsetting him. This is a heavy burden, albeit unspoken, to place on the shoulders of a daughter. Though in one sense Emma Woodhouse has one of the happiest family lives of all the heroines, in another her middle of life threatens to be unfulfilled except for duty because of a helpless and demanding father who, for all his fondness, never asks himself what would be best for Emma.

7. MERRY WIDOWS

Although Mrs Jennings of *Sense and Sensibility* is the only one of Austen's widows to whom the adjective 'merry' is attached, her mirth is little more than a readiness to laugh at all the young people of her acquaintance and to get all the enjoyment out of her declining years that she can. The conventional 'merry widow' of literature as an unprincipled predator with a voracious sexual appetite and a carefree disregard of conventional morals is too gross to find a place in the kinds of novels Austen published. But in two pieces of fiction unpublished in her lifetime, she explores the situation of older women who have overstepped the boundaries of acceptable behaviour, much to the dismay of their relatives.

The most audacious, amoral, and sexually alluring of any Austen character, Lady Susan Vernon is the chief protagonist of the novella in letters that Jane Austen is thought to have composed in 1793–4 (before she was twenty). Known to us as *Lady Susan,* this work is unlike anything else in Austen's *oeuvre* in several ways: in taking as its main character not a young heroine embarking on life, but an older woman, whose character repels even as it attracts; in being written in letters, and never subsequently recast into direct narrative; and in being short, yet not a fragment, as the story does come to a conclusion, though it is hastily and summarily wound up. Austen thought well enough of her creation to make a fair copy on paper watermarked 1805, and to preserve it all her life, yet she never submitted it for publication. Nor, after her death, did her effective literary executors Cassandra and Henry

Austen. The next generation of the family was also highly reluctant to make the work public, since it offended Victorian sensibilities and might damage their aunt's reputation. Happily, though they did not consider it fit to be published, no one thought to destroy it during all these decades. Eventually, but with many misgivings, James Edward Austen-Leigh appended it to the second edition of his *Memoir of Jane Austen* (1871). The wonder is that today, with the insatiable public appetite for all things Austen and for stories of sexual intrigue, it has not been made into a film. The subject and the characters seem perfect for that medium: another *Liaisons Dangereuses*.

Lady Susan is like a Mary Crawford much more advanced in cynicism and sin and, by virtue of her widowhood, with much more freedom of action. As an unscrupulous and manipulative but glamorous and seductive widow and mother, the character certainly has an eighteenth-century feel about her. The merry widow was a common enough stock character of the period, but one that Austen handles with wit and aplomb belying her own youth and inexperience. It is a highly accomplished and polished piece of writing, remarkable both in conception and in execution for so young an author, the only finished work of any period of her life that does not belong to the courtship genre.

That Lady Susan might be inspired by observation as well as reading has long been mooted by critics. The young Austen had before her the real-life example of her cousin Eliza de Feuillide, a widow who admitted to enjoying flirtation and liberty. Eliza was born in 1761, the child of Mr Austen's sister Philadelphia, and was thus fourteen years Jane's senior. Jane knew her first as the wife of the French minor aristocrat the Compte de Feuillide and, after his guillotining, as his widow. Eliza became a regular visitor to Steventon Rectory, especially enjoying life there when the family was involved in amateur theatricals, in which she excelled. The child Jane watched as her glamorous cousin toyed with two of her brothers: James (also widowed, and four years Eliza's junior) and Henry, ten years younger. Both wished to marry her, but she was reluctant to exchange 'the homage of half a dozen' for 'subjection and the attachment of a single individual'.[1] Unlike Fanny Price in a similar situation in *Mansfield Park*, the onlooker Jane appears to have been fascinated rather than disapproving, since Eliza mentions her 'kind partiality for me' in a letter to another cousin, Philadelphia Walter; possibly it was the older sister Cassandra who was troubled or disapproving, as Eliza confesses her own preference was for Jane.

In a sequence of letters to the same correspondent (which Jane could not have seen), Eliza was perfectly open about her relish for 'dear liberty and dearer flirtation'. Like Mary Crawford, she had an aversion to being the wife of a country clergyman, rejecting James on this count alone, and persuading Henry not to become ordained but to take up a much more fashionable career, in the army. A combination of ductility and persistence on Henry's part won her over, and they seem to have been a happy couple, settling eventually in London where Henry, with the help of his military contacts, took up banking. As a wife Eliza appears never to have forfeited the good opinion of her mature sister-in-law, and she is not known to have done anything really wrong, but as a 'merry widow' in the alluring flesh rather than just in books, as a person quite different from the run-of-the-mill Hampshire neighbours, she had perhaps provided some hints to the young author.

Lady Susan

At thirty-five, Lady Susan Vernon is 'excessively pretty for a lady no longer young'. Within a month of being widowed, she has conducted an affair with a married man right under the nose of his wife, while staying in their home. She has also, by means of flattery and flirtation, detached the suitor of his unmarried sister, as she designs him and his money for her own innocent young daughter. Having caused havoc and misery in one family, she moves on to the country home of her brother- and sister-in-law, where she soon has another conquest in her sights, the young, proud and handsome Reginald De Courcy, brother to Mrs Vernon. It seems he at least will be impervious to her charms, for he has heard all about her mischief, as he tells his sister:

> What a Woman she must be! I long to see her, & shall certainly accept your kind invitation, that I may form some idea of those bewitching powers which can do so much – engaging at the same time & in the same house the affections of two Men who were neither of them at liberty to bestow them – & all this, without the charm of youth.

But Lady Susan is equal to the challenge. Her tactics vary from man to man, and in Reginald's case, instead of subjecting him to the full force of her coquetry, she assumes the mantle of modesty, propriety and victimhood, so that he concludes she has been much maligned.

> There is something about him that rather interests me, a sort of sauciness, of familiarity which I shall teach him to correct. He is lively & seems clever, & when I have inspired him with greater respect for me than his sister's kind offices have implanted, he may be an agreeable Flirt. There is exquisite pleasure in subduing an insolent spirit, in making a person pre-determined to dislike, acknowledge one's superiority.

The epistolary form is perfectly suited to this story, giving us access to each character's private thoughts and motivation. We watch as Reginald allows his preconceptions about her to be overturned, to the great distress of his elderly parents, while Lady Susan glories in her power over him, and at the same time reveals, in letters to her friend, her readiness to sacrifice the happiness of her daughter Frederica by marrying her off against her will to Sir James Martin. This London friend, Mrs Johnson, has a tiresome husband of her own, whose fits of gout, brought on at will it would seem, bring this note of sympathy from Lady Susan:

> There needed not this last fit of Gout to make me detest Mr Johnson; but now the extent of my aversion is not to be estimated. To have you confined, a Nurse, in his apartment! My dear Alicia, of what a mistake were you guilty in marrying a Man of his age! – just old enough to be formal, ungovernable & to have the Gout – too old to be agreeable, & too young to die.

Reginald also muses on the question of age. In the early stages of his succumbing to Lady Susan's charm, he allays his father's fears that he might wish to marry her by saying 'our difference in age must be an insuperable objection'. But this objection, like all the others, is got over as Lady Susan manipulates him into subjection and eventually a longing to marry her. After many convolutions of plot as she moulds him to her will and keeps him dangling, it is only by a chance meeting with the wife of Lady Susan's other lover that, as Reginald puts it himself, 'the spell is removed' and he backs away.

Lady Susan's heartlessness towards her daughter is unforgiveable, but the remainder of her conduct, though manipulative, can be seen as a reasonable strategy given the social conditions in which she has her being. A woman, even a beautiful woman, approaching – or passing – what Jane Austen in *Persuasion* terms the years of danger, will see her main source of power over men slip away from her, until she is all too easy to ignore and marginalize. Lady Susan does not possess that other source of power: money. She has been left with no home, no fortune, no protector, no useful role or occupation. Like Mary Crawford, she has no worthwhile outlet for her considerable abilities. But though she prides herself on her cleverness and eloquence, in reality within a patriarchal system she will always be at the mercy of men – whether endeavouring to evoke their desire or to elude their disapproval, she must play the game on their terms. Before she has been widowed a year, she has married again, and not to the man she loves, Mr Manwaring, for he is married already, not even to the handsome Reginald, but to Sir James Martin, the foolish baronet she had once designed for her daughter.

Abandoning the epistolary form, 'to the great detriment of the Post office Revenue', the narrator suddenly takes the story into her own hands, winding it up in direct narrative, and taking it upon herself to apportion pity and blame among the characters as appropriate:

> Whether Lady Susan was, or was not, happy in her second Choice – I do not see how it can ever be ascertained – for who would take her assurance of it, on either side of the question? The World must judge from Probability. She had nothing against her, but her Husband, & her Conscience.

With the two young people Frederica and Reginald about to be married, and the innocent De Courcys relieved of anxiety, the narrator finally states that while

> Sir James may seem to have drawn a harder Lot than mere Folly merited . . . I confess I can pity only Miss Manwaring, who coming to Town & putting herself to an expense in Cloathes, which impoverished her for two years, on purpose to secure him, was defrauded of her due by a Woman ten years older than herself.

It is fitting that the piece should end with this remark on Lady Susan's age.

An Old Lady Plays the Fool

Lady Susan's is one of the rare examples of female second marriage in Austen's work, and the only one to occur in the course of the narrative. In the fragment *The Watsons,* it is the remarriage of Emma Watson's aunt, offstage, that sets the story in motion. The second marriage of *Sanditon's* Lady Denham is part of her back-story, and that of *Persuasion's* Mrs Clay might never happen.

(If we like playing the game, as we know Austen herself did, of speculating on the future lives of her characters beyond the covers of the book, we might quite plausibly imagine that the delightful Mrs Dashwood, not much more than forty, will allow herself a 'second attachment' when all her daughters have left home; and that warm-hearted Mrs Grant, in her early thirties, may well find herself 'taken in' again, good-humouredly learning to put up with the different set of foibles of another imperfect husband: but we have no authority for such flights of fancy.)

Though so few female characters in Austen's work remarry, those who do demonstrate a variety of inducements. Lady Susan's is the obvious allure of money, a home and position in society from which, no doubt, to embark on further adventures. Lady Denham marries her second husband for a title – and, we might infer, for companionship; she loves talking, so for somebody to talk to, perhaps. But Emma Watson's aunt Mrs Turner seems to have only one possible motivation, and that is sexual desire.

Mrs Turner is, in fact, a most intriguing character, though she remains very much in the background – talked about, but not appearing – of a fragment which was itself abandoned, so she has not received the attention she deserves. Why *The Watsons* was abandoned has taxed critics and commentators and no single obvious reason can be advanced. The fragment dates from Austen's Bath years, and though the death of her father and unsettled home may have caused her to put it aside, that hardly explains why, after preparing *Sense and Sensibility* and *Pride and Prejudice* for the press, she did not continue *The Watsons* before turning to completely fresh work in *Mansfield Park*. Perhaps it is the preponderance of old maids among the *dramatis personae* that dissatisfied the author. Perhaps she simply could not see a way forward for the characters she so vividly brings to life. The hero and heroine seem drawn to each other too quickly, so what is to keep them apart – except, possibly, the sordid question of money? Be that as it may, it is the action of an older woman, Mrs Turner, which sets the plot in motion, and it is because she is the possessor of money that her conduct has such a profound effect.

Having inherited her late husband's whole fortune, she is comfortably circumstanced, while for companionship and interest she has her niece Emma, adopted by herself and her husband since childhood, to whom she has always shown great tenderness and indulgence. Mrs Turner has an 'amiable temper' and it is this, perhaps, which makes her susceptible to male attentions after the death of her husband. She foolishly risks her own financial security, and destroys Emma's present comfort and damages her future prospects, when she is swept off her feet by an Irish army officer. Emma is sent back to live with her own family of unmarried sisters and ailing clergyman father, whose imminent death will deprive them all of a home and income.

Mr Watson has nothing to say about Mrs Turner (presumably the sister of his late wife), perhaps out of delicacy to Emma's feelings, but two other men of the world are very ready to give the male viewpoint. In a passage worth quoting at length as worse and worse details emerge, neighbour Mr Edwards begins by remembering Emma's aunt in her youth:

> "I am pretty sure I danced with her in the old rooms at Bath, the year before I married. She was a very fine woman then – but like other people I suppose she is grown somewhat older since that time. I hope she is likely to be happy in her second choice."
>
> "I hope so, I believe so, Sir," said Emma in some agitation.
>
> "Mr Turner had not been dead a great while I think?"
>
> "About two years Sir."
>
> "I forget what her name is now?"
>
> "O'Brien."
>
> "Irish! Ah, I remember – she is gone to settle in Ireland. I do not wonder that you should not wish to go with her into *that* country Miss Emma; but it must be a great deprivation to her, poor lady! After bringing you up as a child of her own."

"I was not so ungrateful, Sir," said Emma warmly, "as to wish to be anywhere but with her. It did not suit them, it did not suit Captain O'Brien that I should be of the party."

"Captain!" repeated Mrs Edwards. "The gentleman is in the army then?"

"Yes Ma'am."

"Aye – there is nothing like your officers for captivating the ladies, young or old. There is no resisting a cockade, my dear."

"I hope there is," said Mrs Edwards gravely . . . [now thinking of her own daughter].

"Elderly ladies should be careful how they make a second choice," observed Mr Edwards.

"Carefulness – discretion – should not be confined to elderly ladies, or to a second choice," added his wife. "It is quite as necessary to young ladies in their first."

"Rather more so, my dear," replied he, "because young ladies are likely to feel the effects of it longer. When an old lady plays the fool, it is not in the course of nature that she should suffer from it many years."

It is clear in what light this mature married couple regard Mrs Turner's action. That her new husband is in the army, and is Irish, explains a lot to them. Fanny Burney's *Cecilia* and *Camilla* and Robert Bage's *Hermsprong* – all novels of the 1780s or 90s known to have been read by Austen – contain Irish fortune-hunters who prey on English women, while Ireland itself was often deemed to be an uncouth place where residence would be an endurance and an exile, explaining Mr Edwards's comment on that point. (Having married Irishmen, Burney's sister Susan[2] and Austen's niece Louisa Knight[3] did struggle to adapt to the different manners and standards of living there.) The distance was also a useful plot device in making the separation between aunt and niece more complete and final. Emma will not be able to see for herself how happy or otherwise her aunt's new husband makes her.

The Edwards do not mention the financial implications of Mrs

Turner's decision; that second strand of criticism is left to one of Emma's brothers, a self-satisfied attorney, who in his first conversation with his sister, has no compunction in beginning:

> "A pretty piece of work your aunt Turner has made of it! By heaven, a woman should never be entrusted with money. . . .What a blow it must have been upon you! To find yourself, instead of heiress of eight or nine thousand pounds, sent back a weight upon your family, without a sixpence. I hope the old woman will smart for it."
>
> "Do not speak disrespectfully of her – she was very good to me; and if she has made an imprudent choice, she will suffer more from it herself, than *I* can possibly do."
>
> "I do not mean to distress you, but you know everybody must think her an old fool. I thought Turner had been reckoned an extraordinarily sensible, clever man. How the devil came he to make such a will? . . . He might have provided decently for his widow, without leaving everything that he had to dispose of, or any part of it, at her mercy."
>
> "My aunt may have erred," said Emma warmly, "she *has* erred – but my uncle's conduct was faultless. I was her own niece, and he left to herself the power and the pleasure of providing for me."
>
> "But unluckily she has left the pleasure of providing for you, to your father, and without the power. That's the long and the short of the business."

Though Emma defends her aunt from her brother's abuse, she privately acknowledges the imprudence of the older woman's actions. Austen surely wants us to think that only a powerful sexual attraction could induce such rash – and irrational – behaviour.

Most of the fictional widows in the published novels seem to be without either the wish or the means to remarry, and none of them shows interest in a younger man. When Austen tells us in a rather curious statement, 'That Lady Russell, of steady age and character, and extremely well provided for, should have no thought of a second marriage, needs no apology to the public, which is rather apt to be unreasonably discontented when a woman *does* marry again, than when she does not', we need an understanding of the 'old fool' theory of women to explain the public discontent, or scorn. It would certainly seem that, in taking a second husband, a woman who has no need to do so for financial reasons or to provide herself with a home is giving proof of continuing sexual desires too apt to overpower her judgement or her sense of propriety. Of course, the double standard was in operation here, as in so many aspects of relations between the sexes, as men were never similarly castigated for taking a second spouse. Indeed, a man's sexual needs were most respectably accommodated in marriage, so if he lost one wife, he was thought to be doing a good thing in seeking another – and in giving another single woman the chance to be wed.

A wealthy widow of Austen's acquaintance who, in taking a second husband, braved public opinion – and her own parents' disapproval – was Lady Sondes. She was a beauty who had been painted by Reynolds (who charged a hundred guineas to her husband and another hundred guineas to make an exact copy for her father),[4] and she was certainly extremely well provided for without this second marriage, being the only child of the wealthy Richard Milles, MP for Canterbury, and therefore heiress in her own right, besides becoming the widow of another wealthy but this time titled man, Baron Sondes. The mother of seven children, six of whom survived, she took, within three years of the death of her first husband, a second in the person of General Sir Henry Tucker Montresor, with whom she was to have two more children (who died in infancy). At the time of their marriage the couple were both forty-two, but this was his first marriage (after a late start, he was to marry twice more). On the announcement of their engagement, Austen makes the pertinent comment:

> Lady Sondes' match surprises, but does not offend me; – had there been a grown-up single daughter, I should not have

> forgiven her – but I consider everybody as having a right to marry once in their Lives for Love, if they can – & provided she will now leave off having bad head-aches & being pathetic, I can allow her, I can wish her to be happy.[5]

Evidently Austen is going against the general reaction to this marriage in *not* being offended; later she remarks that their friend Martha Lloyd equally 'does not make the least objection to it', as if objections were certainly to be expected from the public at large. Austen's niece Fanny, in fact, a more conventional person, with the added intolerance of youth, wrote to her ex-governess, 'I am rather surprised at her marrying at all with such a family and particularly at her acting so contrary to Mr & Mrs Milles's wishes'.[6]

A mature woman, then, was still expected to conform to her parents' wishes, as well as to take her children into account. The comment made by Austen about the grown-up daughter is interesting in the light of Lady Susan Vernon's continuing attempts to eclipse *her* daughter, Frederica, and Mrs Turner's sad abandonment, under the influence of infatuation, of the girl she had raised as her own daughter. Perhaps too it reflected the common knowledge, which Austen shared, of the Thrale/Piozzi marriage.

For part of the widespread outrage that had met the second marriage of the widowed Mrs Thrale in 1784 had been that she put her own desires ahead of the marriage prospects of her four daughters. Mrs Thrale was the classic case of feeling herself to have the right to marry once in her life for love. Her first marriage, to wealthy brewer Henry Thrale, had been arranged by her mother to save the family fortunes. He was regularly unfaithful to her, and ate and drank to excess. After bearing him twelve children – of whom only the four daughters reached adulthood – and acting as a charming hostess to his guests, including Dr Johnson, Hester Lynch Thrale found herself widowed at the age of forty. Before long, she had fallen in love with her eldest daughter's Italian singing master, Gabriel Piozzi. She was thought to be showing a most unbecoming infatuation or lust that she should get the better of. Her friends, including Fanny Burney and Dr Johnson, cautioned her not to give way to her feelings, and when, after becoming ill with thwarted desires, she married Piozzi anyway, a total breach ensued. The daughters were left behind in England while the newlyweds travelled on the Continent for several years. It was the scandal of the age. "Madam, you are ignominiously married" was Dr Johnson's hurt – and hurtful – reaction to her marriage.[7]

But to return to Lady Sondes: was it common knowledge that her first marriage had not been for love, or is this just a mischievous comment on Austen's part? Is she hinting that the headaches and pathetic behaviour are symptoms of sexual frustration? Later in the same letter, Austen returns to the subject and says of the groom, 'I like his rank very much – & always affix the ideas of strong sense, & highly elegant manners, to a General.' More suggestion, perhaps, that sexual attraction has played its due part in the match. Or at least, that Austen likes to imagine it has.

Her final comment on the match is perhaps not to be taken too seriously. She appears to succumb to the general disapproval when, a month into the marriage, she hears of the couple being settled at the General's house, which happened to be only three miles from Lady Sondes' previous marital home. This is so perfectly reasonable that Jane can only be relishing the opportunity for a joke when she remarks, 'Lady Sondes is an impudent Woman to come back into her old Neighbourhood again; I suppose she pretended never to have married before – & wonders how her Father & Mother came to have her christen'd Lady Sondes.'[8]

That Lady Sondes, or rather Lady Montresor as she had now become, should be considered by anybody as *impudent* for living openly with a second husband in his own house amid her old neighbours and in the same society she had graced as a first wife is surely proof of the stigma attaching to second marriages in women of a certain age.

It is intriguing to consider that in addition to Mrs Turner and her Irish army officer, Austen's aborted manuscript *The Watsons* may contain a second sexually active widow in the character of Lady Osborne. The suggestion that she may be romantically motivated arises not from anything in the fragment of text, where she appears solely in the character of disagreeable, card-playing snob, but in the author's intentions for the continuance of the story, as purveyed via Cassandra to her nieces. If such a long chain is to be believed – and nothing was written down until by James Edward Austen-Leigh in 1871 – 'Much of the interest of the tale was to arise from Lady Osborne's love for Mr Howard, and his counter-affection for Emma, whom he was finally to marry.'[9]

Lady Osborne is 'nearly fifty' and Mr Howard 'a little more than thirty', and moreover he had been tutor to her son, now the grown-up Lord Osborne, so they have known each other for a long time. The age disparity led the Austen scholar R.W. Chapman to wonder whether 'Lady' is a slip of the pen for 'Miss' Osborne, the daughter.[10] While it is true that Lady Osborne is credited with having 'much the finest person' of the females in her party at the public assembly, her daughter is no self-effacing Anne de Bourgh or Miss Carteret, silent young women who hide behind their mothers, but one quite capable of 'lively consultation' with some young men on the ballroom floor, arrogant treatment of Mr Howard's young nephew, with whom she breaks her promise to dance, and 'a broad stare' at Emma when the latter steps in to offer her hand in dance to the mortified boy.

The amorous attentions of a woman so much his senior as Lady Osborne are unlikely to have kept Mr Howard long from seeing his way to marrying Emma. Readers must therefore make up their own minds whether Lady Osborne or Miss Osborne is likelier to have been the heroine's rival in this fragment which is so tantalizingly abandoned, and therefore whether the theme of older women in love was to be developed by Austen in a novel she chose not to complete.

8. FOUR DOWAGER DESPOTS

The conjunction of power and masculinity is of course the norm in Austen's world. But when in special circumstances power falls into female hands, that provides intriguing material for the novelist. Those special circumstances are widowhood allied to wealth. Over the course of her writing career Austen explores the phenomenon in a quartet of autocratic widows, all different from one another but all, in their various ways, made tyrannical, meddlesome and mean by the possession of money.

Mrs Ferrars in *Sense and Sensibility*, Lady Catherine de Bourgh in *Pride and Prejudice* and Lady Denham in the unfinished fragment *Sanditon* all use the power of money to impose their wills on other people; *Mansfield Park's* Mrs Norris, not rich in her own right, but with a supine sister and often absent brother-in-law, appropriates their wealth and status to wield power by proxy. Perhaps only Lady Denham is a true *dowager*, the strict definition of which is a woman whose income derives by legal pre-arrangement from her late husband's estate, the estate (and title, if there is one) having passed on his death to his heir. (This is the situation of yet another widow, Mrs Rushworth who, as Austen tells us, on the marriage of her son takes herself off to Bath 'with true dowager propriety';[1] but pompous as she is, Mrs Rushworth is no despot so makes no further appearance in this chapter.) Both Lady Catherine and Mrs Ferrars appear to have the whole of their late husband's fortune under their own control, while Mrs Norris's husband was not in this league. But more loosely used, the term suits the mixture of self-importance and interference in others' lives which having the control of money has bestowed on the four elderly women examined here.

A Formidable Mother-in-Law

Though Mrs Ferrars cannot exact the deference due to rank of a Lady Catherine or a Lady Denham, her married surname has aristocratic connotations, and either she or her husband has (or had) a brother called Sir Robert. Her property in Norfolk seems regarded by her only as a source of income, not as a home. She prefers to live at the smart London address of Park Street, where she is on the spot to meddle more effectually in her children's concerns. Whether her late husband inherited or earned his money we do not know, but he died 'very rich' and, apart from a few annuities, he has left all his wealth to his widow to dispose of as she chooses. Marriage articles would usually tie up family money in the male line, with provision for the widow for life, whereas the money a man earned in a profession, business or government sinecure was his to do with as he saw fit. Certainly, it was unusual for a man with sons not to leave his fortune, wherever it came from, to the eldest, with smaller provision for the widow and any younger children. Perhaps Mrs Ferrars resembles her daughter Fanny in being able to talk her husband into whatever suited her: not through charm, for she surely never had any, but by exploiting any weakness in his character. If Edward, so different from his brother and sister, has inherited his tenderheartedness from his father, it is quite easy to picture the late Mr Ferrars as fundamentally a kind man (leaving three annuities to old superannuated servants) but not very assertive and, either through love or fear, under his wife's dominion. From whatever combination of circumstances, he was evidently willing to entrust his children's futures to the will and pleasure of their mother.

Austen tells us that a kind mother would make her sons independent, but Mrs Ferrars uses the devices of dependency and disinheritance to try to control their choice of marriage partner and way of living. Robert, the younger, has neither sense nor sensibility to be hurt by his dependency, and spends the greater part of the book in self-satisfied idleness, probably sponging off the mother whose favourite he is. Not that Robert is completely under his mother's thumb, as he proves by acting exactly contrary to her wishes almost, it would seem, for the sake of it, when marrying Lucy Steele. He has no feelings of gratitude or duty to make him hesitate over this step. Edward, infinitely better endowed in heart and mind, more dutiful and honourable in every respect, more conscious of the difficulties that meet him at every turn, is in a depressed state from the time he leaves university, being 'neither fitted by abilities nor disposition to answer the wishes of his mother and sister, who longed to see him distinguished – as they hardly knew what'. Without considering his tastes or abilities, 'his mother wished to interest him in political concerns, to get him into parliament, or to see him connected with some of the great men of the day'.

Elinor, accounting for Edward's dejection of mind and uncertain attitude to herself, puts it all down to 'the necessity of temporising with his mother' and 'the dependent situation which forbad the indulgence of his affection' towards any woman who does not satisfy Mrs Ferrars' ambition. 'She knew that his mother neither behaved to him so as to make his home comfortable at present, nor to give him any assurance that he might form a home for himself, without strictly attending to her views of his aggrandisement.' When Edward pays his visit to Barton, Mrs Dashwood attributes his continuing unhappy demeanour to 'some want of liberality in his mother', and she 'sat down to table indignant against all selfish parents'. Reasoning from the perspective of a loving mother, she urges patience and hope: "Your mother will secure to you, in time, that independence you are so anxious for; it is her duty, and it will, it must ere long become her happiness to prevent your whole youth from being wasted in discontent."

For much of the narrative Mrs Ferrars is felt as a constant but distant presence, a malign figure always to contend with, by Edward principally, but also variously by Elinor and Lucy Steele. Even John Dashwood is frightened by her, or at least by anyone's crossing her. Characters who have never met her are conscious of her standing in their way as "a very headstrong proud woman" and a 'formidable mother-in-law'. The fact that John Dashwood can speak of her coming forward "with the utmost liberality" if Edward marry the woman his mother has marked out for him, Miss Morton with her £30,000, attests not only to Mrs Ferrars' manipulative and mercenary nature but to John's own perverted sense of values, the consequence of being married to Mrs Ferrars' equally mercenary daughter. Because Fanny always behaves exactly as her mother might wish, she is rewarded by, for example, having banknotes to the value of £200 put into her hands by her mother on arrival in London. This might seem an act of generosity, as John Dashwood asserts, yet it is really another example of parental control: Fanny gets the carrot, and Edward the stick.

After such a lengthy build-up, it is only when Elinor and Marianne attend the dinner party given by Mr and Mrs John Dashwood in London that Mrs Ferrars appears in person. At this point, Austen gives one of her few physical descriptions of a character:

> Mrs Ferrars was a little, thin woman, upright, even to formality, in her figure, and serious, even to sourness, in her aspect. Her complexion was sallow; and her features small, without beauty, and naturally without expression; but a lucky contraction of the brow had rescued her countenance from the disgrace of insipidity, by giving it the strong characters of pride and ill nature.

If it is rare enough for Austen to describe a face, it is rarer still for her to adopt the common novelistic device of depicting features as the outward expression of character. More than most people, Mrs Ferrars has the face she deserves.

Remarkably, perhaps, she actually appears only in one scene, and has only three lines of dialogue, all brief: "very pretty"; "Beautifully indeed! But *she* does everything well"; and "Miss Morton is Lord Morton's daughter". This last is described by the narrator as 'a bitter philippic', and is pronounced in an angry voice after 'drawing herself up more stiffly than ever'. Fifteen words only of direct speech, yet her malign influence, implacable will and unpleasant personality are felt throughout the novel, because they are felt by everyone whose lives she touches. It is a masterly portrait, the comedy of which is heightened by so much of her behaviour becoming known to us via the testimony of John Dashwood, whose reports of his mother-in-law are a trembling mixture of admiration and alarm.

If we were in any doubt as to Mrs Ferrars' motives – if we were inclined to give her the benefit of the doubt as to wanting the best for her son, and being misguided rather than unfeeling in trying to promote a marriage with Miss Morton – any such illusion would be shattered when her reaction to Edward's sticking to his engagement to Lucy is made known. Her vindictiveness in making his birthright over to Robert and, even more, her resolution of doing everything in her power to prevent his rise in any profession by which he may seek to provide for himself, are sheer cruelty. No wonder Marianne cries "Gracious God! can this be possible!"

As it happens, however, Mrs Ferrars' ill nature in disinheriting her eldest son works in his favour, for we cannot doubt that being forced into employment, activity and independence is beneficial to Edward Ferrars. Nor is she able to carry out her threats of holding him back once he has embarked on a profession, assisted as he is by Colonel Brandon, who admires his honourable and upright behaviour. We see Edward at the end of the novel settled at Delaford Parsonage with the wife of his choice and it is evident that 'From the ready discharge of his duties in every particular, from an increasing attachment to his wife and his home, and from the regular cheerfulness of his spirits', he would not change places with his younger brother but is perfectly 'contented with his lot'.

Even this modest degree of worldly prosperity and comfort have not come about without some resistance on Mrs Ferrars' part. On their engagement, Edward and Elinor are not quite as much in love as to think that the interest on his £2,000 and Elinor's £1,000, together with the Delaford living, amounting in total to £350 a year, will supply them with the comforts of life. A young couple marrying then had to allow for any number of children who might be born. It is only right that Edward receives *some* portion of his father's wealth and, distasteful as it is for him, he resolves to go to London and make 'mean concessions' via his sister Fanny to his mother.

> After proper resistance on the part of Mrs Ferrars, just so violent and so steady as to preserve her from that reproach which she always seemed fearful of incurring, the reproach of being too amiable, Edward was admitted to her presence, and pronounced to be again her son.
>
> Her family had of late been exceedingly fluctuating. For many years of her life she had had two sons; but the crime and annihilation of Edward a few weeks ago, had robbed her of one; the similar annihilation of Robert had left her for a fortnight without any; and now, by the resuscitation of Edward, she had one again. . . .
>
> What she would do towards augmenting their income, was next to be considered; and here it plainly appeared, that though Edward was now her only son, he was by no means the eldest; for while Robert was inevitably endowed with a thousand pounds a year, not the smallest objection was made against Edward's taking orders for the sake of two hundred and fifty at the utmost; nor was anything promised either for the present or the future, beyond the ten thousand pounds which had been given with Fanny.
>
> It was as much, however, as was desired, and more than was expected by Edward and Elinor; and Mrs Ferrars herself, by her shuffling excuses, seemed the only person surprised at her not giving more.

An unnatural mother to the end, incapable of rejoicing in the wellbeing or integrity of her son, the last we hear of her is when she grudgingly visits the newly married couple in their parsonage: 'Mrs Ferrars came to inspect the happiness which she was almost ashamed of having authorised.'

In discussing the parallel stories of the sisters in *Sense and Sensibility,* critics have failed to make much of the *other* older female relative whose power of disposing of her money after her death exerts an undue influence on a young man's choice of wife. Mrs Smith of Allenham (who may be a widow but is – from descriptions of her – much more likely to be a single lady, awarded the courtesy title of Mrs in acknowledgement of her age) is not mother but cousin to Willoughby – probably a cousin once removed, considering the difference in their ages, for she is 'elderly' and he is 'five and twenty'. He is acknowledged as her heir – provided he does not offend her sense of propriety. There are rival claimants waiting in the wings, whose later actions in telling tales of Willoughby attest to their envy and affront. We do not know the precise degrees of relationship of any of these people, but what is clear is that Mrs Smith has the power of choice over her fortune. Willoughby is probably suspected of charming his way into her favour. He has been paying annual visits of duty to Mrs Smith since before the action of the novel begins, and takes care to conceal from her behaviour of which she would not approve.

Mrs Smith remains an under-developed character, perhaps because Austen judged it would seem like a failure of imagination to give *both* the young men courting the Dashwood sisters the same difficulties to contend with, or at least, to give them the same prominence. There is just sufficient of an echo to be artistically pleasing, and at the same time to portray a society in which the young are hobbled by the opinions and wishes of their elders.

The telling difference between Mrs Ferrars and Mrs Smith is that the latter only wants her young relation to be good, not rich or distinguished. She is introduced to us as 'an elderly lady of very good character' and Willoughby's difficulties – as he later explains to Elinor – begin when she finds out about his seduction of Eliza Williams. "The purity of her life, the formality of her notions, her ignorance of the world – everything was against me", he says. (There are strong suggestions here of a maiden lady.) "In the height of her morality, good woman! she offered to forgive the past, if I would marry Eliza." This, Willoughby will not countenance – poor Eliza is classic damaged goods, as was her mother before her – perhaps she was damaged even before her own pregnancy *by* being the daughter of a disgraced mother, never likely to be sought in marriage by a gentleman – and a total breach ensues: "I was formally dismissed from her favour and her house." Cut off from his expectations, he turns to marriage with a wealthy heiress to make good the deficit, abandoning Marianne in the process. At the end of the novel, now married to Miss Grey, 'his punishment was soon afterwards complete in the voluntary forgiveness of Mrs Smith, who, by stating his marriage with a woman of character, as the source of her clemency, gave him reason for believing that had he behaved with honour towards Marianne, he might at once have been happy and rich'. Mrs Smith might well be pleased that he is respectably married, but this does not negate his offence with Eliza, and it is hard not to suppose that, just like Elinor at Cleveland, the elderly lady has been influenced against her better judgement by Willoughby's open, affectionate manners 'which it was no merit to possess'.

As a person of elderly, spinsterish, uncompromising propriety, Mrs Smith is a sketch of a type not found elsewhere in Austen, except perhaps in Mrs Percival, the righteous maiden aunt of *Catharine, or the Bower;* but that lady receives a much more comic treatment and is given some deliciously absurd lines of dialogue. In *Sense and Sensibility* Mrs Smith's values are not mocked, they are in fact those to which all the worthy principal characters subscribe, and it is a slight waste of a character unique in Austen's *oeuvre* that she interacts with no one but Willoughby in the novel. But from her actions and reported speech we know sufficient of her to appreciate that though her power is similar, her unworldliness and goodness are in stark contrast to the aims and motivations of Mrs Ferrars; and perhaps that is all we need to know.

Patroness of a Parish

Equally determined with Mrs Ferrars to control her relations' matrimonial affairs (though equally thwarted by the true love of those concerned) is *Pride and Prejudice's* Lady Catherine de Bourgh, that controller *par excellence*. There are many differences between these domineering despots. While Mrs Ferrars is small and thin, Lady Catherine de Bourgh is 'a tall, large woman, with strongly-marked features, which might once have been handsome'. While Mrs Ferrars is 'not a woman of many words', whenever Lady Catherine is on the scene, she is talking – whether telling her fellow card-players of their mistakes, relating an anecdote of herself, or determining 'what weather they were to have on the morrow'. She is 'not rendered formidable by silence, but whatever she said, was spoken in so authoritative a tone, as marked her self-importance'. Lady Catherine enjoys meddling for its own sake, meddling with all the world; not a charge that could be laid at Mrs Ferrars' door, whose narrowness of personality is reflected in the narrowness of her concerns.

Like Mrs Ferrars, however, Lady Catherine has a specific match in view – between her nephew Mr Darcy and her daughter Anne – and a specific young woman whose wishes (or as she would see them, pretensions) she would like to thwart – Elizabeth Bennet. But Darcy is too great a man to brook her interference, and Elizabeth is one of the few young people – perhaps the only one – with the spirit to stand up to her. Others, most notably Mr Collins (who owes his benefice to her) take her at her own estimation. He bows, scrapes and praises *ad nauseam* but she is incapable of being sickened by his excess. Even a knight of the realm like Sir William Lucas is so much in awe of her that his self-possession quite deserts him in her company. Her fortune is bolstered by rank, and her love of dictating takes the direction of general meddlesomeness in the affairs of the neighbourhood:

> Elizabeth soon perceived that though this great lady was not in the commission of the peace for the county, she was a most

> active magistrate in her own parish, the minutest concerns of which were carried to her by Mr Collins; and whenever any of the cottagers were disposed to be quarrelsome, discontented or too poor, she sallied forth into the village to settle their differences, silence their complaints, and scold them into harmony and plenty.

Nothing escapes her observation; nothing is beneath her notice. At once petty and arrogant, she has an opinion on everything, from how Charlotte Collins should arrange her cupboards to the entail that will deprive the Bennet sisters of the family home after their father's death – for Mrs Bennet, if she survives her husband, will be one of those whom widowhood hits hard, and this despite being the daughter of a lawyer, who was powerless to protect her future by legal settlement in the event of there being no sons. By contrast Lady Catherine, coming to her husband as the daughter of an earl, was evidently the subject of favourable marriage articles: she has a life interest in her husband's property which will pass to their only child, a daughter. At Lady Catherine's first meeting with Elizabeth, she observes, '"Your father's estate is entailed on Mr Collins, I think. For your sake", turning to Charlotte, "I am glad of it; but otherwise I see no occasion for entailing estates from the female line. It was not thought necessary in Sir Lewis de Bourgh's family."' As we have seen previously, Elizabeth's calm responses to a slew of impertinent questions result in some astonishment on the part of Lady Catherine, who exclaims "Upon my word, you give your opinion very decidedly for so young a person. Pray, what is your age?" and when Elizabeth does not choose to satisfy her curiosity, 'Lady Catherine seemed quite astonished at not receiving a direct answer; and Elizabeth suspected herself to be the first creature who had ever dared trifle with so much dignified impertinence!'

It is when Lady Catherine makes her ill-advised trip to Longbourn to bully Elizabeth into promising not to become engaged to Darcy that the real clash of wills takes place. "My character has ever been celebrated for its sincerity and frankness", she begins in full confidence, but Elizabeth, knowing that she has right and reason on her side, refuses to be intimidated. "Miss Bennet, do you know who I am? I have not been accustomed to such language as this", says Lady Catherine and, after further refusal to be bowed on Elizabeth's part, "You are to understand, Miss Bennet, that I came here with the determined resolution of carrying my purpose; nor will I be dissuaded from it. I have not been used to submit to any person's whims. I have not been in the habit of brooking disappointment." As Elizabeth answers, "*That* will make your ladyship's situation at present more pitiable; but it will have no effect on *me*."

Although Lady Catherine is given much more dialogue than Mrs Ferrars, although she is one of the major comic characters of *Pride and Prejudice* whom readers remember with much delight, and although she translates wonderfully well to stage and screen, she is in fact a much less powerful adversary. That she throws her weight around is true enough, but she never has the ability to affect the heroine's destiny. Only Darcy can do that. Elizabeth does not know how much influence Lady Catherine may have with her nephew, but if it should turn out to be a great deal, Darcy will prove himself unworthy of being loved by her – and won't be worth a regret. But Darcy never does show any symptom of doing what his aunt wishes against his own inclination, nor of even contemplating marriage to his insipid and sickly cousin. Darcy is financially independent. The difference between an Edward Ferrars and a Fitzwilliam Darcy is money.

One advantage over Mrs Ferrars, however, Lady Catherine does possess. While the former is capable of gratification only by the advancement of her family, the latter glories in a much wider sphere of influence. Though she fails equally in her principal object, she can console herself with the deference and obedience of almost every person with whom she comes into contact, from Mr Collins to Maria Lucas to the four nieces of Mrs Jenkinson whom she places out as governesses.

Angry and abusive as Lady Catherine is when the marriage of Darcy and Elizabeth takes place, after a period she is motivated by one of her most powerful characteristics, irrepressible curiosity; and she 'condescended to wait on them at Pemberley, in spite of the pollution which its woods had received, not merely from the presence of such a mistress, but the visits of her uncle and aunt from the city'. *Pride and Prejudice,* just like *Sense and Sensibility,* concludes with some form of reconciliation between the newly-wed couple and the person who has tried to keep them apart, and in both instances it is the female of the youthful pair who urges magnanimity. But who can say whether a little tinge of triumph in displaying their married happiness does not mingle with the more noble and selfless motivations of Elinor and Elizabeth in welcoming their husbands' relations and their own erstwhile antagonists into their marital homes.

Power by Proxy

If Elinor Dashwood and Elizabeth Bennet have to contend with meddling widows among their in-laws, Fanny Price has the misfortune to grow up with one in her own family. From the moment she arrives, a timid child of ten, at Mansfield Park, poor Fanny is persecuted, picked on and put down by her aunt Norris at every opportunity. Only a warped character with a grudge against the world could get her gratification from treating a child in this way. What accounts for Mrs Norris's spitefulness? The eldest of three sisters, in her youth she was considered 'quite as handsome' as the next in age, but failed to achieve an equally advantageous marriage – indeed, almost failed to get a husband at all, until in desperation after half a dozen years she grabbed at a clergyman friend of her rich brother-in-law. (Her good looks may not have sufficiently masked her ill nature among the young men of her acquaintance, especially as her youth passed away.) If marrying neither for love nor money is a bitter disappointment to her, she has also to contend with childlessness while her sisters are self-evidently fertile. No doubt this accounts for the 'angry voice' with which she regularly announces to the Bertrams the arrival of another little Price in the world. With no children to occupy her time and attention, she has little to think about except ingratiating herself with the baronet's family and economizing on the housekeeping budget at the Parsonage, which becomes an obsession. 'Her love of money was equal to her love of directing, and she knew quite as well how to save her own as to spend that of her friends.'

Mrs Norris's attitude to being widowed is to 'console[d] herself for the loss of her husband by considering that she could do very well without him, and for her reduction in income by the evident necessity of stricter economy'. Though her income, calculated by Sir Thomas, is £600 a year – ample for a single person – she wallows in the image of a poor, struggling widow. Having fixed for her new abode on the smallest habitation which could rank as genteel among the buildings of Mansfield parish, her insistence that she keep a spare room for a friend misleads Sir Thomas into thinking she intends to take Fanny to live with her; she is quite startled when Lady Bertram mentions it:

> "Fanny live with me! the last thing in the world for me to think of, or for anybody to wish that really knows us both. Good heaven! what could I do with Fanny? Me! a poor helpless, forlorn widow, unfit for anything, my spirits quite broken down, what could I do with a girl at her time of life, a girl of fifteen! the very age of all others to need most attention and care, and put the cheerfullest spirits to the test. . . . Dear sister! If you consider my unhappy state, how can she be any comfort to me? Here am I a poor desolate widow, deprived of the best of husbands, my health gone in attending and nursing him, my spirits still worse, all my peace in this world destroyed, with barely enough to support me in the rank of gentlewoman, and enable me to live so as not to disgrace the memory of the dear departed – what possible comfort could I have in taking such a charge upon me as Fanny! If I could wish it for my own sake, I would not do such an unjust thing by the poor girl. She is in

good hands, and sure of doing well. I must struggle through my sorrows and difficulties as I can."

"Then you will not mind living by yourself quite alone?"

"Dear Lady Bertram! what am I fit for but solitude? Now and then I shall hope to have a friend in my little cottage (I shall always have a bed for a friend); but the most part of my future days will be spent in utter seclusion. If I can but make both ends meet, that's all I ask for."

Far from seeking solitude and seclusion, Mrs Norris spends most of her days at the Park, usurping her sister's role as mistress and mother. Though Fanny is her chief victim, being almost daily harassed by her, she exerts her power over any social inferior who comes within her ambit, most memorably Dick Jackson, young son of the estate carpenter, her triumph over whom (in preventing his partaking in the servants' midday meal) constitutes one of her boasts unpleasant to her listeners. Towards other inferiors she assumes the role of ostentatious carer, whether nursing a sick maid, treating the old coachman for his rheumatism or promising the gardener at Sotherton a charm for his grandson. In so doing, she tries to allay her own sense of inferiority and to exact gratitude for her ministrations that she seeks in vain from the Bertrams, who take her services and her flatteries as their due.

Though Fanny Price suffers abuse at the hands of this aunt both physically – being denied a fire in her sitting room, for example, or having to walk between the Park and the village twice under a hot sun; and emotionally – being publicly accused of ingratitude and always reminded that she is 'the lowest and the last' in any company, in fact Mrs Norris has power only over the daily comforts of Fanny's life, not over her destiny. She cannot dictate whom she should or should not marry. Quite apart from Fanny's own quiet resolve which no attack can break down, Sir Thomas is too much master in his own house, especially after his return from Antigua when he comes to experience Mrs Norris's presence in his home as an 'hourly evil'. He ponders whether 'time had done her much disservice' or whether only now are his eyes open to her true nature. The punishment meted out to Mrs Norris is exceptionally harsh for Austen, but then this is probably the nastiest character she created. Her ejection (by her author, not exactly by the ever-courteous Sir Thomas) from Mansfield and immurement with the adulterous and thwarted Maria, 'on the one side no affection, on the other, no judgement' condemns her to an end of life devoid of calm and content, the most miserable old age perhaps of any projected in Austen's fiction.

Every Neighbourhood Should Have a Great Lady

In Mrs Norris, Austen shows us a woman whose officiousness, though practised on every possible occasion, operates in a relatively limited sphere owing to her lack of personal wealth and status. The only partially defeated (at the end of the novel) Lady Catherine enjoys a wider range of influence and Lady Denham wider still: a whole town – Sanditon – and three distinct families are subject to the caprices of this 70-year-old woman.

Lady Denham is the widow of a baronet and the undisputed 'great lady' of the neighbourhood, being a major landholder and the colleague in speculation of the nascent resort's other property-holder Mr Parker. They are not wholly in accord. While the entrepreneurial Mr Parker is ever optimistic that his schemes will bring fame and fortune to Sanditon, in the breast of Lady Denham caution and avarice are at perpetual war.

The only character in Austen to be twice widowed, Lady Denham's most pleasing characteristic is her readiness to speak fondly of her two deceased husbands, "poor Mr Hollis" and "my poor dear Sir Harry". But for a very rich woman she is tight with her money, suspicious of hangers-on, risk-averse and petty. Her financial history is given to us in some detail. She was a Miss Brereton, an heiress with £30,000 – as much as Emma Woodhouse, or the desirable Miss Morton whom Mrs Ferrars is so anxious for one of her sons to marry. Since Lady Denham is ill-educated, it is fair to guess that her father's fortune was made in some low trade. The suspicious nature that we see in her as a 70-year-old is perhaps the consequence of a youth spent in wariness of suitors who might be only after her for her money. She was thirty before she married, her first husband being the elderly Mr Hollis, a man of considerable property in Sanditon. She 'so well pleased and nursed him' that his entire fortune is left to her on his death.

Whether the pleasing and nursing are seen as further points in her favour, showing her to have had a sweet nature earlier in her life; or whether she was coolly calculating even in her ministrations, is debatable. The nursing role reminds us of Marianne Dashwood's opinion that a woman marrying over the age of twenty-seven would be entering into a pact whereby she received the status and security of marriage in exchange for fulfilling "the office of a nurse". Miss Brereton, however, with her own fortune, was not in such desperation that she need enter into such a bargain unless she derived some enjoyment from the society of her husband. The balance of probability is that she did feel real affection for him.

After a widowhood of some years Mrs Hollis married Sir Harry Denham, an impoverished baronet. What was her motive? To become the titled great lady of the neighbourhood, undoubtedly – but perhaps also to have someone to talk to. Lady Denham has 'a natural love of talking'. If the baronet's motive was to acquire her money for his own family, as suspected by the neighbourhood, he was thwarted by her insistence on keeping it within her own control when the marriage articles were drawn up. As a shrewd woman of forty or fifty, Mrs Hollis is not going to be parted from her cash. So when Sir Harry dies in his turn, his widow takes her own money back to her own property, Sanditon House – the place she had acquired from Mr Hollis – and boasts that "though she had got nothing but her title from the family, still she had given nothing for it". She is now the dowager Lady Denham, Sir Harry's nephew having inherited the baronetcy, and when that young man marries, his wife will likewise be a Lady Denham. The young Sir

Edward, however, has not inherited a fortune commensurate with the title. To support the lifestyle of a baronet, he will have to marry a woman with money – unless the present Lady Denham chooses to enrich him.

Thus it will be seen that she has three sets of relations with roughly equal claims to inherit money and property after her death, and to receive help while she is still living: the Breretons, whose £30,000 she began with; the Hollises, whose Sanditon estates she now owns; and the Denhams, whose family she was most lately connected with. The interplay of all these hangers-on, with her own reluctance to give anything to anybody, was to provide some of the fun of *Sanditon*.

This back story is conveyed to the heroine of *Sanditon*, Charlotte Heywood, as she travels towards the village, by Mr Parker, whose view of her ladyship is by no means as fawning as John Dashwood's of Mrs Ferrars, still less as Mr Collins's of Lady Catherine, for Mr Parker is an independent man. His views therefore are not immediately discounted, as Mr Collins's views of his patroness are discounted by Elizabeth Bennet, who sees them for the absurdities they are. As it happens, when Charlotte is able to decide from her own observations, she finds that Mr Parker's own good nature colours his judgement. However, until she can arrive at her own assessment, she is given a not unfavourable sketch of Lady Denham's character with which to begin their acquaintance:

> "There is at times," said he "a little self-importance – but it is not offensive; – and there are moments, there are points, when her love of money is carried greatly too far. But she is a good-natured woman, a very good-natured woman – a very obliging, friendly neighbour; a cheerful, independent, valuable character – and her faults may be entirely deputed to her want of education. She has good natural sense, but quite uncultivated. She has a fine active mind, as well as a fine healthy frame for a woman of seventy, and enters into the improvement of Sanditon with a spirit truly admirable – though now and then a littleness

> *will* appear. She cannot look forward quite as I would have her – and takes alarm at a trifling present expense, without considering what returns it *will* make her in a year or two."

When we – and Charlotte – are introduced to her in person, her physical presence, though less individually designated than that of Mrs Ferrars, is more vividly rendered than that of Lady Catherine de Bourgh. Her height is between the two and (at first glance at least) she is more prepossessing than either, showing greater good humour in her verbal and facial expressions:

> Lady Denham was of middle height, stout, upright and alert in her motions with a shrewd eye, and self-satisfied air – but not an unagreeable countenance – and though her manner was rather downright and abrupt, as of a person who valued herself on being free-spoken, there was a good humour and cordiality about her – a civility and readiness to be acquainted with Charlotte herself, and a heartiness of welcome towards her old friends, which was inspiring the good will she seemed to feel.

In this description Lady Denham seems to have something about her reminiscent of both the shrewd and alert Mrs Croft (*Persuasion*) and the downright and cordial Mrs Jennings (*Sense and Sensibility*), and Austen readers may well be prepared to find her equally amiable. But in fact the dominant characteristic of Lady Denham's personality, which soon afterwards emerges, is more reminiscent of Mrs Norris: a love of money so entrenched that it shapes every thought and action of her life.

We already know that, having avoided being in London for many years because she is wary of falling in with the Breretons, she accepts their hospitality at last because a three-day hotel bill outrages her. In other words she would rather run the risk of her nearest blood relations sponging off her – because she thinks she can hold out against that – than pay to stay any longer at the hotel while conducting her business in town. In her first conversations with Mr Parker after the latter's return from Willingdon, she bewails the rise in the price of butcher's meat which she foresees as the consequence of visitors to Sanditon spending freely – though that is exactly what Mr Parker knows is desirable for the place. Lady Denham's calculations are all short-term. As for having a resident doctor in the place, that is anathema to her, and she is still resenting the ten sets of fees paid to "one of that tribe" by her last late husband – and then he died anyway, so they were completely taken in. Callously, she hopes one of the girls from a visiting school turns out to be consumptive, and willing to pay for milk from one of her own asses – but as opposed to that possible profit, they may scratch the furniture. All her thoughts are as petty as this, and Charlotte is rapidly revising her opinion. In their next encounter, she is left for a while alone with Lady Denham and, in a conversation entirely inappropriate to the shortness of their acquaintance and the very great difference in their ages, the older woman boasts:

> "I am not the woman to help anybody blindfold. I always take care to know what I am about and who I have to deal with, before I stir a finger. I do not think I was ever over-reached in my life; and that is a good deal for a woman to say that has been married twice. Poor dear Sir Harry (between ourselves) thought at first to have got more. But (with a bit of a sigh) he is gone, and we must not find fault with the dead. Nobody could live happier together than us – and he was a very honourable man, quite the gentleman of ancient family. And when he died, I gave Sir Edward his gold watch – "
>
> She said this with a look at her companion which implied its right to produce a great impression – and seeing no rapturous astonishment in Charlotte's countenance, added quickly, "He did not bequeath it to his nephew, my dear – it was no bequest. It was not in the will. He only told me, and *that* but once, that he should wish his nephew to have his watch; but it need not have been binding, if I had not chose it."

"Very kind indeed! very handsome!" said Charlotte, absolutely forced to affect admiration.

"Yes, my dear – and it is not the *only* kind thing I have done by him. I have been a very liberal friend to Sir Edward. And poor young man, he needs it bad enough; for though I am only the dowager, my dear, and he is the heir, things do not stand between us in the way they commonly do between those two parties. Not a shilling do I receive from the Denham estate. Sir Edward has no payments to make *me*. He don't stand uppermost, believe me. It is *I* that help *him*."

But she will not invite Sir Edward and his sister to spend a week in her house, for then her housemaids would want higher wages. . . . "I have no fancy for having my house as full as an hotel." Charlotte ceases to listen to all her reasons and muses, "She is thoroughly mean. . . . Mr Parker spoke too mildly of her. . . . I can see no good in her. . . . Thus it is when rich people are sordid." With her fussing about her housemaids and the price of butcher's meat, Lady Denham displays something of Dr Johnson's (uncharacteristically misogynistic) dictum that 'When female minds are imbittered [sic] by age or solitude, their malignity is generally exerted in rigorous and spiteful superintendence of domestic trifles'.[2] Most such females, of course, had no power *but* over domestic trifles. Mrs Norris is a prime example. Lady Denham has a larger sphere of influence than many, but the pettiness of her mind dictates the pettiness of her concerns.

In the short fragment (twelve chapters) that is *Sanditon*, Lady Denham has quite as much revelatory dialogue as Lady Catherine in *Pride and Prejudice*. Of much lower birth, yet equally outspoken and self-satisfied, and with an array of family members to play off against one another, to all of whom she is more or less resistant, she represents a new departure for Austen. The fascinating new topic of property speculation, too, provides rich material with which to illustrate character. While Mr Parker sees the bigger picture, Lady Denham's mind cannot raise itself above the petty gains and losses that might accrue, and these are wonderfully imagined and grounded in the recognizable world. At the very end of her life, Austen's power of invention was undimmed, not only in the creation of original new characters and new subjects of discourse, but in finding for each an individual voice.

9. NOT THE ONLY WIDOW IN BATH

In *Emma,* the odious Mrs Elton, who has found herself a husband in Bath, tries to persuade Emma to go there for the same purpose: "The advantages of Bath to the young are pretty generally understood," says she, with almost a nudge and a wink. The advantages of Bath to the middle-aged and elderly were no less apparent. Residence in Bath offered those of mature years freedom from the cares of a country property and housekeeping; company on tap; and easy access to medical attention as well as to shops, libraries, concerts and plays. These factors, indeed, are what drew Jane Austen's own parents to the city in 1801 after nearly forty contented but hardworking years of life in a country rectory and farm. If it were so for couples, then how much more might widows – unequal to managing a country estate, perhaps, or displaced from it by the next generation – see in Bath the solution to their problems.

Bath had long been a magnet for those on the make, but by the early nineteenth century its social composition was in the process of changing. Once a place of high fashion, patronized by the rich and famous, it was losing its allure for such people as it slipped unrelentingly down the demographic scale. Now its appeal was to precisely the kind of people Jane Austen knew and wrote about: the minor gentry with a taste for social life and the means to indulge their real or imagined illnesses; the less well-off, especially single women, desperately clinging to their shreds of gentility in a place where living was comparatively cheap; well-funded widows and retired professional men with their families, looking for an agreeable holiday or long-term residence in a sedate and highly stratified environment; and, as ever, a motley assortment of hangers-on and would-be social climbers.

In *Persuasion* the shrewd lawyer Mr Shepherd is skilful enough to direct Sir Walter's thoughts to Bath as a place of residence rather than London: 'It was a much safer place for a gentleman in his predicament: he might there be important at comparatively little expense. . . . Sir Walter and Elizabeth were induced to believe that they should lose neither consequence nor enjoyment by settling there.' And nor do they, for there are far more people to look up to them in Bath than in their country neighbourhood, and there is certainly a lot more to do. Anne might scorn 'the littlenesses of a town' and deplore the fact that her nearest relations can find 'extent to be proud of between two walls, perhaps thirty feet asunder', when they have been used to Kellynch Hall, but in all logic, residence in Bath had much to offer. Her staid and rational godmother and friend Lady Russell is an advocate of Bath, spending winter months there which would be dreary in the country, and finding mental refreshment in meeting up with old friends and getting all the new publications. Driving into Bath, she is greeted by its familiar city noises of traffic and bustling humanity but they do not repel her: 'they were part of the winter pleasures, and her spirits rose under their influence'.

Bath was certainly attractive to widows. A wealthy widow with a small household of servants could lead a life of unimpeachable respectability and comfort, while an impoverished one could look out for opportunities to better the lot of herself or her children. Thus in *Northanger Abbey,* the widowed and not very affluent Mrs Thorpe gambles on the expense of bringing her daughters to Bath for a few weeks, it may be inferred, to give their matrimonial prospects the wider stage which the beauty and resolute stylishness of her eldest girl at least seem to warrant. (If Jane and Cassandra Austen suspected that any such hopes provided an additional motivation in their parents' decision to retire to Bath, it would only have added to their own distaste for the move. To be regarded by their acquaintance in Bath as looking for husbands as their twenties slip away would have been just too demeaning.)

In an almost throwaway line in *Mansfield Park* we read that Mrs Rushworth senior, on leaving her son's house on his marriage, 'removed herself, her maid, her footman and her chariot with true dowager propriety to Bath'. The phrase 'true dowager propriety' indicates that resettling in Bath was a common course of action for such women. Mrs Rushworth is doing what many of her kind had done before. The choice for such displaced women was usually between a dower house on her son's estate, or a town house in Bath or another provincial city, and probably many a daughter-in-law was glad when her predecessor chose the latter. Among Jane Austen's Kent connections were two widows who made opposite choices at this stage of their lives. Her brother Edward's adoptive mother and benefactress, Mrs Catherine Knight, chose to give up her country estate to Edward and his young family and to occupy a more manageable house in the city of Canterbury, with company and amenities on hand. Edward's *wife's* mother, Lady Bridges, decided to remain on family property in the country at the Dower House, Goodnestone, Kent, where she could keep an eye on the next generation. During her visits to Edward, Jane stayed with both ladies from time to time. Both were very comfortably circumstanced, Mrs Knight keeping an income of £2,000 a year when she surrendered the estate of Godmersham to Edward, and Lady Bridges rich enough to afford a lengthy visit to Bath, despite its being at a distance, when she fancied herself suffering from gout. Putting herself under the care of the most eminent medical man, Dr Parry, she was persuaded to extend her visit over the whole winter of 1813–14. 'I suppose he will not mind having a few more of her ladyship's guineas', Jane remarked dryly when she heard what was proposed.[1]

No small part of Bath's attractions for women in their later years was the scope for reliving former glories before a captive audience. Thus, Mrs Rushworth settles in Bath, 'there to parade over the wonders of Sotherton in her evening parties – enjoying them as thoroughly perhaps in the animation of a card table as she had ever done on the spot'. One suspects that Jane Austen herself had attended many such card parties, and been an unwilling listener to many such boastings, at the home of her aunt Leigh Perrot. On 13 May 1801, shortly after moving to Bath, she wrote:

> Another stupid party last night; perhaps if they were larger they might be less intolerable, but here there were only just enough to make one card table, with six people to look over, & talk nonsense to each other. Ly Fust, Mrs Busby & a Mrs Owen sat down with my Uncle to Whist within five minutes after the three old *Toughs* came in, & there they sat . . . till their chairs were announced. I cannot anyhow continue to find people agreeable.

The three named ladies, appearing without menfolk, were presumably widows. Bath was sunk indeed from the period, only two decades earlier, when its most celebrated mature women were the blue-stockings, listened to with respect by their juniors (as the young novelist Fanny Burney listened deferentially in 1780 as Mrs Carter and Mrs Montague held forth in their Bath salons); now, to a critical young mind, women of a similar age merited only the designation old *Toughs*.

Another widow known to Jane Austen through her uncle and her aunt Leigh Perrot was a Mrs Wilhelmina Lillingston who, at the time of the Austens' removal to Bath, resided at 10 Rivers Street – the very street in which Austen would place her own widowed Lady Russell, in *Persuasion,* some fourteen years later. Austen had nothing very kind to say about Mrs Lillingston who, at age sixty to her own twenty-five, must have seemed just another dull old woman, and horribly representative of a breed she was going to have to encounter daily in her new Bath life. 'We have had Mrs Lillingstone [sic] and the Chamberlaynes call on us,' she told Cassandra, who had not yet joined Jane and her mother in Bath, within a day of their arrival on 6 May 1801. The visit was returned on 10 May: 'We met not a creature at Mrs Lillingstone's & yet were not so very stupid as I expected, which I attribute to my wearing my new bonnet & being in good looks.' She met her again in a 'tiny party' of her aunt's on 21 May, and again at the home of mutual friends the Holders on 25 May: 'My evening visit was by no means disagreeable. Mrs Lillingstone came to engage Mrs Holder's conversation, & Miss Holder & I adjourned after tea into the inner Drawingroom to look over Prints & talk pathetically.' The same uninteresting people to meet day after day: the claustrophobia of Bath life comes over vividly.

But either the two Miss Austens became better friends with Mrs Lillingston as they grew to know her better (there is a dearth of letters for the rest of their residence in Bath), or the old woman, who was estranged from her own married daughter, liked or pitied them despite their indifference, because when she made her will in 1805, among many small bequests she left them £50 apiece.[2] Her death occurred in January 1806, just as Mrs Austen (herself now a widow) and her two daughters were preparing to leave Bath. This was one of the very few legacies that ever came the way of Jane Austen, and was by no means a run-of-the-mill occurrence in her life. It certainly must have added cheer to her departure from the city, and it is just possible that this cushion of money helped her to decide, five years later, that she could afford to publish her first novel, *Sense and Sensibility*, on the commission system – that is, that she would bear any loss incurred by the publisher if sales did not cover his costs. (She actually made a profit.) Jane's uncle James Leigh Perrot was Mrs Lillingston's executor and, as such, the person who put the Rivers Street house on the market. It was bought by a Mr Russell and, if she was aware of this, the names may have been Jane's belated tribute of gratitude or atonement when she came to write *Persuasion*.

In leaving Bath shortly into her widowhood, Mrs Austen was going against the trend. The fact was that she could scarcely afford to continue living there, comparatively cheap though it was considered to be. Between the death of Mr Austen (and his income) in January 1805 and the Austen women's departure from the city in July 1806, they moved to a sequence of ever-meaner lodgings until they were glad of the offer to share accommodation and expenses with Jane's newly married brother Francis, and to bear his pregnant young wife company in their Southampton lodgings when the young naval officer went away to sea. If Mrs Austen had hoped her rich, childless brother James Leigh Perrot, who with his wife spent six months of the year in Bath and the other six on his country estate in Berkshire, would help her out in widowhood, she was disappointed, and found herself relying on her sons instead. To be nearer her eldest and favourite son James, in Hampshire, became the object of her desires. There was nothing to keep the three women in Bath, and the two younger ones certainly left it with 'happy feelings of escape'.[3] Though it had not been an easy or a fulfilling period for her, Jane Austen's five-year residence in the city had furnished her with a new depth of understanding and a wider range of human circumstances, including perhaps more people in the later stages of their lives, to draw upon in the novels she was yet to write.

'Females and Invalides'

Fearing herself to be sliding into the ranks of Bath's many impoverished all-female households did not necessarily make Austen more sympathetic to their common plight. In some instances it had the opposite effect of making her recoil in distaste. In *Emma,* Mrs Partridge is, the heroine guesses disparagingly, 'some vulgar, dashing widow who, with the help of a boarder, just made shift to live!' At least Mrs Partridge goes into company and mingles with the lower gentry (precisely what Emma Woodhouse has against her) but a Bath landlady of a slightly lower order is Mrs Speed in *Persuasion,* who runs the boarding house in Westgate Buildings where Mrs Smith lodges. Anne Elliot fails to notice whether it is

Mrs Speed, or her maidservant, or her sister Nurse Rooke who opens the door when she calls on Mrs Smith, so much beneath her notice are such women – notwithstanding that Anne is the most sensitive, least snobbish of heroines. Though Anne surely said thank you as she passed inside, she must have 'looked through' the person to whom she was speaking. Mrs Smith herself, sunk by poverty and ill health, is not above making a friend of Nurse Rooke, a working woman with a fund of common sense and experience. When Anne understands this, she does not cavil – though neither does she reproach herself for her earlier blindness. Both sisters – Mrs Speed and Nurse Rooke – are of good character. They have located themselves in Bath because of its earning opportunities. Its steady influx of sick visitors brings them work: one in providing lodgings and the other in nursing services. In one sense they are better off than Mrs Smith, in that they can keep the proceeds of their honest labours. Mrs Smith has her gentry status to guard and, in need of money though she is, cannot afford – in a social sense – to be known to work for payment. The small craft items she makes as therapy and pastime while bedridden are sold not for her own benefit, but for charity.

Mrs Smith and Mrs Clay are the two impoverished widows of *Persuasion* whose circumstances are similar but whose struggles are viewed very differently by Austen. They are linked in the reader's consciousness when Sir Walter, finding out about Anne's visits to her old school friend, voices his scorn:

> "A widow Mrs Smith lodging in Westgate Buildings! A poor widow barely able to live, between thirty and forty; a mere Mrs Smith, an everyday Mrs Smith, of all people and all names in the world, to be the chosen friend of Miss Anne Elliot, and to be preferred by her to her own family connections among the nobility of England and Ireland! Mrs Smith! Such a name!"
>
> Mrs Clay, who had been present while all this passed, now thought it advisable to leave the room, and Anne could have said much, and did long to say a little in defence of *her* friend's

> not very dissimilar claims to theirs, but her sense of personal respect to her father prevented her. She made no reply. She left it to himself to recollect, that Mrs Smith was not the only widow in Bath between thirty and forty, with little to live on, and no surname of dignity.

Anne loathes Mrs Clay and we take our responses from the normally reliable Anne. Her loathing arises from perceiving that Mrs Clay is on the make, insinuating herself into Elizabeth Elliot's regard by obsequiousness and flattery, and angling to become Sir Walter's second wife. Deplorable tactics no doubt, but what choice does Penelope Clay have in life but to try for a second marriage? Were she to work, as we have seen, she would lose status. Returning to her father's roof as a widow with two small children is a temporary accommodation, but is this what a woman in her thirties, 'certainly altogether well-looking' and possessed of 'an acute mind and assiduous pleasing manners' must settle for? Can we blame her for wanting more? Love and romance as well as security and social elevation might be within her grasp, and even her abandonment of her children for months on end might be excused if a second marriage and settled home be viewed as in their interests too. In fact Sir Walter shows no sign of regarding Mrs Clay as anything more than a camp follower, and Anne's apprehensions on that score seem unwarranted, as well as founded rather uneasily on snobbery. For if they *were* to marry, what would be so dreadful in that? In point of character and intelligence, Sir Walter hardly deserves better. When Mrs Clay gives up on Sir Walter to go off with the much younger and more attractive Mr Elliot, we may question her morals, but not her heart. There is palpable physical attraction here, and she is willing to take the risk of being merely a discardable mistress to snatch again at youth and romance. There is a life force in Mrs Clay which, if we view her dispassionately, without the disapproval that Anne and her creator bring to bear, is not unattractive.

Meanwhile Mrs Smith displays excellent qualities of resilience, cheerfulness and fortitude, which Anne admires and so do we. Mrs

Smith (Christian name undisclosed, though Anne must think of her by the name she would have known when they were at school together) – is of all Austen characters the one most aware in herself of change in outlook wrought by the passage of time. She looks back on herself when "very young" as living only for enjoyment, associating with people equally young and thoughtless, without any strict rules of conduct. "I think differently now," she tells Anne; "time and sickness and sorrow have given me other notions". The contrast with Elizabeth Elliot is striking. The two women are much the same age, and both begin with good looks and a sense of their own superiority, but whereas 'twelve years had transformed the fine-looking, well-grown Miss Hamilton, in all the glow of health and confidence of superiority' into a more thoughtful person with a better knowledge of her own place in the world, Elizabeth is 'still the same handsome Miss Elliot that she had begun to be thirteen years ago'. It is true that Elizabeth has 'some regrets and some apprehensions' but they are purely selfish regrets and apprehensions: time has not taught her to look beyond herself as it has Mrs Smith, who tries to help local families with her handiwork and who is interested in all classes of persons. While Mrs Smith has matured with experience and adversity, there has been no equivalent enlargement in Elizabeth Elliot's understanding or sympathies.

Not that Mrs Smith is a paragon. Unlike Mrs Clay, she makes no sexual play for anybody – as an invalid confined to two rooms, she does not have much opportunity. But needs must, Mrs Smith is in a desperate plight, and she is not without cunning of her own. She is quite willing to see her friend Anne marry a man with a dubious moral history if it will bring benefit to herself.

> "Let me plead for my – present friend I cannot call him, but for my former friend. Where can you look for a more suitable match? Where could you expect a more gentlemanlike, agreeable man? Let me recommend Mr Elliot. I am sure you hear nothing but good of him from Colonel Wallis; and who can know him better than Colonel Wallis?"

> "My dear Mrs Smith, Mr Elliot's wife has not been dead much above half a year. He ought not to be supposed to be paying his addresses to anyone."
>
> "Oh! if these are your only objections" cried Mrs Smith, archly, "Mr Elliot is safe, and I shall give myself no more trouble about him. Do not forget me when you are married, that's all. Let him know me to be a friend of yours, and then he will think little of the trouble required, which it is very natural for him now, with so many affairs and engagements of his own, to avoid and get rid of as he can; very natural perhaps. Ninety-nine out of a hundred would do the same. Of course, he cannot be aware of the importance to me. Well, my dear Miss Elliot, I hope and trust you will be very happy. Mr Elliot has sense to understand the value of such a woman. Your peace will not be shipwrecked as mine has been. You are safe in all worldly matters, and safe in his character."

This is, of course, the precise opposite of what Mrs Smith knows to be the truth, which she reveals when finally convinced that Anne will not be marrying her cousin. After the shocking history of Mr Elliot comes tumbling out, with corroborating evidence and much bitterness, Anne thinks to question her friend's earlier recommendation, but Mrs Smith brushes off her insincerity: "My dear, there was nothing else to be done." That is not quite true: she could have done and said nothing, at least until Anne is actually married. Mrs Smith is not punished by her author for jeopardizing Anne's happiness in this way – a conscious stratagem which, if successful, would have been another case of woeful persuasion. To the contrary, she is accorded the honour, unique in Austen's novels, of sharing the last paragraph of 'happy ending' with the heroine.

An older woman, followed and flattered for her rank rather than her own merits (which are nil) is the Irish Viscount's widow Lady Dalrymple, whose regular visits to the city seem to be made principally for the adulation she receives. Her unmarried daughter of unspecified age, Miss Carteret, is her mere hanger-on. We also hear of a Lady Alicia among the Elliots' and Lady Russell's friends, a woman whose Christian-name title indicates rank higher than the widow of a baronet or knight, rank that obtains from being the daughter of an earl or a duke. Spinsters, widows and widowers are commonly portrayed by Austen as having questionable motive and enjoyment in coming to Bath. More honest enjoyment is ascribed to older married people who happen to find themselves in the city, whether Mrs Musgrove, the centre of a family grouping come to Bath for a quick jaunt of shopping and play-going, whose hotel sitting room is the scene of 'ease and animation' briefly interrupted by the 'cold composure' and 'heartless elegance' of the Elliots' entry; or the Crofts, brought to Bath in quest of a cure for the Admiral's gout. Anne is mortified by the difference her father and sister's presence make to the Musgrove circle; and she observes the self-sufficiency of the Crofts with great pleasure:

> They brought with them their country habit of being almost always together. . . . Anne saw them wherever she went. Lady Russell took her out in her carriage almost every morning, and she never failed to think of them, and never failed to see them. Knowing their feelings as she did, it was a most attractive picture of happiness to her. She always watched them as long as she could, delighted to fancy she understood what they might be talking of, as they walked along in happy independence, or equally delighted to see the Admiral's hearty shake of the hand when he encountered an old friend, and observe their eagerness of conversation when occasionally forming into a little knot of the navy, Mrs Croft looking as intelligent and keen as any of the officers around her.

Later, Admiral Croft tells Anne what she could not know merely by observation, that for all the pleasure of these morning jaunts and having "plenty of chat" in the streets, the part of the day they really prefer is when "we get away from them all, and shut ourselves in our lodgings, and draw in our chairs, and are as snug as if we were in Kellynch, ay, or as we used to be even at North Yarmouth and Deal." In other words, the Crofts make their own happiness wherever life takes them, so long as they can be together. Luxury and show are nothing to them. They love to remember their earlier life together, hardships and all. The plain-spoken Admiral continues, "We do not like our lodgings here the worse, I can tell you, for putting us in mind of those we first had at North Yarmouth. The wind blows through one of the cupboards just the same way." The Crofts are one of the few couples whose fond remembrance of their own past enables us to glimpse them as the same people, only younger. This is rather touching.

A similarly devoted couple were Jane's own parents, enjoying their well-deserved retirement in Bath. Their grand-daughter, Anna Austen Lefroy, stayed with them at 4 Sydney Place in 1802 when she was nine; many years later she remembered how they 'seemed to enjoy the cheerfulness of their Town life, and especially perhaps the rest which their advancing years entitled them to, which, even to their active natures, must have been acceptable. I have always thought this was the short Holyday of their married life.'[4] Mr Austen had been considered an extremely handsome man in his youth and, with his bright dark eyes and benevolent expression, 'he was still handsome when advanced in age'. His hair by this time was perfectly white, yet 'very beautiful and glossy, with short curls above the ears', and Anna could 'well remember at Bath ... what notice he attracted, when on any public occasion he appeared with his head uncovered.'

(Mrs Austen in old age perhaps could not vie for looks with her husband, yet at the moment of her death a strange effect occurred. According again to Anna, 'when it was over the very wrinkles seemed smoothed out of her face and the beauty of youth restored to it.'[5] But this was not to happen for another quarter of a century.)

In 1815 another real-life couple, General d'Arblay and his wife, the novelist Fanny Burney, now in their sixties, and living on a very small income, chose Bath as their place of residence. Like the Crofts, they spent as much time as possible together, and after a morning in town, loved to shut themselves up in their lodgings to talk, write and read. Fanny, whose first visit to Bath had been in 1780, extolled the city on every return visit: its beautiful views, its amenities, its broad pavements and fine buildings. And its cheapness: 'It has a thousand coaxing recommendations to folks of small pecuniary means'.[6] She would happily have spent the remainder of her life there, but when her husband died three years later, she shifted her focus to providing a home for their only son, reluctantly but selflessly acknowledging that such a home must be in London: 'Bath is not a place for a young man to begin life in: it is too confined to females and invalides.'[7]

The Victorian age would confirm both trends – the social acceptability, even desirability, of delicate health in the gentry class; and the preponderance of all-female households in Bath. The 'Bath chair' was invented to cater for this clientele, to be sat in by one woman who fancied herself too ill to walk, and pushed by another who was her paid companion, or a poor relation, perhaps. The French spelling *invalide* adopted by Burney was an affectation heralding the gentrification of chronic malady. Jane Austen did not spell the word so, but her niece Caroline, writing as a middle-aged Victorian lady, recalled her last visit to her ailing aunt at Chawton, and being taken upstairs to visit her in her bedroom: 'She was in her dressing-gown, and sitting quite like an invalide in an arm chair.'[8]

Typical of Bath's population in the decades following Jane Austen's death was in fact Fanny's half-sister Sarah Harriet Burney, a less well-known novelist and a poor spinster, with barely £100 a year secure income. From 1834 to 1841 – now an old lady, of course – she occupied a room in a ladies' boarding house in Henrietta Street where she disdained her housemates for their petty-mindedness and narrow experience of life. Even Fanny, erstwhile lover of Bath, did not think her sister would be happy in the city, accurately predicting to another sister that 'She will tire of its monotonous composure.'[9]

By the census of 1851, there were 3,980 widows to 1,086

widowers in the city, and 10,767 spinsters (at least a quarter of them domestic servants) to 4,057 bachelors.[10] Though Jane Austen herself never saw Bath after 1806, she had discerned the beginning of this trend in its social composition, and was grateful to make her own escape. She continued to receive reports of the city from visiting friends and relations, and in the novels she created subsequently, Bath appears not as the place of fun and frivolity it is in *Northanger Abbey* but increasingly as the choice of the old and dreary. Mrs Rushworth the dull dowager, Lady Dalrymple the titled nonentity, Sir Walter Elliot the indebted baronet, Mrs Smith the poor invalid and Mrs Clay the fortune-hunter are among the characters she brings to Bath, balanced it has to be said by the charming, unaffected Crofts and the rational but old-fashioned Lady Russell. Austen's Bath is not without its young people but it is an appropriate stage for so many of her older ones.

10. AGE AND MONEY

The financial implications of growing older could be considerable in a society that knew neither health service, welfare benefits nor fiscal redistribution. Though the passage through life might bring about a transformation, for better or worse, in the matter of worldly wealth, more often it intensified either the chronic poverty or the rising affluence of the individual or the family unit.

There are many examples of increasing prosperity in the novels, enough to suggest the nation at large becoming richer through the enterprise of its inhabitants. Mr Weston and Mr Cole, both characters in *Emma*, are among those who have risen in affluence by dint of their own efforts in business. In the same novel, John Knightley is rising in his profession as lawyer, and Robert Martin is increasing in prosperity as a hard-working, intelligent farmer, interested in new agricultural methods. In *Sense and Sensibility*, the low-born Mr Jennings has made sufficient fortune in trade to leave his widow very comfortably provided for, while in *Pride and Prejudice*, Mr Gardiner makes sufficient income in his line of business to be quite reasonably suspected of having more money than his idle brother-in-law Mr Bennet to settle Wickham's debts; and Charles Bingley's father has amassed enough by the same means to enable his son to live without any profession or contamination by trade. Many of the naval characters have made fortunes from the capture of French ships, or 'prize money' (or as Sir Walter Elliot says, "bringing persons of obscure birth into undue distinction, and raising men to honours which their fathers and grandfathers never dreamt of").[1] Heiresses who have come by their fortune via their fathers' trading success include in *Persuasion* the late Mrs Elliot, in *Sense and Sensibility* Mrs Willoughby and in *Sanditon*, the Miss Brereton who married Mr Hollis. But there were exceptions to this upward trend.

For men it was usually the vagaries of their profession or a stroke of ill health which reduced their earning power. In *Persuasion,* Captain Harville is lame from a severe wound, and is forced to live in very straitened circumstances. When Admiral Croft hopes he will have the good luck to live to see another war, it is presumably the reduction of income during peacetime which he deplores. Many naval men were turned off on 'half pay' after the peace of 1815, Jane's two sailor brothers among them. Charles, the younger, had not built up the cushion of capital which his brother Frank had amassed, which included a thousand guineas presented to him by the East India Company for convoying their ships, as well as navy pay and prize money. In 1811, when Charles returned from a long posting at sea with his first wife and young family, Cassandra wrote to a cousin, 'I am afraid they will find themselves very poor', and she was saying the same thing to the same person twenty-one years later (Charles having now a second wife and second crop of babies): 'I wish he were richer, but fortune has not yet smiled on him.'[2]

It was not for want of effort on his part. In 1820 he was reduced to accepting a job with the Preventive Service, or Coast Guard, at Padstow in Cornwall. Mrs Austen described his duties: 'He is to ride along the Coast to a certain distance, 12 miles on one side of the Town and 15 on the other, if any smuggling Vessels appear, he sends out his Boats & Men, but does not go himself.'[3] As Brian Southam writes in his book *Jane Austen and the Navy*, 'It was a job usually kept for superannuated naval officers and seemed a sad end to his career',[4] but Charles was only forty. In 1826, through his own initiative, he gained another command, which took him abroad for four years, and ended when he fell from a mast in a gale and received a severe injury to the chest. His seafaring days however were not over. The later part of his career was more distinguished, as he rose, like his brother, to the rank of Admiral, though rather late in life, and he never enjoyed Frank's degree of wealth.

An even more dramatic playing out of the wheel of fortune was the failure of brother Henry's bank in 1815; from being a rich man in London, all his worldly goods were forfeit and to support himself he became ordained. For a while he survived as a curate on a mere fifty-two guineas a year. 'Dreams of affluence',[5] he wrote, were over for him, though that was not strictly true as with a characteristic mixture of enterprise and sycophancy he gradually rose again – if by no means to the levels he had once enjoyed. Cassandra's previously mentioned letter of 1832 describes Henry as living 'on his little piece of preferment' and having 'nothing to wish for but a trifling increase of wealth and better health for his wife'. Not all of Henry's attempts to increase his wealth bear too much scrutiny – surviving letters show that he was inclined to beg multiple livings from distant rich relations,[6] and to attempt to call in favours from his former high-born acquaintance – but to do him justice, even when rebuffed, he always remained cheerful. Both he and Charles resembled *Persuasion's* Mrs Smith in possessing that resilience in adversity which Jane Austen called 'the choicest gift of heaven'.

The Austen brothers, in their different ways, were resourceful, energetic men who could be counted on whenever their fortunes ebbed to come up with some new strategy to try. Women enjoyed far less scope to affect their own worldly wealth. For them, so much was chance. Of course, marriage might aggrandize them from almost nothing to consequence and privilege, as it does Elizabeth Bennet, Jane Fairfax and others including Miss Maria Ward of Huntingdon; or it might plunge them down into grinding poverty as it does Maria's sister Frances – but at least these were changes to some extent under their own control. Completely beyond their control was the fact of widowhood which, while it certainly brought unaccustomed financial independence and power to some, to others was the sad harbinger of struggle and penury. With the death of her husband at the start of *Sense and Sensibility*, Mrs Dashwood is deprived of the comfortable home and most of the income that she has been used to. Taking up the offer of a small cottage on her cousin's estate in a distant county, she comforts herself with pipedreams. "Perhaps in the spring, if I have plenty of money, as I dare say I shall, we may think of building", she tells her daughters. "I shall see how much I am beforehand with the world in the spring, and we will plan our improvements accordingly." The narrator remains sceptical that 'all these alterations could be made from the savings of an income of five hundred a year by a woman who never saved in her life'.

Mrs Smith in *Persuasion* has fallen further than most, from a rich young wife who lived only for pleasure to 'a poor, infirm, helpless widow' – almost from youth to age in a span of twelve years: 'She had been used to affluence; it was gone.' Thoughtless extravagance on the part of her husband, followed by his death, the confused state in which he left his affairs, and her own subsequent ill health, have transformed her into one of the most poverty-stricken characters portrayed by Austen. Mrs Smith in her Bath lodgings, the Dashwood women in their rented cottage, and the Bates mother and daughter living above a shop in *Emma* are three all-female households coping with the constant spectre of poverty made more poignant by memories of a time when they took more comfortable circumstances for granted.

In Highbury it is common knowledge, because Mr Weston says so, that Mrs Bates the widow of a clergyman "has barely enough to live upon". Mr Knightley describes her middle-aged daughter as having sunk from the comforts that she was born to, and being likely to sink yet further if she live to her own old age, perhaps because the small amount of money the women have put by is being gradually diminished by living expenses or contingencies. Miss Bates's middle years are devoted to the care of an ailing mother, and to making a small income go as far as possible.

Medical attention was an incalculable expense that could sabotage the budget, and was almost certain to increase with age and infirmity. In his sympathy for their predicament, Mr Perry the apothecary would prefer not to charge his old neighbours the

Bateses for his services, but Miss Bates is well aware that he has a family to keep and "is not to be giving away his time". In the course of the novel it happens that in the Bates household only Jane Fairfax is ill, but in time Mrs Bates and then Miss Bates will very likely require more than home-made medicines. Mrs Smith, whose journey to Bath in quest of health exacerbates her pain and leaves her for a period bedridden, finds herself on arrival with 'the absolute necessity of having a regular nurse, and finances at that moment particularly unfit to meet any extraordinary expense'. She has probably calculated that she can just about afford the cost of the journey and lodgings and regular submersion in the hot bath, but had not reckoned on having to be nursed with the additional expenditure entailed. In *Sanditon,* Sir Harry Denham parts with ten sets of fees to doctors before dying anyway of his complaint. His widow is still complaining of this waste of money several years later.

A drawn-out illness, fatal or otherwise, was a real drain on resources. As yet, no bills for attendance in Jane Austen's own last illness have emerged, but recent research has brought to light some medical records relating to the least known of her brothers, George.[7] Disabled in some way, including probably mentally, as a child he was not brought up with the rest of the family and there is no mention of him in Jane's surviving letters. It has long been known that he spent his later years being cared for by the Culham family of the Hampshire village of Monk Sherborne, and it is probable that he spent his entire life in their cottage, providing them with a useful additional source of income to that which Charles Culham earned as a thatcher. Towards the end of his life, quarterly payments of £15 were being made for George's upkeep by the Austens, later the Knights, with additional sums for special clothing needs.

These sums may have been relatively small, but over George's seventy-two years of life, they amounted to quite a drain on family resources, which however does not appear to have been questioned or begrudged. Private asylums for paying patients did exist, but George's disabilities were evidently not of a nature which made him impossible to look after in a normal home – just not the normal home of the Austens. Pauper lunatics might have their fees paid for by the parish, or be put in the workhouse, where their treatment would almost certainly be harsh and misguided; but George was not to be classed with paupers, fortunately for him. The most recent research has revealed bills for eighteen doses of medicine and sixteen visits by local doctor Charles Lyford (a cousin of the Giles Lyford who attended Jane in Winchester), during George's last year of life.

He died on 17 January 1838, a full two decades after Jane. On his death certificate his occupation is given as gentleman and the cause of death as dropsy. The accoutrements for his funeral, though by no means grand, far exceeded those that the usual village person would have known, costing over £5. In sickness and in death, therefore, George continued to be funded by his birth family, his physical needs compassionately attended to, his gentility scrupulously maintained, even if they never or rarely saw him.

Rural Poverty

'Whenever any of the cottagers were disposed to be quarrelsome, discontented or too poor', we read in *Pride and Prejudice*, Lady Catherine de Bourgh 'sallied forth into the village to settle their differences, silence their complaints, and scold them into harmony and plenty'. Plenty indeed was what these poor people never knew. Among the labouring classes, little or no medical help could be afforded, domestic comforts were beyond reach, and old age could be the miserable and painful end to a lifetime of hard work. For all its celebration of agricultural prosperity and the interdependence of community, *Emma* reveals more than any other Austen novel glimpses of the dark side of life in rural England. Emma herself, with a great deal more compassion and good sense than Lady Catherine, pays visits of charity to a family suffering from 'sickness and poverty together'. Further on the margins of the village and of society, some are driven to pilfering, others to begging; while an honest old man like John Abdy, clerk to the parish for twenty-seven years, but now "bedridden, and very poorly with the rheumatic gout in his joints", has no pension, no livelihood, no means of ending his life in dignity, but must turn to parish relief if he is not to be a drain on the son who has his own family to maintain. If Mr Perry *does* attend him, it will be as an act of charity. The contrast in every respect between John Abdy and the other old man of the village, the pampered Mr Woodhouse, is extreme.

In *Mansfield Park*, the old coachman suffers from rheumatism which the amateur Mrs Norris, in her own words, has "been doctoring him for ever since Michaelmas". She visits him "up in his room" which suggests he has quarters above the stables, and his insistence on driving through his pain may suggest either fear of dismissal, or determination to go on working for his keep as long as possible out of self-respect.

It was expected of the gentry that they would continue to maintain faithful servants who had given a lifetime's service after their capacity for work was over in old age. In his will, Edward Ferrars' father leaves annuities to three "old superannuated servants" which his widow, less generously disposed, finds tiresome to discharge.[8] Sometimes it is not their capacity for work so much as their role in the family which has reached its natural end; yet from gratitude and common humanity, good employers continue to provide board and lodging. Such is the case in *Persuasion,* where the faithful old nursery maid Sarah is described as 'one who having brought up all the children, and seen the very last, the lingering and long-petted Master Harry, sent to school after his brothers, was now living in her deserted nursery to mend stockings and dress all the blains and bruises she could get near her'.

In the family of Jane's wealthiest brother, Edward Knight, the nursemaid Susannah Sackree, who joined the household on the birth of the first of their eleven children, was kept on for the rest of her life, long after they had all grown up. Known to Jane Austen as Sackree, and to the children in her care as Cakey, she was treated almost like one of the family. 'I am sorry to find that Sackree was worse again when Fanny wrote,' Jane reported in February 1813; 'she had been seized the night before with a violent shivering & Fever, & she was still so ill as to alarm Fanny, who was writing from her room.' The picture of the 20-year-old mistress of Godmersham keeping watch over the ill servant while she writes letters is a pleasing one. Yet she was *not* one of the family, and it was the habit of the Austen ladies to slip her ten shillings at the end of their visits. Sackree lived to be ninety, and was buried in the local churchyard with a handsome memorial stone provided by the family to mark her grave.

Another valued old servant of the Austen family was John Bond, the bailiff who managed the farm for Jane's father, and who was instrumental in maximizing the farm profits which contributed so much to the household economy of Steventon Rectory in Jane Austen's childhood when, with boarding pupils as well as family and servants, there was a very large number of mouths to feed. 'John Bond begins to find himself grow old, which John Bonds ought not to do, and unequal to much work', Jane reported to Cassandra when he was sixty-two, but the remark was premature. In fact he lived to be eighty-seven and he continued to give good service. When the Reverend George Austen retired to Bath, one of his concerns was to find John Bond new employment, as James, his successor in clerical duties at Steventon, did not take on the farm. But James tells the touching story of John Bond's subsequent life as part of his long last poem, *The Economy of Rural Life.*[9] Bond's new master, writes James, 'placed him in a cottage tight and warm' where he seemed likely to live out his days with his wife. But when John was seventy the cottage burned down, and instead of saving his own 'goods and chattels' in the short time available, he rushed to save his master's horse and 'so he lost his little all'.

'Tis somewhat late at three score years and ten / to start afresh in life' wrote James sympathetically and so he offered to take John and Ann Bond to live in Steventon Rectory, where the grateful old man enjoyed 'a healthful & a green old age' and repaid the kindness with all the devoted service of which he was capable. John and his wife outlived James himself, both dying in 1825. Unlike James's own wife and daughter, who had to vacate the Rectory within weeks of his death, the Bonds seem to have remained there under the next two incumbents, Henry Austen and William Knight. George Austen, who had been so anxious for Bond's welfare when he himself left Steventon, would have been deeply pleased that his grandson housed the faithful servant to the end, and conducted his funeral service.[10]

In the same poem, James Austen gives a picture of what rural poverty was like for the majority: 'The hut, mud floored & damp, & thinly thatched;/The chamber without chimney, straw-stuffed bed/ And curtainless – where lie the sick and old.' He expresses a wish that 'the pampered sons of luxury & indulgence' could witness such scenes.

Wealth and Wills

Death is not quite the end of many a life history, as influence very often extends beyond the grave via the will. Except for the very poorest, there are material artefacts to disperse, which will keep the deceased's memory alive. Little Mary Price is remembered by her family far more for the silver knife – her sole treasured possession, a christening present – which she has left behind, and which forms a bone of contention between two of her sisters, than for her own self.[11] The much richer Sir Harry Denham in *Sanditon* has time during his protracted dying to tell his soon-to-be widow that he would like his gold watch to go to his nephew Sir Edward. Lady Denham is unable to forget her own generosity in carrying out this dying wish which was not legally binding.

In the novels, three families of sisters face being deprived of their fair share of family money and property by the customs of primogeniture, the law of entail or the vagaries of somebody's will. Most famously, the five Bennet sisters will lose their home on the death of their father who is powerless to prevent its being inherited by a cousin, Mr Collins, in default of a son of his own.[12] In *Persuasion*, though Sir Walter Elliot has three daughters, again it is a male cousin, William Walter Elliot, who is his lawful heir. Neither of these eventualities has happened by the end of the respective narratives, and as the heroines make good marriages to the men they love, the question of inheritance slips out of the scene. But it is very much present at the beginning of *Sense and Sensibility*, where in the third paragraph:

> The old gentleman died; his will was read, and like almost every other will, gave as much disappointment as pleasure. He was neither so unjust, nor so ungrateful, as to leave his estate from his nephew; but he left it to him on such terms as destroyed half the value of the bequest. Mr Dashwood had wished for it more for the sake of his wife and daughters than for himself or his son; but to this son, and his son's son, a child of four years old, it was secured, in such a way, as to leave to himself no power of providing for those who were most dear to him, and who most needed a provision, by any charge on the estate, or by any sale of its valuable woods. The whole was tied up for the benefit of this child.

Old Mr Dashwood's will drives the entire plot of *Sense and Sensibility*. Another novel is concluded rather than begun with an inheritance. At the end of *Northanger Abbey*, it is 'the unexpected accession to title and fortune' of the unnamed young man who has long admired Eleanor Tilney which induces her father's good humour and clears the way to the marriage of the hero and heroine, Henry Tilney and Catherine Morland. Eleanor's husband in fact inherits a viscountcy, making Eleanor a viscountess: the highest rank of any living Austen character.

On the occasions when a woman inherits money in her own right, it almost simultaneously places her in some danger. Miss King, in *Pride and Prejudice*, inherits £10,000 from a grandfather, and thereby becomes the focus of George Wickham's matrimonial interest – though as it happens, he entangles himself with Lydia and loses sight of his intended prey. Miss Grey's £50,000 make her a temptation to Willoughby which he has not integrity enough to resist. These story threads – and there are others – show the effect on the younger generations of family money filtering down from the old.

Wills and inheritance played a large part in Austen family history. Conscious of family money that never seemed to come their way, Jane wrote to Cassandra wryly in July 1808, 'Indeed, I do not know where we are to get our Legacy – but we will keep a sharp look-out.'

This remark was made in the context of a further vast inheritance that was at that time accruing to an already rich uncle, the brother of her mother. Nothing illustrates better the unequal division of wealth between the sexes than the respective incomes and property of brother and sisters James, Jane and Cassandra Leigh, children of a clergyman without much fortune of his own. (There was another brother, Thomas, but as an 'imbecile' he was cared for in a similar way to George Austen.) At the age of sixteen James added Perrot to his surname under the provision of the will of his great-uncle Thomas Perrot, from whom he inherited considerable property in Oxfordshire, some of which he went on to exchange with the Duke of Marlborough for land in Berkshire, on which James Leigh Perrot and his bride Jane Cholmeley – herself an heiress – remodelled the house Scarlets, which became their beloved country home. Meanwhile his sisters each received just £200 of the Perrot fortune and £1,000 on their father's death – a mere fraction of what brother James inherited. When she was widowed in 1805 and left with very little income, Mrs Austen might reasonably have expected some help from her brother. After all, Mr Leigh Perrot's fortune had fallen into his lap; he had not had to work for it, it came to him through the line of descent he shared with his sister. (By then his other sister was dead.) Living part of the year in Bath, he must have witnessed Mrs Austen's plight. The

£1,000 from her father, which had been set aside as her widow's portion, brought in just over £100 a year, and without help from her sons, she and her daughters would have been destitute. An allowance of a few hundred a year would have made little difference to James Leigh Perrot but a world of difference to his sister, with whom he always appeared on good terms. She lingered in Bath for a year and a half after her husband's death, perhaps hoping he was just being a little tardy in coming forward, but eventually gave up expecting anything from him and moved to Southampton to amalgamate households with her son Frank.

At about the same time, James Leigh Perrot inherited a second considerable fortune, though only after a great deal of negotiation, as he was one of three legal claimants to the estate of Lord Leigh of Stoneleigh Abbey in Warwickshire. To buy out his interest, his relation James Henry Leigh raised a mortgage of £20,000 to be paid to James Leigh Perrot, and made him a yearly allowance of £2,000 payable for his own life and that of his wife. These were huge sums for an ageing man with no family, who had scarcely been able to spend all his first fortune. As his own wife wrote later, 'Alas! Ill health was then making the considerable addition of Fortune of less & less use to us.'[13] Yet still no allowance was made to his sister, though £100 a year was spared for James Austen. Mrs Austen was pleased for any of her children to get anything, but it was her younger, poorer children, particularly Cassandra, Jane and Charles, for whom she wished a legacy which would make them comfortable in their own middle and old age. As nothing had been forthcoming in his life, she not unnaturally turned her hopes for their ultimate security towards her brother's will, as her children well knew.

A bitter disappointment was in store for them all. When the will was opened on the death of James Leigh Perrot in March 1817, it was discovered that his house at Scarlets, with furniture, horses, carriages and lands in the parish of Wargrave, were to go to his wife and her heirs, together with his house 49 Great Pulteney Street, Bath, and all its contents. Mrs Leigh Perrot was also to have £10,000 plus all plate, jewels, linen, china, books and monies in both houses and in Hoare's Bank. This part of his fortune was hers to dispose of as she wished in her own will. The remainder of his property was to be held by his nephew James Austen in trust, paying the income to Mrs Leigh Perrot for her lifetime; after her death, this remainder was to go to James, apart from £6,000, which was to be divided between such of Mr Leigh Perrot's Austen nephews and nieces still alive at the time of her death.[14] The luxury itemized in the will is in bitter contrast to the strict economy which had to be practised at Chawton Cottage, especially after Henry's bankruptcy had reduced Mrs Austen's income from her sons.

James Leigh Perrot died when his niece Jane was suffering her own illness. 'I am ashamed to say that the shock of my Uncle's will brought on a relapse,' she wrote to her brother Charles, 'I am the only one of the Legatees who has been so silly, but a weak Body must excuse weak Nerves. My Mother has borne the forgetfulness of *her* extremely well; – her expectations for herself were never beyond the extreme of moderation.'[15] Jane added that her mother 'heartily wishes her younger Children had more, & all her Children something immediately'. Mrs Austen made the excuse for her brother that he had probably expected to outlive her, and it was true she had complained of ill health all her life – but then so had he, taking the waters in Bath every year for his gout.

Mrs Leigh Perrot survived her husband by nineteen years, outliving Mrs Austen, James and Jane. The old woman did make an allowance, for various periods, to her sister-in-law, to James, to James's widow and to James's son, but all were modest sums and all were extended or withdrawn at whim. On the occasion of one such withdrawal, James's son wrote to his father, 'I have long thought too meanly of her, to be much astonished by any fresh instance of want of feeling or of hypocrisy.'[16] James Austen never did inherit the property to which he had been brought up, albeit tacitly, as heir; and although it went eventually to his son, it was only after he and others had endured considerable caprice on the part of his great-aunt, with attempts to control other people's behaviour, or punish them for it, reminiscent of Jane Austen's dowager despots.

11. THE DANGEROUS INDULGENCE OF ILLNESS

The first indication in Austen's letters of anything amiss with her health appears in September 1816, when she responds to an evident enquiry from Cassandra, then in Cheltenham: 'Thank you – my back has given me scarcely any pain for many days.' She adds, 'I have an idea that agitation does it as much harm as fatigue, & that I was ill at the time of your going, from the very circumstance of your going', though the sisters had very often been separated, and this had never happened before. To allay Cassandra's worries, she assures her, 'I am nursing myself up now into as beautiful a state as I can.' A few lines later, having mentioned the death of a distant acquaintance, Jane writes, 'I treat you with a dead Baronet in almost every Letter.' She was determined not to take illness and death any more seriously than she had hitherto in her life.

Considering the state of medicine of the time, Austen had been lucky to enjoy pretty good health all her life, her only recurring complaints being occasional pain in the side of her face and weakness in her eyes, which she once characterized impatiently as 'a sad bore to me'. In childhood she had nearly died of a fever caught at school (a fever serious enough that her aunt *had* died of it after arriving, together with her sister Mrs Austen, to snatch their daughters away); and in 1806 she had caught whooping cough as an adult when staying with a family of cousins, a disease that is dangerous and exhausting at any time of life. But the Austens were a hardy breed, not one of them lost in infancy, which was quite remarkable for the period. Mrs Thrale, whose children were contemporaneous with Mrs Austen's, lost eight of her twelve before they reached adulthood, despite being wealthier. Of Jane's siblings, Edward experienced a period of ill health in 1799, which sent him to Bath for treatment, but thereafter lived on in apparent good health until 1852; and Henry was dangerously ill in 1815, but recovered both in body and spirits and enjoyed an active life until his death in 1850. Had Cassandra suffered any ailments there would surely be some mention in the letters, some sympathetic enquiry of Jane's, but there is just one reference, coming in April 1805: 'I am heartily glad that you can speak so comfortably of your own health & looks. . . . Could travelling fifty miles produce such an immediate change? You were looking so very poorly here'. After that there is no hint of anything to worry about in Cassandra's health, and she lived another forty years.

Mrs Austen seems to have been considered by her daughters as something of a hypochondriac during the period of Jane's early letters to Cassandra, with her various symptoms liable to be mocked, but she lived to be eighty-seven, 'a great age for a person who had been ailing all her life', as Cassandra was to write to a cousin, adding, 'her constitution was certainly a wonderful one'.[1] Jane's father, having enjoyed good health all his life, had succumbed to a short, sharp illness in 1805, at the age of seventy-four.

So Jane herself had every reason to hope and believe that hers was just a passing complaint, and for as long as she could she assured every correspondent that she was getting better. In January 1817 she told her niece Anna, at the end of a letter about many other things, that 'I feel myself getting stronger than I was half a year ago, & can so perfectly well walk to Alton, or back again, without the slightest fatigue that I hope to be able to do both when Summer comes.' To another niece, Fanny, she wrote the following month 'I am almost entirely cured of my rheumatism; just a little pain in my knee now & then, to make me remember what it was, & keep on flannel. Aunt Cassandra nursed me so beautifully!' And on 13 March, to the same correspondent, 'I am got tolerably well again, quite equal to walking about & enjoying the Air; & by sitting down & resting a good while between my Walks, I get exercise enough.' The Austen ladies had acquired a donkey and a donkey carriage for getting about, but Jane had a scheme, she continued to Fanny, for riding on the donkey when the weather grew more springlike, so that she could accompany Cassandra on her walks, without the trouble of getting the carriage out. Her optimism was unfounded, her illness inexorable, though it proceeded in fits and starts, and by 23 March she was forced to admit to Fanny:

> I certainly have not been well for many weeks, & about a week ago I was very poorly, I have had a good deal of fever at times & indifferent nights, but am considerably better now, & recovering my Looks a little, which have been bad enough, black & white & every wrong colour. I must not depend upon being ever very blooming again. Sickness is a dangerous Indulgence at my time of Life.

The discolouration of skin reported by Austen is one of the distinctive symptoms of her otherwise difficult to diagnose slow deterioration, which has led present-day commentators to suggest she was suffering from Addison's disease, now treatable, a tuberculosis of the adrenal glands, though non-Hodgkins lymphoma has been suggested as an alternative. The medical knowledge of the day was powerless to do anything for her. Nobody knew whether she would recover and go on to live a long life, or continue to decline. In the autumn of 1815, after all, she had helped nurse her brother Henry through a mysterious illness that seemed to put him so much in danger that at one point all available brothers and sisters were called to his bedside: yet he had apparently fully recovered (though it is now thought that he may have passed tuberculosis on to Jane, and then gone into long remission himself. At this distance it is little more than educated guesswork). At the time there seemed no reason why Jane should be less lucky. She was not ready to give up hope, nor to burden those who loved her with gloomy prognostications. In this determination, she was perhaps motivated by a conscious desire to behave differently from – better than, as she saw it – her mother. If she had indeed always deplored her mother's quest for sympathy, she could now demonstrate how a sick person ought to behave. This perhaps is what lies behind the oft-quoted story, first recorded by her niece Caroline, that in her illness Aunt Jane never would take to the sofa, even when her mother was not using it, but put three chairs together to put her feet up and claimed they were all she desired. Is this the stratagem of the martyr or the stoic?

To the young niece Caroline, she maintained the cheerful mode, writing the following day, 'I have taken one ride on the Donkey & like it very much – & you must try to get me quiet, mild days, that I may be able to go out pretty constantly. – A great deal of Wind does not suit me, as I have still a tendency to Rheumatism.' But on 6 April she wrote to her brother Charles that 'I have really been too unwell the last fortnight to write anything that was not absolutely necessary. I have been suffering from a Bilious attack, attended with a good deal of fever.' She had seemed to be better, but the devastating news of her uncle's will had brought on a relapse followed by a partial recovery: Cassandra's return from their uncle's funeral had the effect of making her feel better that morning, enabling her to write to Charles, 'I live upstairs for the present however & am coddled'. Three weeks later she made her own will.

A Little Sea-Bathing

By 'writing anything that was not absolutely necessary' Austen meant replying to letters; but on 18 March she had also laid aside her literary work, the beginning of a new novel known to us as *Sanditon*. It is testament to her earlier determination to be well again that she had embarked on a wholly new work in January 1817, and even more remarkable that she chose as its setting a fishing village with ambitions to become a resort of health and leisure, and a cast of characters many of whom are obsessed with their state of health. She had always found hypochondria despicable in the sense that it denoted an absorption in self, and now that she was experiencing a grave illness of her own she seemed determined to confront it by wringing every drop of humour from the subject.

Health, in *Sanditon,* is in the first place a means of making a profit for the chief land-holders of the area, the thoroughly healthy Mr Parker (except when he sprains his ankle on a wild goose chase) and the even more robust, 70-year-old Lady Denham. In their different ways, to further such a project they inevitably have to be motivated by some cynicism, though his is ameliorated by his engaging enthusiasm, almost childlike, for the place of his birth; and hers is aggravated by thoroughgoing meanness of spirit and purse. But even the villagers are catching on to the idea that money may be made from the quest for health: smartening up their cottages, advertising lodgings and, if they are shopkeepers, dealing in more fashionable wares. Mr Parker observes all this with deep satisfaction, but Lady Denham is more ambivalent, wanting the value of her holdings to rise, but fearing that the price of provisions will rise likewise. Austen herself is ambivalent in a different way: an increase in prosperity is good for the country, but a commercial approach to all human transactions is not.

In itself this scenario would be funny and piquant enough, but to increase the comedy Austen then introduces a set of characters who, in their exaggerated character traits, seem simultaneously to hark back to the absurdities of her own Juvenilia, and look forward to the fiction of Dickens. Truly Dickensian, surely, are Diana, Susan and Arthur Parker, characters who, in their broad brush strokes, it is impossible to imagine appearing in the supremely delicate 'little bits of ivory' which we know as Austen's mature fiction, the novels begun and completed at Chawton. What unites these Parker siblings is obsession with health carried to an absurd level. As John Wiltshire points out in his book *Jane Austen and the Body,* these characters' preoccupation with their bodies monopolizes their imaginations and directs their actions every hour of the day.

'Invalids indeed – I trust there are not three people in England who have so sad a right to that appellation' as the most active of them, Diana, claims, though adding, 'My sister's complaints and mine are happily not often of a nature to threaten existence *immediately*.' Austen sums up:

> Some natural delicacy of constitution in fact, with an unfortunate turn for medicine, especially quack medicine, had given them an early tendency, at various times, to various disorders – the rest of their suffering was from fancy, the love of distinction and the love of the wonderful. They had charitable hearts and many amiable feelings – but a spirit of restless activity, and the glory of doing more than anybody else, had their share in every exertion of benevolence – and there was vanity in all they did, as well as all they endured.

The down-to-earth heroine, Charlotte Heywood, spending the evening at their lodgings, finds them all crouched over a fire despite its having been a very fair English summer day. Susan sits with salts in her hand, and takes drops two or three times from one of several phials 'already at home on the mantlepiece [sic]' while the youngest sibling Arthur, whom Charlotte had expected from his sister's comments to be puny, turns out to be fat, greedy and indolent, buttering his toast and swigging his cocoa with relish, while claiming to be suffering from nerves. Austen not only has fun describing the various excesses of the family, but takes care to point up Charlotte as the right-minded observer who has very little sympathy for their imaginary complaints. In the case of Susan, 'Charlotte could perceive no symptoms of illness which she, *in the boldness of her own good health*, would not have undertaken to cure, by putting out the fire, opening the window, and disposing of the drops and the salts by means of one or another'. And when she takes her place next to Arthur, '*such was the influence of youth and bloom* that he began even to make a sort of apology for having a fire'. [My italics in both cases.] "The sea air is always damp," he tells her, "I am not afraid of anything so much as damp", to which she replies that she never knows whether the air is damp or dry as "it always has some property that is wholesome and invigorating to me".

Because *Sanditon* exists in manuscript it is possible to see that revisions made by Austen are not, on the whole, intended to curb a regretted exuberance of first thoughts but to broaden the humour and enhance the eccentricities of her characters to the point of incredulity, on a par with the comic exaggerations of her Juvenilia. For example, in the letter which precedes Diana's arrival in Sanditon, Austen first wrote:

> Two years ago I happened to be calling on Mrs Sheldon when her coachman sprained his foot as he was cleaning the carriage and could hardly limp into the house – but by the immediate use of friction alone, steadily persevered in (and I rubbed his ancle [sic] with my own hand for four hours without intermission) he was well in three days.

Austen subsequently amended this to make it not *more* believable but *less,* increasing the four hours continuous rubbing to six.[2] Diana Parker is as officious and patronizing as – though more kind-hearted than – Mrs Norris, who doctors the old coachman at Mansfield through one winter.

It is poignant to reflect that in creating the self-indulgence and self-delusion of these characters Austen is working not *in the boldness of her own good health* or under *the influence of youth and bloom* but as a dying woman. Critics have been unable to agree – for there is no way of telling – whether this late departure from the fiction of probability formerly adhered to is a stylistic innovation that would have been developed had she enjoyed good health, or her way of amusing herself through a period of bedrest with work that she had no intention of publishing, or a fierce response on her part to the horrible reality of a fatal illness at a time when she had everything to live for.

Sanditon is the culmination of Austen's lifelong tendency to mock imaginary invalids. "A little sea-bathing would set me up for ever", claims the nervous, irritable Mrs Bennet in *Pride and Prejudice,* when what she chiefly craves, readers understand, are the social gaieties of Brighton and the array of potential husbands for her daughters she envisages encountering there. In attempting – quite unsuccessfully, of course – to fool her husband into believing it his duty to fund a visit to the seaside for the sake of her health, perhaps she genuinely fools herself about her desires, for her self-knowledge is as minimal as her self-control. Most visitors to the seaside would have gone there with mixed motives of health and pleasure. The Austens themselves, in their annual jaunts to the coast from 1801 to 1805, did not have any particular ailments to address, and went chiefly to enjoy sea breezes and sea views, liberty and landscape; but nobody minds feeling that their surroundings may be doing them good: and we know that Jane bathed and enjoyed it so much that she stayed in too long and overtired herself. Perhaps Mrs Bennet *is* hard done-by in being denied any change of scene.

In the two novels written immediately before *Sanditon,* Austen combines ideas about the efficacy of sea-bathing with mainly comic portraits of real and imagined illness. *Emma's* Mrs Churchill, the most imperious of Austen's invalids, will have her place in the next chapter. In the same novel, Mr Woodhouse is not so much a hypochondriac as a valetudinarian, the word Austen uses for him. Frightened of eating and of leaving home though he is, believing that sea bathing once nearly killed him, and fond of consulting the apothecary Mr Perry at every opportunity, Mr Woodhouse does not flaunt any specific symptoms of ill health or try to elicit sympathy by whinging, à *la* Mary Musgrove, about his ailments. Perhaps he doesn't have to. The neighbourhood is long accustomed to enquiring after his health and consulting his comfort on all occasions. Moreover, he manages to restrict his daughter's activities more effectively than other fathers, even Sir Thomas Bertram, by exercising the power of feebleness of mind, body and spirit. It has to be admitted, however, that Emma colludes in this, presumably because, perversely, her father's helplessness augments her own sense of power. She is simultaneously parent to her father, and his captive, always at his beck and call and ready to shed real tears at the very thought of leaving him. Cultivating the character of dutiful daughter is good for her public credit and her private self-esteem, but the lack of even a shred of internal rebellion suggests some failure in her own courage to encounter life and change. Considered this way, Emma Woodhouse is more timid than Fanny Price.

While Mr Woodhouse may try the patience of John Knightley (and some readers), at least he never takes to the sofa (like Mary Musgrove) or remains in bed (like Mrs Bennet) in order to manipulate others. His fussing rather takes the form of tender solicitude for the health of all his acquaintance, a more amiable characteristic. In this he is resembled by his elder daughter, who with her husband sacrifices a summer holiday in their home village in order to take their five children to Southend for the sake of 'little Bella's sore throats'. That Isabella Knightley is mildly handled by Austen is because her hypochondria mainly takes the form of excessive care for her children; and, while of the Woodhouse sisters, Emma is shown to be the better potential mother – too well-judging to administer 'false physic' – Isabella, though timid and over-protective, is admirable in comparison with that other young mother, *Persuasion*'s Mary Musgrove. It is her *own* health which obsesses Mary, and for this she cannot be forgiven. Isabella's assertion to her father, "excepting those little nervous headaches and palpitations which I am never entirely free from anywhere, I am quite well myself", is in quite a different register from Mary's "I am so ill I can hardly speak", and "my sore throats are worse than anybody's". Isabella, for all her palpitations, is fundamentally unselfish: she will even walk through the snow to get back to her children, asleep in her father's house. When Mary's little boy has a real accident, she first panics and is unable to attend to him and then, when he seems to be recovering, she is happy to leave him in the care of Anne, and to go out to dinner and enjoy herself. This pattern of behaviour is repeated when another relation has an even more severe accident, Louisa Musgrove's fall at Lyme Regis: Mary's reaction is first hysteria, then self-importance and finally insouciance, leaving Anne, again, to put aside ego and to do the right thing for the patient.

Mary leaves her children for weeks on end without a second thought when other enjoyments offer. For all her claims of delicate health, she happily bathes at Lyme in *November.* Mary evidently puts instant gratification before reasonable care for her health, failing to consider that were she even to catch a mild cold, this would be an additional burden for those who are looking after Louisa in Lyme. Mary is no monster, yet her every action is self-centred, whether focusing on her health or forgetting all about it in the pursuit of pleasure. Mary's fictional predecessor is Fanny Dashwood of *Sense and Sensibility,* a young wife and mother in rude health when things go her way – as they generally do – but one who falls into hysterics and screaming fits at bad news, drawing everyone's attention to herself and her own sufferings at a time when the grave plights of others should be the focus of attention. Fanny Dashwood inhabits a novel about sensibility, and it hardly needs pointing out that at times she is a ghastly parody of Marianne, an example of the depths of self-absorption to which the cultivation of sensibility can lead when not accompanied by Marianne's fundamental sincerity and sense. Marianne repents jeopardizing her own health; her sister-in-law repents nothing. The eighteenth-century concern with sensibility was to become the nineteenth-century cultivation of chronic ill health in those who could afford to be ill, and have others running round after them.

Two clerical doctors of advancing age, Dr Grant of *Mansfield Park* and Dr Shirley of *Persuasion*, are portrayed in relation to health issues, and again, it is selfishness or otherwise that concerns Austen. Dr Grant, fond of the good things of life, uses claims of indisposition to manipulate his wife, careless of her feelings or of how he may inconvenience anybody. On the night of the full rehearsal of *Lovers' Vows,* 'Dr Grant, professing an indisposition, for which he had little credit with his fair sister-in-law, could not spare his wife.' "Dr Grant is ill", Mary Crawford announces with mock solemnity. "He has been ill ever since he did not eat any of the pheasant today. He fancied it tough – sent away his plate – and has been suffering ever since." Thus by emotionally blackmailing his wife to stay at home, he spoils the enjoyment of half a dozen young people (that the enjoyment is not entirely innocent is by the bye): 'The comfort of the whole evening was destroyed'; while Fanny Price finds herself suddenly plunged into the dilemma of whether she should overturn her conscientious refusal to act. Would it really have been too much for Dr Grant to say 'You go, dear. I'll be all right with my book and the fire and the servants to bring me a little supper'? For such acts of inconsideration he will, before the narrative end, be duly punished by his author, denied the well-deserved old age pictured for the worthy Dr Shirley.

Henrietta Musgrove may have an ulterior motive in wishing Dr Shirley, her local clergyman, to retire to the seaside (and to appoint a curate, the cousin whom Henrietta wishes to marry), but that does not negate either her genuine concern for the elderly man's health, reflecting the goodwill of the whole community whom he has faithfully served; or the pleasing picture of a healthful old age contained in her enthusiastic outpourings to Anne as they walk along the beach at Lyme. (Note the subtly different voices of Henrietta and Mary Crawford in speaking about these older men – the one naïve and transparent, the other cynical and playful, wonderful examples of Austen's ventriloquism. Though nothing is implausibly exaggerated, neither young woman could be mistaken for the other.)

> "Oh! yes – I am quite convinced that, with very few exceptions, the sea air always does good. There can be no doubt of its being of the greatest service to Dr Shirley, after his illness, last spring twelvemonth. He declares himself that coming to Lyme for a month did him more good than all the medicine he took; and that being by the sea always makes him feel young again. Now, I cannot help thinking it a pity that he does not live entirely by the sea. I think he had better leave Uppercross entirely, and fix at Lyme. Do not you, Anne? Do not you agree with me, that it

is the best thing he could do, both for himself and Mrs Shirley? She has cousins here, you know, and many acquaintance, which would make it cheerful for her, and I am sure she would be glad to get to a place where she could have medical attendance at hand, in case of his having another seizure. Indeed I think it quite melancholy to have such excellent people as Dr and Mrs Shirley, who have been doing good all their lives, wearing out their last days in a place like Uppercross, where, excepting our family, they seem shut out from all the world."

In fact, the Shirleys have not left Uppercross by the end of the novel, but remain doing good in their country village, 'wearing out their last days'. What a contrast to that other family in the novel, Sir Walter Elliot and his eldest daughter, who have never 'done good' but who skip lightly off from what should be the scene of their duties in the country to live vacuous lives in Bath – and they don't even have the excuse of ill health.

Gout and Decrepitude

During Jane Austen's lifetime, English seaside resorts like the imaginary Sanditon and the real Weymouth, Sidmouth and Lyme were usurping the inland spas as places where visitors hoped to find a cure for their physical ailments. But Bath, the first and pre-eminent of such spas, continued to draw an assortment of invalids and imaginary invalids to its lodgings, pump rooms and baths. One real invalid of Jane Austen's acquaintance briefly seeking a cure in Bath was the Reverend Richard Buller, a young man of her own age who had been a pupil of George Austen's at Steventon Rectory, and who, thanks to his own father's having been Bishop of Exeter, held three Devon livings, including the one where he resided, Colyton with its lovely Tudor Vicarage. The Austens almost certainly visited him there on their first West Country holiday in 1801 – and probably again from Lyme in 1803 and 1804.

Despite living so close to the sea, it was to Bath that Richard Buller resorted in the extremity of ill health. Jane wrote from Gay Street to Cassandra on 9 April 1805:

> We heard with much surprise that Mr Buller had called while we were out. He left his address, & I am just returned from seeing him & his wife in their Lodgings, 7 Bath St. His Errand, as you may suppose, is health. It had often been recommended to him to try Bath, but his coming now seems to have been cheifly [sic] in consequence of his sister Susan's wish that he would put himself under the care of Mr Bowen. – Having so very lately heard from Colyton & that account so tolerable, I was very much astonished – but Buller has been worse again since he wrote to me. – His Habit has always been billious [sic], but I am afraid it must be too late for these waters to do him any good; for tho' he is altogether in a more comfortable state as to Spirits & appetite than when I saw him last, & seems equal to a good deal of quiet walking, his appearance is exactly that of a confirmed Decline.

She was right, and he died on 19 December 1806, aged just thirty. Had Jane married him – and there is evidence that he was very fond of her, growing up with her at Steventon Rectory in an intimacy which had caused Tom Fowle to fall in love with Cassandra – she would have been another clerical widow left, perhaps, with small children. Possibly it was longstanding doubts about his health which had made Jane or her parents discourage any special affection on his part; the woman who *did* become his wife was not without jealousy of Jane.[3] It was certainly not the unhealthiness of his lovely Devon parish that caused Richard Buller's decline, since the next two incumbents of Colyton were very long-lived and divided almost a century – until 1903 – there between them.

Though the medical profession and promoters of Bath's waters often claimed that they would cure almost every complaint, the most common illness for which middle-aged and elderly people of the leisured classes travelled to the city was gout. An 1804 guide for the invalid to the watering places of Great Britain recommended Bath for sufferers of gout 'worn out with the inefficacy of other medicines'.[4] Now recognized as a form of arthritis, caused by a build-up of uric acid, it struck mainly in the toe or heel and could make the sufferer feel 'as if the part were stretched, burnt, squeezed, gnawed or torn to pieces' according to another popular health manual of the day.[5] The connection with alcoholic indulgence has now been discounted, but a lifetime of eating, drinking and minimal exercise often preceded gouty symptoms in the Regency period, possibly because the more hardworking sections of the population had neither time nor money to attend to bodily sufferings and consequently either put up with them or succumbed. Indeed, in Austen's fiction, there is one poor character who *does* have to put up with his gout, in his case 'rheumatic gout in his joints' which leaves him bedridden and 'very poorly' in his old age: John Abdy senior, clerk for twenty-seven years to the late Reverend Mr Bates in *Emma,* now with insufficient money – not only to seek medical treatment – but even to live, without help from the parish.

At the other extreme of wealth, Jane's uncle James Leigh Perrot was the archetypal sufferer of gout in many respects. Firstly, he was a man of complete leisure, who could eat and drink as much as he liked and exert himself as little as he liked, quite unlike his busy brother-in-law the Reverend George Austen. Secondly, since Mr Leigh Perrot could do exactly as he liked, it followed that he had plenty of leisure for fancying himself unwell, and total freedom to arrange his life round his complaints and their cure. Consequently, he chose to live for six months of every year in Bath, forsaking the mansion in the country which he professed to love. In Bath, he drank from the pump twice a day, since Jane – who was much fonder of this uncle than of his wife – mentions walking out with him 'when my uncle went to take his second glass of water'.[6] On various other occasions she mentions his walking with a stick and wearing flannel. He seems to have cosseted himself, by which means he lived to be eighty-two.

The official guide to Bath of 1800 advises:

> The water should always be drunk hot from the pump, or else at your lodgings as warm as it can possibly be procured. . . . The water is generally drank in the morning fasting, between the hours of six and ten, that it may have time to pass out of the stomach; though some drink a glass about noon. The quantity generally taken in a day is from one pint to three, though some drink two quarts.

Though gout is and was much more common in men, Jane Austen knew at least one elderly woman who took a course of treatment in Bath for the complaint, Lady Bridges. In September 1813, with a son, daughter-in-law, daughter and grand-daughter, she travelled from Kent and took lodgings at 1 Henrietta Street on the corner with Laura Place. The first report, passed from Jane, who was staying in Kent with her brother Edward (son-in-law to Lady Bridges), to Cassandra at Chawton, explained:

> Lady Bridges drinks at the Cross Bath, her son at the Hot, and Louisa is going to bathe. Dr Parry seems to be half-starving Mr Bridges, for he is restricted to much such a diet as James's bread, water and meat, and is never to eat so much of that as he wishes, and he is to walk a good deal – walk till he drops, I believe – gout or no gout. It really is to that purpose. I have not exaggerated.[7]

A month later, Jane reported, 'Lady B continues very well & Dr Parry's opinion is that while the water agrees with her she ought to remain',[8] although Louisa was inclined to put her mother's good health down to being out of doors so much, rather than to the water. They were about to come home when, early in November, 'a fit of Gout came on last week. . . . Dr P. says it is a good sort of Gout and her spirits are better than usual, but as to her coming away, of course it is all uncertainty.'[9] Three days later:

> My brother has had a letter from Louisa . . . they are to spend the winter in Bath. . . . Dr Parry wished it – not from thinking the water necessary to Lady B – but that he might be better able to judge how far his treatment of her, which is totally different from anything she is used to, is right; & I suppose he will not mind having a few more of her Ladyship's guineas. His system is a lowering one. He took twelve ounces of Blood from her when the Gout appeared, & forbids wine etc. Hitherto the plan agrees with her. She is well satisfied to stay.

But for some reason the younger people had had enough of Bath, and those that could – Henry Bridges and his wife – departed. It is easy to imagine the elderly widow thrilling to the authoritative demeanour of the doctor, while the younger people lost patience. Caleb Hillier Parry used some of the fees which he took off his rich patients in property speculation, being actively involved in the development of Camden Crescent, Sir Walter Elliot's prestigious – and precarious – address (the terrace was never completed because of landslip).

In her fiction, Austen has plenty of gouty characters. They can be useful plot devices. Mr Allen, in *Northanger Abbey,* is 'ordered to Bath for the benefit of a gouty constitution' – most fortunately for the young country neighbour the Allens invite to accompany them, as Catherine Morland must meet a hero somewhere, for there is none in her own village. Another neighbour of the Allens, Dr Skinner, 'was here for his health last winter, and came away quite stout' [i.e strong and healthy]. The hero whose path crosses Catherine's is in Bath likewise because of its benefits to the health of an older person, his father General Tilney, though as his daughter Eleanor explains to Catherine, 'My father can seldom be prevailed on to give the waters what I think a fair trial . . . and as he is now pretty well, is in a hurry to get home.'

In *Persuasion* Lady Russell, without being apparently ill, 'drinks the water' when she is in Bath every winter – perhaps as a precaution. In the same novel Admiral and Mrs Croft turn up in

Bath. Sir Walter Elliot asks Anne:

> "And pray what brings the Crofts to Bath?"
> "They come on the Admiral's account. He is thought to be gouty."
> "Gout and decrepitude!" said Sir Walter. "Poor old gentleman."

As well as presumably taking the waters, Admiral Croft – just like Henry Bridges – is 'ordered to walk to keep off the gout'. Far from being decrepit, he and his wife are seen by Anne every day walking the streets of Bath, for 'Mrs Croft seemed to go shares with him in everything, and to walk for her life to do him good'. This presents 'a most attractive picture of happiness' to Anne, though it eventually results in a blister for Mrs Croft which, for a while, confines her indoors.

Anne's other friend in Bath, Mrs Smith, is there for her health, though she can ill afford it. She has been 'afflicted with a severe rheumatic fever, which, finally settling in her legs, had made her for the present a cripple. She had come to Bath on that account, and was now in lodgings near the hot baths.' Mrs Smith bathes in, rather than drinks, the warm mineral water which rises at a constant temperature in several locations in Bath. The Hot Bath, the King's Bath and the Cross Bath had all been rebuilt in the eighteenth century, and each had its associated pump. The King's Bath, closest to the Abbey, was the most fashionable, and here the finest Pump Room was enlarged and remodelled in the 1790s into a social meeting place opening on to the Abbey Churchyard, and containing the book of new arrivals which Isabella Thorpe and Catherine Morland so avidly consult, while the pumps at the other sites were merely for drinking the waters.[10]

Mention of visiting Bath for health is not confined to the 'Bath' novels. In *Emma,* Mr Woodhouse has tried the waters of Bath 'more than once, formerly; but without receiving any benefit', as his daughter tells Mrs Elton. That obnoxious woman, who is proud of her familiarity with the city, can hardly believe it. "I assure you, Miss Woodhouse, where the waters do agree it is quite wonderful the relief they give. In my Bath life, I have seen such instances of it!" Later in the novel she recommends Bath for the ailing Mrs Churchill.

In the short novel in letters, *Lady Susan,* Mrs Johnson exultantly tells her friend that her husband 'is going for his health to Bath, where if the waters are favourable to his constitution & my wishes, he will be laid up with the Gout many weeks. During his absence we shall be able to chuse our own society, & have true enjoyment'. But her next letter laments,

> Mr Johnson has hit on the most effective manner of plaguing us all. – He had heard I imagine by some means or other, that you were to be soon in London, & immediately contrived to have such an attack of the Gout, as must at least delay his journey to Bath, if not wholly prevent it. – I am persuaded the Gout is brought on, or kept off at pleasure . . . three years ago when I had a fancy for Bath, nothing could induce him to have a gouty symptom.

Whether through lack of funds, lack of desire, insufficient belief or motivation, not all Austen's sufferers from gout get to Bath. Two stay-at-home clergymen are the Reverend Mr Norris of *Mansfield Park*, who suffers from 'gouty complaints' in the years before his death, and the elderly and penurious clerical father in *The Watsons,* who numbers among his several ailments 'a gouty foot'. Mr Watson can be 'a little peevish under immediate pain' but he is one of the few Austen characters whose bodily pain seems genuine. The peevishness is not habitual and he has better days when his quiet presence in the house is soothing to Emma: 'if ill, [he] required little more than gentleness and silence; and, being a man of sense and education, was, if able to converse, a welcome companion'. She develops the habit of sitting with him 'in his chamber' every evening, glad to get away from the less congenial company below.

This invalid father is quite different from Mr Woodhouse, who cannot meet his daughter Emma in conversation either rational or playful. Indeed, Mr Watson is almost too sensible a father for a heroine and as such, in the interest of her trials and development, he must die. Meanwhile his infirmity is put to good narrative use.

On one occasion Mr Watson relates to Emma and her eldest sister, Elizabeth, how on a rare visit outside his home, he recently encountered "a pretty steep flight of steps up to the room we dine in – which do not quite agree with my gouty foot – and Mr Howard walked by me from the bottom to the top, and would make me take his arm. It struck me as very becoming in so young a man." Mr Howard was designed to be the hero of *The Watsons* and this testimony from Emma's sensible father is as valuable an indication of character as, for example, Mr Darcy's praise from his housekeeper. Attractive young men must not be judged solely on how they treat attractive young women – something more is required if the heroine is to arrive at a true evaluation of their worth. This picture of a younger man courteously helping one older and frailer is reminiscent of the Mr Knightley/Mr Woodhouse relationship, though in their case they are longstanding friends and neighbours, whereas Mr Watson has never seen Mr Howard before in his life – which only makes his help more commendable. In such ways Austen uses illness to reveal more than the casual reader might think.

A Poor Honey

In her letter of 26 March 1817 to her young niece Caroline, Jane Austen described herself as 'a poor Honey at present'. 'A poor Honey' was her term for a female hypochondriac overzealous in her care for her own health. She had known many, and as we have seen had created many, all subtly different, in the course of her life. She had used the term about an acquaintance in September 1813, at the peak of her own good health and professional success, *Mansfield*

Park having just been completed and *Pride and Prejudice* published and well received only months before. Writing to her brother Frank, serving at sea, she gave news of a young married couple:

> They have been all the summer at Ramsgate, for her health, she is a poor Honey – the sort of woman who gives me the idea of being determined never to be well – & who likes her spasms & nervousness & the consequence they give her, better than anything else. – This is an illnatured sentiment to send all over the Baltic.[11]

Austen herself was not of course 'a poor Honey' but a seriously ill woman by the spring of 1817. Her last preserved letter from Chawton was written to her friend Anne Sharp on 22 May, to give her the news she was shortly moving to lodgings in Winchester where better medical attention would be on hand. She had been 'very ill indeed' and had been confined to her bed since 13 April, 'with only removals to a Sopha'. But she claimed to be 'getting well again, & indeed have been gradually tho' slowly recovering my strength for the last three weeks. . . . My head was always clear, & I had scarcely any pain; my chief sufferings were from feverish nights, weakness & Languor.' After paying tribute to the kindness of all her family, she concluded, 'In short, if I live to be an old Woman I must expect to wish I had died now, blessed in the tenderness of such a Family, & before I had survived either them or their affection.'

Two days later she was conveyed in her brother James's carriage, with Cassandra beside her, brother Henry and nephew William Knight accompanying them on horseback through the rain, the sixteen miles to Winchester, still clinging to the belief, as she wrote to James's son James Edward three days later from their lodgings, that 'I am gaining strength very fast'.[12]

12. NOTHING TO DO BUT TO DIE

Austen had long observed that for many people, illness was the ultimate way to control others. From Dr Grant's 'indisposition', which enables him to take out his disappointment on his wife, to Mary Musgrove's taking to her sofa to elicit the sympathy of her sister; from Fanny Dashwood's hysterics to Mrs Bennet's nerves; from Mr Woodhouse's 'gentle selfishness' to the way Mrs Churchill keeps her nephew dancing attendance, claims of illness enable people to get their own way, and are often accompanied by complaints that nobody takes their ailments seriously. But with Mrs Churchill, there is a twist in the story. Mrs Churchill dies. Mrs Churchill must have been more gravely ill than people had given her credit for. Her death comes as a shock not only to those who know her or know of her, but to the reader, for it is the only death to occur within the narrative of an Austen novel:

> The following day brought news from Richmond to throw everything else into the background. An express arrived at Randalls to announce the death of Mrs Churchill. Though her nephew had had no particular reason to hasten back on her account, she had not lived above six-and-thirty hours after his return. A sudden seizure of a different nature from anything foreboded by her general state, had carried her off after a short struggle. The great Mrs Churchill was no more.
>
> It was felt as such things must be felt. Everybody had a degree of gravity and sorrow; tenderness towards the departed,

> solicitude for the surviving friends, and, in a reasonable time, curiosity to know where she would be buried. Goldsmith tells us, that when lovely woman stoops to folly, she has nothing to do but to die; and when she stoops to be disagreeable, it is equally to be recommended as a clearer of ill-fame. Mrs Churchill, after being disliked at least twenty-five years, was now spoken of with compassionate allowances.[1]

Austen treats death as she does every other subject, with clear-eyed realism and dry jest. As omnipotent narrator, she allows herself liberties which would be improper in her characters themselves. Humour is not one of the responses of her most right-minded characters, such as Mrs Weston and Emma (both of whom knew Mrs Churchill only by repute). Mrs Weston 'sat sighing and moralising . . . with a commiseration and good sense true and steady'. Emma is at first as grave, but not quite as steady as her older friend: 'The character of Mrs Churchill, the grief of her husband – her mind glanced over both with awe and compassion, and then rested with lightened feelings on how Frank might be affected by the event, how benefited, how freed'. Emma's musings take a rational sequence endorsed by her author: due acknowledgement of the passing of a life, as much concern for the bereaved as for the dead soul, and before long turning to the prospects of the next generation.

Death as a *dieu ex machina* suddenly easing the path towards matrimony of hero and heroine is not a device in which Austen often indulges. On the final page of *Northanger Abbey*, it is true, the death of some previously unknown viscount enables Henry Tilney and Catherine Morland to marry, as contrived an ending as in any conventional novel – contrived however by a very knowing author. Austen undercuts the device in a different way in *Mansfield Park*, where the convenient death of Dr Grant at the end of the story does not revolutionize Fanny Price's prospects, only enhances them by giving her a better home and larger income. At the same time, the manner of Dr Grant's death – brought on by overeating – fits nicely with the character we have come to know, completes the portrait very satisfactorily, doles out his just deserts, and is simultaneously absurd and convincing. Quite a lot to be achieved by an apparently throw-away line forming only part of a long sentence – but such is Austen's economy.

The death of Tom Bertram would do more good for Fanny, but his moral reformation is much more in Austen's line, and we are given to believe much more pleasing to Fanny herself. Contributing to its serious, even solemn tone, *Mansfield Park* is the only novel in which ideas about the hereafter find a place. When Tom is gravely ill, Fanny experiences a 'keener solicitude' even than wishing him to recover for his family's sake: she considers 'how little useful, how little self-denying his life had (apparently) been' and it is clear she is worried that his soul might not be fit for Heaven. (That Jane Austen's mind was deeply imbued with this belief is evident from a comment made during a respite in her own illness: 'The Providence of God has restored me – & may I be more fit to appear before him when I <u>am</u> summoned, than I sh^{d} have been now!')[2]

In dealing with the novel's two adulterers, Austen banishes Maria from social and family life and then writes of Henry: 'That punishment, the public punishment of disgrace, should in just measure attend *his* share of the offence, is, we know, not one of the barriers which society gives to virtue. In this world, the penalty is less equal than could be wished; but without presuming to look forward to a juster appointment hereafter. . . .'

'In this world' is opposed to the afterlife; and although some commentators have read this passage as Austen 'looking forward' in history to a fairer society free from the 'double standard' then obtaining, the correct reading is that while not being so presumptuous as to pre-empt the final judgement, which is God's and God's alone, the narrator trusts that men and women will stand before Him on equal terms.

In the same novel, the protocol surrounding death is illustrated when the news of the demise of Lord Ravenshaw's grandmother puts an end to the home theatricals at Ecclesford. Tom Bertram's friend the Honourable John Yates, who was to have taken part, laments:

> "To be sure the poor old dowager could not have died at a worse time. . . . It is impossible to help wishing that the news could have been suppressed for just the three days . . . and being only a grandmother, and all happening two hundred miles off, I think there would have been no great harm, and it *was* suggested, I know; but Lord Ravenshaw, who I suppose is one of the most correct men in England, would not hear of it."

Yates, who self-evidently has few scruples when his own gratification is concerned, brings the acting itch to Mansfield, and sets in train the disasters that their own selfishness induces in almost all the young people. A far-off death has great consequences indeed. The threads are brilliantly interwoven: having escaped death himself, Tom's post-reformation reflections include self-reproach that he was accessory to his sister's downfall 'by all the dangerous intimacy of his unjustifiable theatre'.

There are other interesting deaths in other novels but, like that of Lord Ravenshaw's grandmother, they are kept very firmly off stage. Many of them occur at the very beginning of a novel as part of its exposition, or even before the action starts, to surface at a later date. That is the case with Colonel Brandon's first love in *Sense and Sensibility*. Eliza Williams, in falling prey to a sequence of illegitimate childbirth, prostitution and consumption, is an example (albeit one with extenuating circumstances) of Goldsmith's fallen woman who has nothing to do but to die. By the mores of the late eighteenth century, it is unthinkable that Brandon could rescue and marry her and nurse her back to a full life. Like so many eighteenth- and nineteenth-century heroines – from Clarissa Harlowe to Maggie Tulliver to Tess Durbeyfield, from Marguerite Gautier to Emma Bovary to Anna Karenina – Eliza has sexually transgressed and must die. If it is odd to find Austen being so conventional, it must be borne in mind that Eliza Williams is a very minor, non-speaking character, hardly more than a plot device; that *Sense and Sensibility* has not in every respect quite broken free from the sentimental literature that gave it birth; and that Marianne Dashwood is very firmly *not* allowed to die as the result of an (admittedly unconsummated) love affair. ('It is no creed of mine', Jane Austen wrote robustly to a niece, 'that such sorts of Disappointments kill anybody'.)[3]

In addition to these examples, many are the late husbands of Austen's widows, or parents of the heroes and heroines, but they are shadowy characters, long deceased. Having only one parent living was a common enough circumstance at the time, and there are some characters who have very credibly lost both parents at an early age, including Jane Fairfax, Mary Crawford and Georgiana Darcy. Emma Woodhouse has an indistinct memory of her mother's caresses; Anne Elliot and Eleanor Tilney, who were of school age when their respective mothers died, remember and mourn their loss, but apart from their both being patient, virtuous ladies who had much to bear within their husbands, neither Lady Elliot nor Mrs Tilney is individualized.

Mrs Tilney's death, however, though happening nine years before the action of *Northanger Abbey*, is described in retrospect by one of her surviving children more fully than Mrs Churchill's and is the only actual description of a death in any of the novels:

> "My mother's illness . . .the seizure which ended in her death, *was* sudden. The malady itself, one from which she had often suffered, a bilious fever – its cause therefore constitutional. On the third day, in short, as soon as she could be prevailed on, a physician attended her, a very respectable man, and one in whom she had always placed great confidence. Upon his opinion of her danger, two others were called in the next day, and remained in almost constant attendance for four and twenty hours. On the fifth day she died. Frederick and I (*we* were both at home) saw her repeatedly; and from our own observation can bear witness to her having received every

> possible attention that could spring from the affection of those about her, or which her situation in life could command. Poor Eleanor *was* absent, and at such a distance as to return only to see her mother in her coffin."

Revisiting the circumstances of Mrs Tilney's death in speech and thought brings about an *éclaircissement* between Catherine and Henry. Death is never gratuitous in Austen; it always has some function to perform in terms of plot or character. In an age when infant mortality was high, a rare child death in the comedy of Austen's fiction is that of little Mary Price in *Mansfield Park*, while in *Persuasion*, grown up but young people whose premature deaths form part of the survivors' consciousnesses include Dick Musgrove and Fanny Harville. In all three cases, it is the nature of the grief in those they leave behind – its durability or otherwise, its authenticity or otherwise – that interests Austen. Fanny Price would not pain her mother by alluding to the death of her sister, which happened some years ago, yet to her astonishment she finds that when Mary is mentioned by others, her mother is too much occupied by her household cares and her superfluity of children to have any feelings to spare for the one who died. Poor Dick Musgrove had been 'scarcely at all regretted when the intelligence of his death abroad had worked its way to Uppercross' but now, two years later, his mother looks over his letters again and, forgetting his faults after the lapse of time, she is thrown 'into greater grief for him than she had known on first hearing of his death'. Austen, usually celebrated for her ability to cut through cant, has for some critics and readers become unacceptably cruel in her harshness towards 'thick-headed, unfeeling, unprofitable Dick Musgrove' and his mother, indulging in 'large fat sighings over the destiny of a son, whom alive no one had cared for'.

Captain Benwick's grief at first seems not only more genuine but more rational, as his dead fiancée Fanny Harville was 'a most superior creature'. Benwick makes a great show of being a bereaved person, cultivating a gloomy, romantic appearance, avoiding common small talk but eager to discuss poetry with Anne, and repeating with 'tremulous feeling the various lines which imaged a broken heart, or a mind destroyed by wretchedness'. Austen never trusts excessive show of feeling, however, and sure enough, before long Benwick has fallen in love with another woman, Louisa Musgrove. It is Fanny's brother, Captain Harville, who keeps her longer in memory, and his exchange with Anne Elliot on the subject of enduring love, "when existence or when hope is gone" as she so eloquently puts it, is one of the most tender passages in this or any other Austen novel. Fanny Harville's death enables Anne to articulate her own feelings for the man she has never ceased to love, and moreover to be overheard by him, since she cannot tell him directly. This denouement comprised Austen's second thoughts on the way to end her novel, the first having no reference whatsoever to Fanny; these second thoughts are not only far more moving, they are artistically superior. It has often been noticed by critics that in bringing the Musgrove family to Bath, the replacement chapters draw together elements from the early part of the story. Less often noticed is that this conclusion also makes Fanny Harville's death an intrinsic part of the pattern in the carpet, in which second chances and second attachments are woven into a realistic and satisfying whole.

Mourning and Funerals

On Mrs Churchill's death her brother-in-law Mr Weston, who has never taken her illnesses seriously, makes amends by resolving 'that his mourning should be as handsome as possible', while his wife sits sewing, 'sighing and moralising', as we have seen, 'over her broad hems'. The editors of the Cambridge University edition of *Emma* compare this passage with one in Susan Ferrier's 1818 novel *Marriage*, where the ladies prepare their mourning clothes 'by dressing crape; reviving black silk; converting narrow hems into broad hems'. Even two decades later, when the fashionable silhouette was quite different, the custom persisted, as they also cite

Catherine Gore's 1836 novel *Mrs Armytage; or Female Domination* in which the Duchess of Spalding's mourning dress is 'all crape and broad hems'. The suggestion by these editors is that broad hems on an otherwise plain black dress would allow for a decorative touch, but much more likely is that a broad hem of black crape fabric would be added to ordinary clothes to denote mourning – not of course in a widow, for whom nothing less than full mourning would suffice, but when the deceased was not a close relation. It would be rather like adding a black armband today, and a lot cheaper and easier than a complete change of clothes. The black hem or border would have been easily removable at the end of the mourning period. Costume historian Penelope Byrde supports this view.[4]

The Dashwood women must all have been in full mourning at the beginning of *Sense and Sensibility*, though this is never depicted in film versions. The only other persons said to be wearing any sign of mourning in an Austen novel are those acknowledging the very recent death of Mr Elliot's wife in *Persuasion*. He himself wears crape round his hat, he has a 'servant in mourning' to drive his curricle and even his cousin Elizabeth is 'wearing black ribbons' when we first encounter her, an extraordinary circumstance considering she never met the late Mrs Elliot and has always regarded her scornfully as being 'of inferior birth'. Presumably Anne and Mary must be wearing black ribbons likewise, as they stand in the same relationship to the deceased. In such a hidebound family as that of Sir Walter Elliot, it is hard to imagine that such tokens were optional.

Black-edged writing paper was another convention. There is no instance in the novels, but 'I have forgotten to take a proper-edged piece of paper', wrote Jane to her brother Charles shortly after the death of their uncle James Leigh Perrot in 1817.[5] In *Emma*, the long letter of explanation which Frank Churchill writes to his stepmother following Mrs Churchill's death, would certainly have been on black-bordered paper, but Austen does not choose to be explicit. Contemporary readers would have taken it for granted.

Doing the right thing was paramount. When Mr Leigh Perrot died, his nephew the Reverend Edward Cooper, who felt even more bruised by the will than the Austens, since he was excluded altogether – despite being the same degree of relationship – wrote to Jane, 'Will you be kind enough to send us word, when you write, what is the period for the mourning, as we would wish to do the same as you do. As for the little boys we conclude that one suit of black will be sufficient for them.'[6]

Jane Austen's own letters make several mentions of mourning clothes. If she can make a joke she will, as on the occasion when she meets an old acquaintance in Bath wearing such deep mourning that either his mother, his wife or himself must be dead.

Most of her remarks on the subject, however, are practical. Wearing mourning for a member of the royal family was expected, but irksome, and stretched the budget of those with a small dress allowance like herself. In 1805 she wrote, 'I suppose everybody will be in black for the D[uke] of G[loucester]. Must we buy lace, or will ribbon do?'[7] When Queen Charlotte's brother, the distant Duke of Mecklenburg-Strelitz, died in 1814, Jane wrote of 'this 6 weeks mourning'.[8] She was in London at the time and informed Cassandra, 'Almost everybody was in mourning last night, but my brown gown did very well. . . . I have determined to trim my lilac sarsenet with black sattin [sic] ribbon just as my China crape is, 6d width at bottom, 3d or 4d at top. With this addition it will be a very successful gown, happy to go anywhere.' Broad hems to the rescue at little expense. A king's death would be more worthy of being marked than that of a king's brother-in-law. In 1811, when George III seemed likely to die (though in fact he lived, under his son's Regency, until 1820) Jane wrote that she had gone shopping with her niece Anna and a friend: 'Their business was to provide mourning against the King's death; & my Mother has had a Bombasin bought for her.'[9] With mourning de rigueur for the royal family as well as for one's own distant family connections, people must often have felt that they were never *out* of mourning. Three months after the death of one relation, Jane wrote to a brother, 'Our mourning for her is not over, or we should now be putting it on again for Mr Tho[mas] Leigh.'[10]

Bombazine was a heavy blend of silk and wool with a matte surface. Crape was the other traditional mourning fabric, gauzier than bombazine, therefore suitable for hat bands, caps, veils and trimmings on gowns and bonnets. The death of a family member occasioned a longer period and more complete set of mourning, as a mark of respect for the departed, though for the non-wealthy, this involved some ingenuity. In October 1808, on hearing of the likely demise of a distant relation, Jane wrote that her mother 'is preparing mourning ... she has picked her old silk pelisse to pieces, & means to have it dyed black for a gown',[11] although the old lady lingered on for another six months. Mrs Austen's efforts were not wasted, however, as tragically, only a few days later, the sudden death of a much nearer relation, Jane's sister-in-law Elizabeth Austen, followed the birth of her eleventh child. Cassandra, who had been staying in Kent to assist the young family during Elizabeth's confinement, requested Jane send what she could from their home in Southampton, as Jane replied:

> Your parcel shall set off on Monday ... I shall send you such of your Mourning as I think most likely to be useful, reserving for myself your Stockings & half the velvet ... I am to be in Bombazeen & Crape, according to what we are told is universal here. ... My Mourning however will not impoverish me, for by having my velvet Pelisse fresh lined & made up, I am sure I shall have no occasion this winter for anything new of that sort. – I take my Cloak for the lining – & shall send yours on the chance of its doing something of the same for you – tho' I believe your Pelisse is in better repair than mine. One Miss Baker makes my gown, & the other my Bonnet, which is to be silk covered with Crape.[12]

Except for the very rich, burial would take place in the parish church where the death occurred. Mrs Churchill, of course, is rich, which is why the Highbury gossips speculate as to where the funeral will be. Later it transpires that her body is taken back to Yorkshire, a long way from Surrey where she dies. She will, presumably, be laid to rest in the family tomb or vault, where her husband will first go to pay his respects, and then, eventually, join her. Elizabeth Austen, as the wife and sister of wealthy men, was given a funeral with no expense spared although, dying as she did at home, there was no cost incurred in conveying the body.

As the Godmersham family were not particularly showy, presumably the arrangements accorded with what was expected for people in their station in life. Strangely, to our minds, Jane Austen expressed the sincere hope that the widower, her brother Edward, would not attend. Writing the day before the funeral,[13] she envisaged the 'mournful party' gathered at Godmersham in the evening rather than thinking of them at the church by day. Whether Edward was there is not recorded, but a recent scholar, Linda Slothouber, has discovered bills marking the occasion, which was unimaginably lavish:

> Ceremonial attendants included the undertaker, an assistant, 18 underbearers with truncheons, two mutes, and a featherman. The mutes, carrying staves swathed in black fabric, stood alongside the house entrance prior to the funeral and then walked in the procession. The featherman supplied plumes of black ostrich feathers for the horses drawing the hearse.[14]

Twenty-two mourning cloaks were hired for the day for the underbearers and other functionaries, including the rector, the undertaker, two physicians, and five Godmersham upper servants: the butler, gardener, housekeeper, nursemaid and lady's maid. The butler and gardener, as well as nine further male servants, received new hats, hatbands, scarves, suits and hose. The female upper servants and a further ten maidservants received hoods, hose and enough fabric to clothe themselves sombrely for the duration of the mourning period (perhaps a year): 14¼ yards of muslin specifically for making shawls, 60 yards of calico and 71 of printed calico; 50 yards of bombazett, 20 yards of jaconet muslin (probably all black) and 20 yards of serviceable brown Holland fabric, the whole probably sufficient to provide three outfits per maidservant. Presumably the housekeeper worked out the quantities required. All the above-named servants, plus the carpenter who made the coffin and the bricklayer who prepared the vault, were given gloves to keep, that is, fifty-four pairs in all; and a further six pairs of gloves of superior black silk were presumably designated for family mourners, who otherwise supplied their own clothes. This may imply that six family members (all male) followed the coffin, in which case Edward was surely among them, together with a brother and brothers-in-law.

Elizabeth's eldest sons, aged fourteen and thirteen, were not brought home from school (they went to stay with their grandmother in Southampton, nearer to their school in Winchester than Kent, to be comforted in their first grief) and the younger ones would certainly not have been present; neither would daughter Fanny nor sister-in-law Cassandra, though they were in the house. Gentlewomen then did not attend funerals, as they were considered too stressful for the female mind and body to bear.

Not a Mind for Affliction

The working population were tougher. On 25 March 1817, not so very far off death herself, Jane wrote in her usual humorous vein to Fanny Knight, describing a village funeral:

> Old Philimore [erstwhile landlord of Miss Benn] was buried yesterday, & I, by way of saying something to Triggs, observed that it had been a very handsome Funeral, but his manner of reply made me suppose it was not generally esteemed so. I can only be sure of one part being very handsome, Triggs himself, walking behind in his Green Coat. – Mrs Philimore attended as cheif [sic] Mourner, in Bombasin, made very short, and flounced with Crape.

Jane Austen's attitude to the death of others ranged between the insouciant, the pragmatic and the heartfelt. Her chief desire seems to have been to avoid cant. If the deceased person was of no particular interest to the Austens, then she would seize the opportunity to make a joke. One of her most famous quips, often quoted against her, concerns a Mrs Hall of Sherborne being 'brought to bed of a dead child some weeks before she expected, owing to a fright. – I suppose she happened unawares to look at her husband.'[15] Less forgivably, perhaps, a tragic death in the family also became the subject of a witticism, though not until a few months after the event. Her cousin Jane Cooper, with whom she had been at school and at whose wedding to Captain Williams of the Royal Navy in Steventon Church Jane Austen had been witness, was killed when she was thrown out of the light carriage she was driving on the Isle of Wight. She was only twenty-seven. This must have been a great shock to the Steventon family, but as the Austen sisters were together at that point, no letters record Jane's reaction until five months later when Jane Cooper's brother Edward was offered the living of Hamstall Ridware in Staffordshire. Despite the large families of the period, it happens that the Austens had only three first cousins: Jane and Edward Cooper, and Eliza de Feuillide, who had recently turned herself into a sister-in-law by marrying Henry Austen. Writing to Cassandra on 21 January 1799 to convey the news of Edward Cooper's removal, Jane could not resist a droll remark: 'Our first cousins seem all dropping off very fast. One is incorporated into the family, another dies, and a third goes into Staffordshire.' This does seem remarkably unfeeling, and it is somewhat surprising that it escaped Cassandra's later excisions.

On 8 April 1798 at the age of twenty-two, it fell to Jane to write the family letter of condolence when her father's half-brother William Walter died. In addressing his daughter Philadelphia she reached for the conventional phrases:

> . . . the loss of so kind & affectionate a Parent, must be a severe affliction to all his Children, to yourself more especially, as

> your constant residence with him has given you so much the more constant & intimate knowledge of his Virtues .... the Goodness which made him valuable on Earth, will make him Blessed in Heaven.

It is possible that the Austen parents regarded the writing of this sort of letter as part of a gentlewoman's training, and Cassandra's being away from home at the time suggested to them that this would be a good exercise for Jane in keeping her wit under wraps.

When her own father died seven years later, she had to send the news from Bath to her brother Frank, on board ship – and she was obliged to repeat the story of his sudden death in a second letter, since after posting the first it was found that he was in a different port from the one they had originally supposed. These two letters, of 21 and 22 January 1805, show her again struggling to be natural. 'The loss of such a Parent must be felt, or we should be Brutes', has long struck critics as somewhat odd, as if she is telling herself what she should be feeling. 'Heavy as is the blow, we can already feel that a thousand comforts remain to us to soften it', is another locution which does not quite seem to come from the heart. Giving a truer picture, perhaps, of the realization of what she had lost are two sentences in the second letter: 'The Serenity of the Corpse is most delightful! It preserves the sweet, benevolent smile which always distinguished him.' It was as if her father's death had stunned her, for it had certainly been unexpected, and she had not known how to react. The aftermath seems to have been a time of personal growth for her, and what followed was an increase in empathy. Just a few months later, when Martha's mother Mrs Lloyd lay dying, and Cassandra was staying with Martha, Jane wrote to the former with perfect sincerity, 'May her end be peaceful & easy, as the Exit we have witnessed!' She added, 'The Nonsense I have been writing in this & my last letter, seems out of place at such a time; but I will not mind it, it will do you no harm, & nobody else will be attacked by it.'[16]

It was four years after the death of her treasured older friend and Steventon neighbour Mrs Anne Lefroy before she was moved to write a poem commemorating the sad event. Mrs Lefroy had been thrown from her horse on 16 December 1804, Jane's twenty-ninth birthday. It is a stilted, solemn, religious poem in thirteen stanzas, unlike anything else that has come down to us from Austen's pen; but nobody could deny that it is heartfelt:

The day, commemorative of my birth,
Bestowing Life & Light & Hope to me,
Brings back the hour which was thy last on Earth.
Oh! bitter pang of torturing Memory![17]

And so on. The vocabulary, with its talk of angels and bliss and heaven, is uncharacteristic, but reminds us of the strong religious beliefs that underlay Austen's world view, but which she kept for private consolation.

In the letters, it is the balance between feeling and common sense which prevails. The death of Edward's wife Elizabeth, as we have seen, elicited much true sympathy for the widower and bereaved children from Jane; but that did not prevent her adding briskly to Cassandra, 'We need not enter into a panegyric on the departed.' Three months after another sister-in-law, Eliza de Feuillide Austen, died in April 1813 after a long struggle – probably with breast cancer, like her mother – Jane sent a thoughtful account to Frank of how the widower Henry was coping:

> Upon the whole his Spirits are very much recovered. – If I may so express myself, his Mind is not a Mind for affliction. He is too Busy, too active, too sanguine. – Sincerely as he was attached to poor Eliza, moreover, & excellently as he behaved to her, he was always so used to be away from her at times, that her Loss is not felt as that of many a beloved Wife might be, especially when all the circumstances of her long & dreadful illness are taken into account. – He very long knew that she must die, & it was indeed a release at last.[18]

It sounds as if Jane approved and perhaps shared Henry's pragmatism – almost his impatience to put the past behind him and get on with life. Her earlier insouciance, not unusual in a young person, had matured into a more compassionate attitude to death, but she was never tempted to become maudlin.

The exception to the family's robust attitude to death was James Austen. In his last poem he mused with characteristic melancholy on 'the short and quickly passing years' and on how 'When this brief scene is over as it must/Pass some few years, to all who tread life's stage . . .'.[19] In their mother, a combination of realism, religion and humour in the face of approaching death was marked. Living to be eighty-seven, and outliving most of her contemporaries, she remarked wryly to a visiting grandson, 'Ah, my dear, you find me just where you left me – on the sofa. I sometimes think God Almighty must have forgotten me; but I daresay He will come for me in His own good time.'[20] Many years earlier, recovering from a brush with death in 1804, Mrs Austen had celebrated by writing two comic stanzas simultaneously making fun of herself and tenderly paying tribute to the love and prayers of her husband, and the practical care of her daughters and doctor for bringing her through. In its combination of wit and feeling, it is a more accomplished poem than Jane's on Mrs Lefroy, or James's verbose meanderings.

In the twelve years between her father's death (within a month of Mrs Lefroy's) and her own mortal illness, Jane Austen experienced no serious bereavement, a quite remarkable circumstance given the medical deficiencies of the period. Sisters-in-law had died, and a few distant relations, but no sibling, no other dear friend. Death had given her a wide berth, only to come suddenly much too close.

When her own death became inevitable, Jane faced it with the Christian fortitude and resignation which had been instilled into her as a child. That she could do this was all the more poignant, and all the more admirable, in that, as her niece Caroline described, in slightly sentimental terms, she had in 1817 every reason to cling to life: 'Though she had passed by the hopes and enjoyments of youth, yet its sorrows were also left behind – Autumn is sometimes so calm and fair that it consoles us for the departure of Spring and Summer – and thus it might have been with her.'[21]

Not that Jane Austen gave up hope of being cured almost to the very end. She agreed to leave her beloved Chawton for Winchester precisely because she believed she could get well under the care of Mr Lyford of that city; had she (or he) been hopeless, she would surely have remained to die in the familiar surroundings of home, with the comfort of being buried in the village graveyard where her sister might one day join her. Instead, the family found the money for Winchester lodgings and medical attendance, and three days after settling in she wrote to a nephew:

> I will not boast of my handwriting; neither that nor my face have yet recovered their proper beauty, but in other respects I am gaining strength very fast. . . . Mr Lyford says he will cure me, & if he fails I shall draw up a Memorial & lay it before the Dean & Chapter, & have no doubt of redress from that Pious, Learned & disinterested Body.[22]

Her last surviving letter, written the following day (28 May) to a friend in London, says 'My attendant is encouraging, and talks of making me quite well. . . . I have been out once in a sedan-chair, and am to repeat it, and be promoted to a wheel-chair as the weather serves.'

It was a cruel aggravation of her decline that it took place as the burgeoning life of summer made its presence increasingly felt. She had always been particularly sensitive to the seasons. In mid-June came a crisis which brought anxious brothers to her bedside, and she made a point of taking Holy Communion from James and Henry while she could still follow the meaning of the words. She rallied and lingered for one more month, and then as Cassandra wrote to Fanny Knight on 20 July,

> Her complaint returned, there was a visible change, she slept

> more & much more comfortably, indeed during the last eight & forty hours she was more asleep than awake. Her looks altered & she fell away, but I perceived no material diminution of strength & tho' I was then hopeless of a recovery I had no suspicion how rapidly my loss was approaching.... When I asked her if there was anything she wanted, her answer was she wanted nothing but death.

Jane Austen was buried in Winchester Cathedral early on the morning of 24 July 1817, attended by three brothers and a nephew. From the first floor bay window in College Street, Cassandra 'watched the little mournful procession the length of the Street & when it turned from my sight . . . I had lost her for ever'.

She had, however, retained some of Jane's hair, to be set into rings and brooches for those who had loved her.[23]

CONCLUSION

Had Jane Austen been granted her three score years and ten – or more – how would she have fared in old age? Professionally, she would surely have grown in both output and reputation. If, as I believe, the three novels she had written at Chawton show an advance in artistic control over her material as well as greater profundity of feeling, promising even more for the future, equally the fragment left unfinished at her death, *Sanditon*, proves there was no waning in her powers of invention. It is idle, perhaps even impertinent, to question the directions which her fiction might have taken, but that it would have developed, to the delight of future readers, can admit of little doubt. Whether she would ever have deviated from the courtship genre to make older characters the focus of a story is just one intriguing possibility. Did she have a *Cranford* in her? Or a 'Condition of England' novel? As well as her own increasing maturity of mind and experience, the evolving spirit of the times and new directions in fiction would have been brought to bear on an exceptional literary intelligence that had always been alive to currents around her. As for her reputation, that grew slowly but steadily anyway after her death, so with a greater presence in the publishing marketplace, there can be no doubt of increasing appreciation in enthusiastic readers and thoughtful critics. Her earnings, too, must have grown.

And her personal life? She would probably have found it harder to keep it wholly private and to avoid the ramifications of fame. But that aside (and dismissing the idea of late marriage – which seems highly unlikely though the examples of Philadelphia Walter and Martha Lloyd show that it was not impossible), we can only go by how Cassandra's own old age worked out.

'Single Women have a dreadful propensity for being poor' is one of Jane Austen's most quoted and heartfelt remarks. For most of her life she had no money of her own and no opportunity to earn any; she was acutely conscious of having no means of support beyond what her kind brothers could afford to spare from their own family commitments, and of how precarious their own incomes could be. When she did at last earn money from her books it brought her a deeply satisfying mixture of pleasure, relief and self-esteem. But she spent hardly any of her earnings, hoarding them against the day when she and Cassandra might be old and poor. She had seen what that could mean in the wretched circumstances of unprotected spinster neighbours Miss Murden in Southampton and Miss Benn in Chawton, as well as all the struggling women in Bath. For Jane, that day never came, and on her death she left almost everything to Cassandra.

Her estate was worth £782, mainly in government stock. After funeral expenses of £92 and legacies and expenses of £129, Cassandra was left with £561, on which she paid legacy duty of three per cent, or £16.16s.8d.[1]

The rather remarkable thing is that Cassandra, who never earned any money of her own, grew more and more comfortably circumstanced as her life went on. In addition to several small legacies of £50 each, over the years she inherited £1,000 from her fiancé Tom Fowle, the £561 from Jane, £600 on the death of her mother (a few days after Jane's death Mrs Austen had altered her will to make Cassandra her sole beneficiary) together with the further sum of £437, being one-fifth share of the old South Sea Annuities in which Mr and Mrs Austen had invested all the money which came to them from their own parents and which was written into their marriage settlement.

Then, in 1833, her aunt Jane Leigh Perrot, as if to make amends for earlier disappointments, settled the large sum of £3,000 on

Cassandra. Three years later, on the death of that aunt, a further £1,000 came to Cassandra in accordance with her uncle's will.[2]

In addition, she received £515.17s.6d as posthumous royalties from the publisher John Murray, who remaindered the last 282 of Austen's books in 1820, and closed his account with her executors. In 1833 another publisher, Bentley, purchased the copyrights from Cassandra for £250, and brought out a cheap new edition in his 'Standard Novels' series. Jane's pen had thus provided her beloved sister with a total of £1,326 for her old age.[3]

Cassandra continued to live rent-free in Chawton Cottage (where from the moment of her mother's death she was known as Mrs Austen),[4] to be supplied with firewood from her brother's Chawton estate (now occupied by his eldest son) and to spend months at a time visiting her now very numerous relations. As her income from investments increased, it considerably outstripped her modest expenditure. The future which Jane had feared and perhaps pictured for herself and her sister never came to pass.

Cassandra's own will is proof of how worldly goods had accrued to her; proof too of the network of family affections.[5] So well had she husbanded and invested her money that, at her death in March 1845, the bank calculated her probate at £16,000. She left £1,000 to each of her brothers Edward, Henry and Frank, with £1,000 to Anna Lefroy as the descendant of James, and £1,000 outside of the family to Caroline Elizabeth Fowle: Cassandra scrupulously returning to the Fowle family, in the person of one of its unmarried daughters, the £1,000 which Tom Fowle had left her nearly fifty years earlier. Her residual legatee was her poorest brother, Charles, who thus came into more than £10,000, rather late in his own life, but very welcome in helping to make his own children comfortable. Numerous small pieces of jewellery and personal objects were listed by Cassandra to go to various nieces, as were the precious papers left by Jane. Cassandra's clothes were bequeathed to her female servants, who were probably grateful for anything to augment their own meagre stock – even if the garments were predominantly black and old-fashioned.

Though in one sense Cassandra must have been lonely, being the last remaining of the four inhabitants of Chawton Cottage, she did exactly what Emma Woodhouse foresaw that she herself would do as a single woman in later age: she occupied herself with needlework, and often had a niece or great-niece to stay with her. She practised charity in the village, took an active interest in the village school and cultivated her garden. Neighbouring Chawton Great House was occupied by one nephew, Edward Knight II, and his large family; and Chawton Rectory by another, the bachelor Charles Knight; so there was no lack of support and cheerful company around her. She was a respected member of the village squirearchy, in effect.

Her increasingly complex financial affairs are suggested in an entry made in Charles Knight's diary for March 1843: 'I went to Alton to appeal for At Cassra against her Income Tax assessment.'[6] Indeed if, as we saw in Chapter 5, Marianne Knight in middle age was to sink from being Emma Woodhouse to being poor Miss Bates, at the same stage of life Cassandra Austen experienced a shift in the opposite direction. No longer the poor relation, she became a woman of substance. Jane would have been the same – even more so if, as is likely, she had enjoyed further literary success.

Cassandra's health seems to have been good until the stroke from which she died suddenly, in 1845. 'She is a very great loss to us all, & to all the parish, for whom she had been doing good and living among them almost uninterruptedly for 35 years', recorded Charles Knight in summing up the year. Within the very different lifespans allotted to them, the sisters had admirably fulfilled, in the words Jane Austen uses in *Persuasion*, the ideal of becoming 'not unworthy member[s]' of the 'little social commonwealth' into which they had found themselves transplanted in 1809.

Apart from the sad loss of Jane, Cassandra's old age was in fact a secure and comfortable one. If only she had been able to share it with her sister.

NOTES

References to Jane Austen's novels and literary fragments are from *The Cambridge Edition of the Works of Jane Austen*, general editor: Janet Todd, Cambridge University Press, 2006, 9 vols: *Juvenilia, Sense and Sensibility, Pride and Prejudice, Northanger Abbey, Mansfield Park, Emma, Persuasion, Later Manuscripts, Contexts.*

References to Jane Austen's letters are from *Jane Austen's Letters*, ed. Deirdre Le Faye, Oxford University Press, 4th edn, 2011.

References to *Austen Papers* are from the privately printed 1942 manuscript by R.A. Austen-Leigh.

Introduction

1. Letter, 8–11 April 1805
2. Letter, 21–23 April 1805
3. Letter, 27–28 December 1808
4. Prayers, *Later Manuscripts*
5. Letter, 9 December 1808
6. Letter, 6–7 November 1813

Chapter 1: The Loss of Youth and Beauty

1. *Emma*
2. *Mansfield Park*
3. *Mansfield Park*
4. Letter, 30 August 1805
5. Letter, 30 April 1811

6. *The Mirror of the Graces,* 1811, reprinted as *Regency Etiquette,* R.L. Shep Publications, 1997
7. Letter, 6–7 November 1813
8. *My Aunt Jane Austen,* Caroline Austen, new edition published 1991, The Jane Austen Society
9. Deirdre Le Faye, 'Recollections of Chawton' in *Times Literary Supplement*, 3 May 1985
10. *My Aunt Jane Austen*
11. Letter, 15–16 September 1815
12. Lefroy MS, quoted in Deirdre Le Faye, *Jane Austen: a Family Record*, British Library, 1989
13. *Pride and Prejudice*
14. *Mansfield Park*
15. *Austen Papers*, letter from Philadelphia Walter, 23 July 1788
16. Austen-Leigh archive, Hampshire Record Office 23M93/86/3 quoted in Deirdre Le Faye, *A Chronology of Jane Austen and her Family*, Cambridge University Press, 2006
17. Letter, 8–9 February 1807
18. Note to Letter, 8-9 September 1807
19. Peggy Hickman, *A Jane Austen Household Book*, David & Charles, 1977
20. Mary Augusta Austen Leigh, *James Edward Austen Leigh: A Memoir*, 1911
21. *Austen Papers*, letter from Eliza de Feuillide, 30 December 1796
22. *An Account of Several Valuable and Excellent Genuine Patent Medicines*, 1790 quoted in *Persuasion*, Vol.II, Chapter 4
23. *Persuasion*
24. Lefroy MS, quoted in Deirdre Le Faye, *Jane Austen: a Family Record*
25. *Pride and Prejudice*

Chapter 2: My Time of Life

1. Deirdre Le Faye, 'Anna Lefroy's Original Memories of Jane Austen' in *The Review of English Studies*, August 1988
2. Letter, 3 November 1813
3. Mary Augusta Austen Leigh, *James Edward Austen Leigh: A Memoir*
4. James Austen, *The Complete Poems of James Austen*, ed. David Selwyn, The Jane Austen Society, 2003
5. *Austen Papers*, letter from Jane Leigh Perrot, March 1835
6. *Mansfield Park*
7. *Persuasion*

8. *Sense and Sensibility*
9. *Austen Papers,* letter from Henry Austen, undated
10. *Emma*
11. *Persuasion*

Chapter 3: Parent Against Child

1. Lawrence Stone, *The Family, Sex and Marriage in England 1500–1800,* Penguin, 1977
2. *The Loiterer,* Robert L. Mack (ed.), Edwin Mellen Press, 2006
3. *Juvenilia*
4. *Emma*
5. *Persuasion*
6. *Northanger Abbey*
7. *Pride and Prejudice*
8. *Mansfield Park*
9. *Persuasion*
10. *Emma*
11. *Pride and Prejudice*
12. *Sense and Sensibility*
13. *Mansfield Park*
14. *Mansfield Park*
15. *Persuasion*
16. *Pride and Prejudice*
17. *Persuasion*
18. *Emma*
19. Letter, 7–9 October 1808
20. Letter, 30 October 1815
21. Letter, 15 July 1816
22. *Mansfield Park*

Chapter 4: Old Wives

1. John Wiltshire, *Jane Austen and the Body,* Cambridge University Press, 1992
2. *Pride and Prejudice*
3. *Mansfield Park*
4. *Mansfield Park*
5. *Emma*
6. *Persuasion*
7. *Emma*

8. *Emma*
9. *Mansfield Park*
10. *Northanger Abbey*
11. *Pride and Prejudice*
12. Caroline Austen, *Reminiscences*, The Jane Austen Society, 1986
13. Bellas MS, quoted in Deirdre Le Faye, *A Chronology*
14. *Austen Papers*, letter from Cassandra Austen, January 1832
15. *Emma*
16. Hazel Jones, *Jane Austen and Marriage*, Continuum, 2009
17. Austen Papers, letters from Tysoe Saul Hancock, 1771 and 1773
18. *Emma*
19. Letter, 2 September 1814
20. *Austen Papers*, letter from Cassandra Austen, August 1811
21. 'The Memoirs of Francis Austen', unpublished manuscript, quoted in Maggie Lane, *Jane Austen's Family through Five Generations*, Robert Hale, 1984
22. *Austen Papers*, letter from Jane Leigh Perrot, October 1828

Chapter 5: Old Maids

1. Letter, 29 January 1813
2. Claire Tomalin, *Jane Austen: a Life*, Viking, 1997
3. Letter, 16 February 1813
4. "Old Philmore" and Miss Benn's "Wretched Abode", Jane Hurst, in the Jane Austen Society *Annual Report*, 2003
5. Letter, 25 March 1817
6. Letter, 20 February 1816
7. Deirdre Le Faye (ed.), *Fanny Knight's Diaries*, The Jane Austen Society, 2000
8. Letter to Anna Lefroy, quoted in Deirdre Le Faye, *A Chronology*
9. David Selwyn, *Jane Austen and Children*, Continuum, 2010
10. Letter, 22 May 1817
11. Letter, 26 October 1813
12. Letter, 12 October 1813
13. Letter, 13 March 1817
14. *Emma*
15. *Pride and Prejudice*
16. *Persuasion*
17. *Austen Papers* letter from Mrs George Austen to Mary Lloyd, November 1796
18. *Emma*
19. *Later Manuscripts*

20. Quoted in Devoney Looser, *Women Writers and Old Age in Great Britain, 1750–1850*, The Johns Hopkins University Press, 2008
21. Letter to Sir William Elford, December 1814 in *A Life of Mary Russell Mitford*, A.G. L'Estrange, 1870
22. *Pride and Prejudice*
23. *Later Manuscripts*
24. Letter, 30 April 1811
25. Devoney Looser, *Women Writers and Old Age in Great Britain, 1750–1850*
26. *Persuasion*
27. Caroline Austen, *Reminiscences*
28. Diary of William King-Hall quoted in Deirdre Le Faye, *A Chronology*
29. Maggie Lane, *Jane Austen's Family*
30. Chris Viveash, 'James Edward at Oxford' in *The Jane Austen Society Annual Report*, 2008
31. Sophia Hillan, *May, Lou and Cass: Jane Austen's Nieces in Ireland*, Blackstaff Press, 2011
32. Hampshire Record Office 18 M61/Box 88
33. Margaret Wilson, *Almost Another Sister*, Kent Arts & Libraries, 1990

Chapter 6: Still a Very Fine Man

1. *Sense and Sensibility*
2. *Persuasion*
3. *Pride and Prejudice*
4. *Emma*
5. *Sense and Sensibility*
6. *Emma*
7. *Persuasion*
8. Fanny Caroline Lefroy, 'Family History', quoted in Deirdre Le Faye, *Jane Austen: a Family Record*
9. Letter, 20–22 February 1807
10. Knatchbull Family Papers, Centre for Kentish Studies, U951 F20
11. Margaret Wilson, *Almost Another Sister*
12. Letter, 13 March 1817
13. *Persuasion*
14. *Emma*

Chapter 7: Merry Widows

1. Deirdre Le Faye, *Jane Austen's Outlandish Cousin: the Life and Letters of Eliza de Feuillide*, The British Library, 2002
2. Philip Olleson, *The Journals and Letters of Susan Burney*, Ashgate, 2012
3. Sophia Hillan, *May, Lou and Cass: Jane Austen's Nieces in Ireland*
4. Margaret Wilson, 'Lady Sondes, her portrait and her marriages' in *The Jane Austen Society Annual Report*, 2005
5. Letter, 28 December 1808
6. Letter from Fanny Knight, 11 January 1809, Centre for Kentish Studies, U951
7. Kate Chisholm, *Wits and Wives: Dr Johnson in the Company of Women*, Chatto and Windus, 2011
8. Letter, 30 January 1809
9. James Edward Austen-Leigh, *A Memoir of Jane Austen*, 1871
10. R.W. Chapman (ed.), *Jane Austen's Minor Works*, Oxford University Press, 1954

Chapter 8: Four Dowager Despots

1. *Mansfield Park*
2. Samuel Johnson, *The Rambler*, quoted in John Wiltshire, *Jane Austen and the Body*, Cambridge University Press, 1992

Chapter 9: Not the Only Widow in Bath

1. Letter, 6–7 November 1813
2. Deirdre Le Faye, 'A Persecuted Relation: Mrs Lillingston's Funeral and Jane Austen's Legacy' in *Bath History*, Volume 7
3. Letter, 30 Jun–1 July 1808
4. Lefroy MS, quoted in Deirdre Le Faye, *Family Record*
5. Fanny Caroline Lefroy, 'Family History', Hampshire Record Office 23M93/85/2 quoted in Deirdre Le Faye, *A Chronology*
6. Maggie Lane, *A City of Palaces: Bath Through the Eyes of Fanny Burney*, Millstream, 1999
7. Maggie Lane, *A City of Palaces*
8. Caroline Austen, *My Aunt Jane Austen*
9. Maggie Lane, *A City of Palaces*
10. Maggie Lane, *A Charming Place: Bath in the Life and Novels of Jane Austen*, Millstream, 1988

Chapter 10: Age and Money

1. *Persuasion*
2. *Austen Papers,* letters to Philadelphia Whitaker, 18 August 1811 and 20 January 1832
3. Letter from Mrs Austen to Anna Lefroy, 21 February 1820, Lefroy Ms, quoted in Deirdre Le Faye, *Family Record*
4. Brian Southam, *Jane Austen and the Navy,* Hambledon, 2000
5. Deirdre Le Faye, *Family Record*
6. *Austen Papers*, Letter November 1828
7. Robert Bearman, 'Henry Austen and the Cubbington Living' in *Persuasions,* Volume 10
8. Linda Slothouber, 'A Dreadful Day: Two Austen Funerals' in *The Jane Austen Society Annual Report*, 2013
9. James Austen, *The Complete Poems of James Austen*
10. Deirdre Le Faye, 'James Austen's poetical biography of John Bond' in *The Jane Austen Society Annual Report*, 1992
11. *Mansfield Park*
12. *Pride and Prejudice*
13. *Austen Papers*, Letter March 1835
14. Le Faye, *A Chronology*
15. Letter, 6 April 1817
16. *Austen Papers,* Letter 1 May 1818

Chapter 11: The Dangerous Indulgence of Illness

1. *Austen Papers*, letter February 1827
2. Janet Todd and Linda Bree, 'Introduction' in *Later Manuscripts,* Cambridge University Press, 2008
3. Maggie Lane, 'Richard Buller' in *The Jane Austen Society Annual Report*, 2001
4. William Nisbet, *A Medical Guide for the Invalid, to the Principal Watering Places of Great Britain*, quoted in *Later Manuscripts*
5. William Buchan, *Domestic Medicine,* 1800, quoted in *Later Manuscripts*
6. Letter, 5–6 May 1801
7. Letter, 16 September 1813
8. Letter, 14–15 October 1813
9. Letter, 3 November 1813
10. *Northanger Abbey;* Maggie Lane, *A Charming Place*
11. Letter, 25 September 1813
12. Letter, 27 May 1817

Chapter 12: Nothing to Do but to Die

1. *Emma*
2. Letter, 27 May 1817
3. Letter, 18 November 1814
4. Penelope Byrde, *Jane Austen Fashion*, Excellent Press, 1999; private conversation
5. Letter, 6 April 1817
6. *Austen Papers*, Letter 7 April 1817
7. Letter, 30 August 1805
8. Letter, 5–8 March 1814
9. Letter, 6 June 1811
10. Letter, 3–6 July 1813
11. Letter, 7 October 1808
12. Letter, 15 October 1808
13. Letter (continuation), 16 October 1808
14. Linda Slothouber, 'A Dreadful Day: Two Austen Funerals'
15. Letter, 27–28 October 1798
16. Letter, 8–11 April 1805
17. David Selwyn (ed.), *Collected Poems and Verse of the Austen Family*, Carcanet Press, 1996
18. Letter, 3–6 July 1813
19. James Austen, *The Complete Poems of James Austen*
20. James Edward Austen-Leigh, *A Memoir of Jane Austen*
21. Caroline Austen, *My Aunt Jane Austen*
22. Letter, 27 May 1817
23. Letters from Cassandra to Anne Sharp (28 July) and Fanny Knight (29 July) in *Jane Austen's Letters*

Conclusion

1. Deirdre Le Faye, *Family Record*
2. Hoare's bank records: www.hoaresbank.co.uk/documents/Feb13-Jane Austen.pdf
3. Jan Fergus, *Jane Austen: a Literary Life*, Macmillan, 1991
4. *Austen Papers*, Letter 14 February 1827
5. Le Faye, *A Chronology*
6. Jane Hurst, 'Aunt Cassandra, a Very Great Loss to Us All,' *The Jane Austen Society Annual Report*, 2010

BIBLIOGRAPHY

Austen, Jane *The Cambridge Edition of the Works of Jane Austen,* general editor Janet Todd, Cambridge University Press, 2006, 9 vols

Le Faye, Deirdre (ed.), *Jane Austen's Letters*, 4th edn, Oxford University Press, 2011

***

Adkins, Roy and Lesley, *Eavesdropping on Jane Austen's England*, Little Brown, 2013

Austen, Caroline, *My Aunt Jane Austen: a Memoir,* 2nd edn, The Jane Austen Society, 1991

—*The Reminiscences of Caroline Austen,* The Jane Austen Society, 1986

Austen, James, *The Complete Poems of James Austen*, ed. David Selwyn, The Jane Austen Society, 2003

Austen, James and Austen, Henry, *The Loiterer,* ed. Robert L. Mack, Edwin Mellin Press, 2006

Austen-Leigh, James Edward, *A Memoir of Jane Austen and Other Family Recollections*, ed. Kathryn Sutherland, Oxford University Press, 2002

Austen-Leigh, Mary Augusta, *James Edward Austen-Leigh*, privately printed, 1911

Austen-Leigh, R.A., *Austen Papers*, privately printed, 1942

Barchas, Janine, *Matters of Fact in Jane Austen*, The Johns Hopkins University Press, 2012

Byrde, Penelope, *Jane Austen Fashion*, Excellent Press, 1999

Chisholm, Kate, *Wits and Wives: Dr Johnson in the Company of Women*, Chatto & Windus, 2011

Fergus, Jan, *Jane Austen: a Literary Life*, Macmillan, 1991

Hillan, Sophia, *May, Lou and Cass: Jane Austen's Nieces in Ireland*, Blackstaff Press, 2011

Jane Austen Society, *Annual Reports*, The Jane Austen Society, 1949–2013

Jones, Hazel, *Jane Austen and Marriage,* Continuum, 2009

Kaplan, Deborah, *Jane Austen Among Women*, The Johns Hopkins University Press, 1994

Lane, Maggie, *A Charming Place: Bath in the Life and Novels of Jane Austen*, Millstream, 1988

—*A City of Palaces: Bath Through the Eyes of Fanny Burney*, Millstream, 1999

—*Jane Austen's England*, Robert Hale, 1986

—*Jane Austen's Family*, Robert Hale, 1984

Le Faye, Deirdre, *A Chronology of Jane Austen and her Family*, Cambridge University Press, 2006

—*Fanny Knight's Diaries*, The Jane Austen Society, 2000

—*Jane Austen: a Family Record*, 2nd edn, Cambridge University Press, 2004

—*Jane Austen's Outlandish Cousin: the Life and Letters of Eliza de Feuillide*, The British Library, 2002

Looser, Devoney, *Women Writers and Old Age in Great Britain 1750–1850*, The Johns Hopkins University Press, 2008

Mullan, John, *What Matters in Jane Austen?*, Bloomsbury, 2012

Selwyn, David, *Jane Austen and Children,* Continuum, 2010

—*Jane Austen and Leisure*, Hambledon, 1999

Selwyn, David (ed.), *Collected Poems and Verse of the Austen Family*, Carcanet Press, 1996

Southam, Brian, *Jane Austen and the Navy*, Hambledon, 2000

Stone, Lawrence, *The Family, Sex and Marriage in England 1500–1800,* Penguin, 1977

Sturrock, June, *Jane Austen's Families*, Anthem, 2013

Tomalin, Claire, *Jane Austen: a Life*, Viking, 1997

Wilson, Margaret, *Almost Another Sister*, Kent County Council, 1990

Wiltshire, John, *Jane Austen and the Body,* Cambridge University Press, 1992

INDEX

Many of Jane Austen's family and acquaintance changed their names either on marriage or for inheritance purposes. Here they appear under the last name by which they were known, with cross-reference to former names. Where two or more generations share the same forename, unless there is a distinguishing title their relationship to Jane Austen has been added for clarity.